# BANISH YOUR INNER CRITIC

*Silence the Voice of Self-Doubt to Unleash
Your Creativity and Do Your Best Work*

Denise Jacobs

Cover Artwork: Americo Morales
Author Photo: Scott Redinger-Libolt
Cover & Layout: Elina Diaz, Roberto Núñez

For permission requests, please contact the publisher at:
Mango Publishing Group
2850 Douglas Road, 3rd Floor
Coral Gables, FL 33134 USA
info@mango.bz

For special orders, quantity sales, course adoptions and corporate sales, please email the publisher at sales@mango.bz. For trade and wholesale sales, please contact Ingram Publisher Services at customer.service@ingramcontent.com or +1.800.509.4887.

Banish Your Inner Critic: Silence the Voice of Self-Doubt to Unleash Your Creativity and Do Your Best Work

Library of Congress Cataloging
ISBN: (paperback) 978-1-63353-471-1, (ebook) 978-1-63353-472-8
Library of Congress Control Number: 2017906492
BISAC category code SEL009000 SELF-HELP / Creativity

Printed in the United States of America

## DEDICATION

For my sister Diane and my mother Deloria.
May they both continue to see, own, and fully stand
in the power of their phenomenal creative selves.

"Every creative person I know, from designers to CEOs, suffers from the inner voice that tells us we're not good enough, we're not special enough, and darn it, nobody likes us. While a little humility is a good thing, too much self-doubt can keep you from achieving what you were put on earth to accomplish. Being your best, authentic self is the only way to fulfill your dreams and leave the world better than you found it. Denise Jacobs can guide you away from your self-imposed naysayers and set you on the path to achieving the serene self-confidence you deserve. Nobody charts this terrain better than she does."

*- Jeffrey Zeldman, studio.zeldman & An Event Apart*


"We are our own worst enemy and harshest critic when it comes to expressing ourselves. Fear holds us back from reaching our potential and gaining the recognition we deserve. That is why I am so excited about Denise's book. Banish Your Inner Critic is the book I have been waiting for. A book I believe will inspire a new generation to step out of the shadows and shine."

*- Paul Boag, author of User Experience Revolution*


"Creativity will be the universal skill of the future in both business and in life. Banishing your inner critic is an ability everyone will need to work on. Denise is a creativity coach, who goes deep into the reasons why we commonly think we are not creative. She then gives us real solutions for how to overcome those hurdles, and bring out the inner creative inside of us. If you are looking to rekindle your creative instinct, have I got the book for you!"

*- Jason Cranford Teague, Futurist Author & Speaker*

"Banish Your Inner Critic: Great book! Easy to read and fun to use. Denise Jacobs has done a wonderful job of taking the complexity of self, and creating a system for each of us to access our creativity and release our creative power. Denise breaks down the inner critic into types and guides each reader through the process to access her distinctive creative self. Banish Your Inner Critic provides knowledge, insight, tools and practice for getting unstuck and expressing full creative potential. Plus, reading Denise's book is like spending time with her, and she's an inspiring delight."

*- Rebecca Stockley, Co-Founder of BATS Improv in San Francisco CA, www.improvlady.com*

"Denise brings a practical approach to silencing the voice in your head determined to undermine your ability to work. Banish Your Inner Critic is a manual for finding the destination, direction, and drive to succeed at life. As a remote worker I frequently find myself with self-doubt and rampant imposter syndrome. I now have the tools to purge those blockers from my mind and be the creative person I know I am."

*- Aaron Douglas, Mobile Software Lead, Automattic (& WordPress.com)*

"Banish Your Inner Critic is a must-read for everyone who has ever had self-doubt. As I read Denise's book, my head nodded in agreement and heralded a whole heap of 'ah-ha' moments for me. This is Denise at her creative best. I encourage you, Dear Reader, to go deep to banish your inner critic!"

*- Kylie Hunt, Workplace, Productivity & Happiness Specialist*

"With creativity comes periods of self-judgment that cause anxiety or paralysis. For designers, there is always this critical voice inside that questions what we are doing from time to time. However, whether you are a creative professional or not, everyone has the potential to be creative. In this book, Denise Jacobs empowers readers to silence their inner critic and unlock their potential to be their best creative self."

- *Andy Vitale, UX Design Principal, 3M Health Care*

"There is an Inner Critic in all of us and it may be the thing that is stopping us from reaching our full creative potential. In this delightful book, Denise openly shares her own struggles with self-criticism, making us feel like we aren't alone. She gives us permission to own it, the tools to get unblocked, and get on the path to a more creative self."

- *Jessie Shternshus, Founder of The Improv Effect and Author of Ctrl Shift: 50 Games For 50 \*\*\*\*ing Days Like Today*

"It's harder than ever to turn down the voices and channels vying for your attention; even when you do, you may find your own inner critic ready to thwart your creative efforts. But Denise Jacobs offers compassionate and practical guidance for overcoming those doubts, channeling your focus, and getting down to creating."

— *Kate O'Neill, founder of KO Insights and author of "Pixels and Place: Connecting Human Experience Across Physical and Digital Spaces"*

"The high tech world has created an epidemic of impostor syndrome. People doubt themselves. You can disagree when others doubt you, but when you doubt yourself, who's going to defend you? Take your power back! In this book, author Denise Jacobs gives you the practical tools you need to own the room by owning your self. Banish that inner devil's advocate and become as powerful as you can be."

*- **Alan Cooper**, Software Alchemist, co-founder of Cooper, and Author*

# TABLE OF CONTENTS

*"Banish your inner critic to Madagascar on an expedition to search for rare lemurs."*

— **Marelisa Fabrega,** *writer & blogger (inspired by SARK, Make Your Creative Dreams Real)*

# INTRODUCTION

## ARE YOU DOING YOUR BEST WORK?

You're feeling the pressure to perform: you're on a tight deadline, and there is a lot riding on your ability to come up with something great.

But, try as you might...nothing. You can't think, you can't problem-solve. You're uninspired. Generating new or interesting ideas?

You wish!

Why?

Because you

- shoot down your ideas before they even have a chance
- call yourself a failure because others around you are succeeding
- discount your ideas because they aren't 100 percent original
- tell yourself that you're just not creative at all
- have a hard time valuing what you create
- can't imagine creating without anguish and effort, so you make it true...

Unsurprisingly, you, my friend, are completely creatively blocked.

And then, when you tune into your internal self-talk, you find a steady torrent of self-chastisement, internal insults, and put-downs:

- "Why can't you come up with anything?!"
- "Wow – so you've got a master's in marketing and this is all you got?!"
- "You're an idiot! Think, for chrissakes!"

Yikes!

Your creative paralysis is all the more frustrating because you've been on the other side. You've had moments when you danced at the intersection of your skills, interests, natural abilities, and aptitudes. You were excited, completely engaged, and seemed to be an endless fount of ideas and solutions. You felt completely knowledgeable, powerful, and competent. Whatever it was that you were doing, you totally nailed it. The experience was fantastic.

For many of us, creating is a tortured process. The torture, however, is not inherent in creating itself, but instead comes from the fears we have around our ability to create. The constellation of our fears manifests as the Inner Critic. This psychological construct can trick us into believing the very worst about ourselves and our ability to create or do anything else of value in the world. It blocks the amazing ideas we have inside from coming out. The Inner Critic keeps us from accessing and expressing the very thing we desire: the flow of our creativity.

Based on several years of research on the creative process, articles written and presentations developed and delivered around the world, survey feedback, coaching clients, and most importantly, talking with conference and workshop attendees and other creatives of all sorts in multiple industries, I know that the Inner Critic is *the* largest block to creativity that exists.

To create, we need to acknowledge the Inner Critic and the damage it does to our work life, personal life, and general well-being.

To create lasting change, however, we really need to learn how to break its power over us so we can regain our capacity to create.

I wrote this book because I want you to be able to work better, produce more, and create with a higher level of excellence than you already do. By identifying and disempowering the various forms of the Inner Critic that plague us, we can remove the barricades standing between us and our full creative expression. This book will help you do just that.

However, I also wrote this book because I feel your pain. I know the topography of self-criticism personally: I have struggled with a particularly mean and relentless Inner Critic that has made me miserable at for most of my life. Because of my own Inner Critic, I have traveled far and wide in the lands of self-judgment and self-doubt, dismissing the creativity that I did have, believing that my work wasn't good enough, and being so focused on what others were doing that I couldn't see my own strengths or progress.

Imagine being able to create without the internal mental friction of the Inner Critic. Doesn't that sound wonderful? It's not just a pipe dream – it can be done. I know because I've experienced it myself.

You see, not only do I write this book from the standpoint of someone who was unsure that she was truly creative; I also write it from the standpoint of someone who has finally silenced her Inner Critic, who embraces and owns her creativity, and who now feels unstoppable.

## TRIUMPHING OVER MY OWN INNER CRITIC

There are those who, by either good fortune or hard work, are not afflicted by self-doubt and don't seem to have much of an Inner Critic at all. And then there are the rest of us: we who struggle daily to maintain a modicum of self-assurance as we go through our work and personal lives because of the barrage of self-critical inner dialogue that is our constant companion.

I used to be in this latter group – until I had an experience that changed my life. Let me tell you what happened.

When I wrote my first book, *The CSS Detective Guide*, the experience did not start out all sunshine and Santa Claus. I landed a book contract from a serendipitous meeting at a tech conference party, and I was thrilled to be on track to achieving my two big life goals:

1) Becoming an author, and

2) Using my expert status to become a speaker.

There was only one problem: I was terrified.

The first two days of my unrealistically aggressive schedule (four and a half months to write a 250-page tech book) found me sobbing on my couch. And let me be clear about this: I wasn't sniffling quietly and dabbing at my eyes with a tissue. Oh no. I *blubbered* while sitting on the side of my couch, as my tears flowed onto the plush sage green fabric of the pillow I clutched to my chest. My fears of not knowing enough, looking stupid, being judged, being a fake and a fraud, and not being good enough all plagued me to the point of near-paralysis. Finally, on the third day I bucked up, put on my big-girl pants, and finally sat down to the very hard work of...researching. You know, the incredibly advanced and rigorous task of looking up articles on the web, reading them, and then earmarking relevant information to put in my book. Yes, it's true: I had worked myself up into an emotional froth over something that I could practically do in my sleep. As a friend of mine would say: Crazypants!

During the next eight months of writing my book (because doing it in four and a half months was completely untenable), I came up against that inner critical voice that tried to block my ideas and creatively paralyze me almost daily. This voice told me every day that

- my ideas were stupid

- even though I had taught this subject for five years at a college level, that I wasn't enough of an expert on it

- my web designs were amateur and simplistic

- people would judge me negatively and criticize my book for not being in-depth, complete, or advanced enough

That's right: every day.

The way I often describe the experience is that instead of exercising creativity, I practiced its evil twin: destructivity. With every fearful thought of not being expert enough, not knowing enough, wondering if my writing was any good, and doubting my ability to design websites, I tore myself down. To try to build myself up, each day I had to focus on what was directly in front of me and do my best to ignore my anxieties about my perceived deficiencies. But they were still there.

Sometime in the fourth month of writing, I'd had enough. I needed to figure out how to turn off (or at least manage) this unending parade of self-critical thoughts. I did a little bit of research on self-criticism and found out about this thing called the Inner Critic. Although I didn't know it, something clicked inside of me, because a few days later, an idea for a presentation came to me in the shower. Still dripping wet and wrapped in a towel, I grabbed pencil and paper to jot down four pages of notes. A few weeks later, I was awakened at 5 a.m. by an idea for a creativity-busting workshop. Something big was brewing in my subconscious.

However, while I was designing the website for *The CSS Detective Guide*, I had a truly magical experience that changed everything.

To have my book's website up before I spoke on a panel at the major tech conference South By Southwest (SXSW) Interactive at the end of the week, I sat down to create my website mockup in Photoshop from a sketch so I could code it more easily. Much to my surprise, my quick sit-down consumed me, so much so that I was an hour and a half late going to a friend's house for dinner. Through the whole evening, I longed to return to my designing, so when I got home at 12:30 a.m., I thought "I'll just do a little bit and then go to bed." 1 a.m., then 2 a.m., and then 3 a.m. rolled by, and I just couldn't stop. With my favorite jazz playing in the background, I was in the high of creative flow as I experimented with color, typography, and layout. It was sheer bliss.

Finally, at 5:30 a.m., still fired up about designing, I stopped because I knew that if I didn't, I would surely get a migraine the next day. Buzzing from the creative juices coursing through me, I did my best to go to sleep.

Waking up again a mere two hours later, I was eager to get back to my creation. My whole body effervesced with energy. In fact, I was beyond blissful: I was euphoric. I felt a continuous rush of excitement and power similar to that of being in love. I felt like I could do anything I put my mind to. I felt like the ultimate version of myself: I felt the full power of my creative potential.

Only in retrospect did I understand why this was such an incredibly powerful peak experience: it was the first time in so long (maybe ever?) that I had experienced creating with no internal self-critical commentary: No thoughts of, "Is this any good?" or questioning my abilities. No comparing my design to those of other people.

No worrying about what other people would think or say about it. For the first time in eight months, I experienced criticism-free creating.

That day I made two monumental realizations:

First, that the absence of my Inner Critic allowed my creativity to flow! Because it was quiet, there was space for my creativity and ideas to come out to play.

Second, that creativity is power, and it's a source of power that each and every one of us has.

Unfortunately, most of us rarely tap into our creative power. Why? For the same reason I sat on my couch and cried for two days instead of starting to write my book. Because of the litany of self-critical thoughts and the self-doubt that they generate. Because of the Inner Critic.

Immediately following those realizations, I had an even deeper epiphany: helping other people reach the feeling of being energized and completely alive by allowing their creativity to flow was what I wanted to do with my life. Why? Because when we remove the blocks, we can access this source of personal power. And when we learn to remove the blocks to more regularly access and channel our creative power, we can transform our lives and the lives of others – and change the world for the better.

I became obsessed: I threw myself into learning about the creative process, specifically how to remove creative blocks. No matter which approach I studied, whether it was based on psychology, neuroscience, productivity, or practicality, they all led back to the same place: the Inner Critic.

Completing my first book did indeed become the springboard for becoming a speaker in the tech industry. Once I had established a good reputation for myself, I shifted to speaking about the creative process, removing creative blocks, and silencing the Inner Critic. As I suspected, the content resonated deeply with audiences. When I took my presentation content a step further by writing an article called "Banishing Your Inner Critic," the response was phenomenal. Hundreds of people posted and shared the article on social media for several days. It even got celebrity attention: on Google+, actress Felicia Day shared the article and vouched for the techniques that I shared. All of the responses validated what I had suspected when the idea for the creativity talk first came to me the shower: the Inner Critic is a problem that everyone has and that *everyone* needs help with.

During the next few years, through the feedback from more talks, keynotes, workshops, several more articles, coaching clients, and heartfelt emails from attendees and readers describing how much the information spoke to them and altered their lives, I knew it was time for me to reach an even wider audience. I knew then that I had to take my content to the next level and make it more accessible to even more people. The indications were clear: it was time for me write a handbook on how to *Banish the Inner Critic*. Through this book, I could help people reclaim their creative power and start achieving more success by silencing their own voice of self-doubt.

# IT'S TIME FOR YOU TO TRIUMPH TOO

You've felt lost and in a stupor, wandering your own wastelands of self-criticism. Fortunately, you are about to (re)discover your Creative Self and your Creative Power, and break yourself out of your Inner Critic-induced trance.

In this book, you will

- learn the origins of the Inner Critic

- discover the one brain function and three skills that you already possess to vanquish your Inner Critic

- learn multiple methods to deal with the fear of being negatively evaluated by others

- discover how to transform highly critical self-talk into that of approval and encouragement

- work on bolstering your sense of self to feel that you and your ideas are good enough

- acknowledge, unblock, and enhance your creativity

- channel your now flowing creativity as a force for positive change in the world

You, my friend, are a pathfinder, and this book is a manual to guide you along the  path of silencing your Inner Critic. Through the pages of this book, I'll be your mentor,  providing you with necessary information to change your thinking habits, and your coach, cheering you on as you release your inner critical thoughts and replace them with thoughts that support your creativity and motivate you to do your best work. Through this process, I've totally got your back.

But the best part is that through using the tools contained in these chapters, instead of being your own worst creative enemy, you'll have your own back too. By the end of this process, you'll only value and respect your creativity more, but you'll also end up liking and appreciating yourself more on the whole. Furthermore, you'll find yourself free from the weight of worrying about what others think, and you'll be able to break away from the restrictions of shoulds, musts, and oughts. You'll escape the trap of comparing yourself to others, and you'll drop the belief that you don't know enough or that you need to figure everything out by yourself.

Are you ready to start looking at the ways your Inner Critic shows up, discovering how to face your fears, bringing mistaken beliefs to the surface of your awareness, and moving beyond them to reach your own unique form of empowered creativity on the other side?

Read on, because we are about to embark on a journey to quiet that insidious Inner Critic so you can unleash your creativity, let your true talents shine, and start doing your best work – and ultimately, live your best life by channeling your creative power for good.

Let's take the first step to a whole new world right now – together.

# HOW TO USE THIS BOOK

This book is your map for the journey back to your Creative Self.

It's jam-packed with approaches for raising your awareness of behaviors and habits that are counter to your creative well-being, best practices to keep you from being creatively blocked from day to day, and techniques for profound and lasting change.

Because it is a road map, to make the best use of it, you need a key and legend, right? This information will help you to better navigate your way through the book and know what you're looking at when you get to it.

## THE CONTENT

Each chapter has a similar structure. Each has an overview of the topics covered, then kicks off with an anecdotal story of someone who is struggling with the particular guise of the Inner Critic covered in that chapter. A checklist of thoughts of people who share that particular form of Inner Critic will help you determine whether and how much you can relate.

Then you'll jump right into the content, exploring various factors that contribute to this form of the Inner Critic, typical challenges and issues that result from it, and ways you can address the potential source of your Inner Critic struggles and move into a new headspace – all supported by research.

From there you'll move on to the best part: one or more relevant exercises to put the concepts immediately into practice and start removing blocks to your creativity.

# Exercises: Creative Doses

Because of the mind's capacity to heal itself through mental training, much in the same way that medicine helps the body heal, the exercises in this book are aptly named "Creative Doses."

The exercises are designed to throw your Inner Critic off guard, confuse it, give it a job, and distract it — all to break the stronghold that it has on your thoughts.

Similar to the way some medicines become more powerful over time, the potency of the Creative Doses is cumulative: the more you use them, the more effective they will become for you in creating a new mindframe.

In some ways, however, the most important thing may not be the exercises themselves but rather the philosophies that underlie them. These four principles are the essence the of the book, the underlying foundations for every exercise.

1) **Change**
It's really the brain's capacity to think differently and consequently change itself – neuroplasticity – that is the true underpinning of this work, and what will facilitate your transformation.

2) **Awareness**
When we think negative thoughts mindlessly, we fall victim to them. However, when we raise our awareness of our thoughts and know when the ones we want to weed out come up, we can take action.

3) **Attention**
Changing the brain is driven by where we place our focus. Our work in this book will rely upon our commitment to shift our attention to focus upon the thoughts that support our creativity and sense of self.

4) **Self-Kindness and Self-Compassion**
You'll find the Inner Critic is born of the habit of self-chastisement. We will actively practice generating and directing the same compassion to ourselves as we would to others, and then actively be more kind and supportive to ourselves. In fact, one way to approach the Creative Dose exercises is to think of them as a kind future self talking to your current self, or even as a kind and compassionate version of your current self talking to your past self.

# Creative Dose Structure

Each section of content has one related Creative Dose, sometimes two. The Creative Doses are tools and techniques that combine various modalities:

- psychology tools

- self-coaching techniques

- mental reframes

- mind-body hacks

- productivity practices

- visualizations

- written exercises/writing assignments

- quizzes

- mindfulness practices

- even improv techniques

While all Creative Doses open with a purpose to prepare you for the upcoming content, you will find the exercises follow several different structures. So that you know what to expect in terms of the brainpower and time needed to devote to them, here is an explanation of each:

1) **Simple**

   What you see is what you get. The exercise is complete as is and has no additional steps, parts, or options, and often can be done in less time than the other exercises in this book.

2) **Steps**

   When you see that an exercise has steps, this means that there are multiple parts, with each part building upon the previous one in the sequence.

3) **Options**

   Exercises with multiple *options* are those in which you have a choice: you can do the work of each option, or you can pick and choose among them. If you do choose to do all of the options, it's not necessary to complete them in any particular order.

4) **Parts**

   Exercises that have parts are substantive: each part could easily stand alone as an exercise by itself. Thus the parts of the exercise could be done independently from one another as separate exercises. Exercises with parts also usually require more time and thought.

5) **Bonus Action**

   Some of the exercises have a "Bonus Action" which takes the exercises even further.

# Online Companions

In several places in the book, there are links to download companion materials to the exercises online. These links are footnoted on the same page so that you can find them easily.

# GUIDELINES FOR SUCCESS

This book is densely packed with *a lot* of information. It will probably take time to digest and assimilate all of it. To get the most out of the content and the process you're about to embark upon, here are some tips for success.

## Choose Your Path

The book is designed so that if you really want to get to the guise of the Inner Critic that affects you the most strongly and learn about the solutions for it, you can go directly to any particular chapter. In fact, there is a quiz in Chapter 2 that will help you identify your predominant Inner Critic guise so you will be able to do just that.

However, I recommend that you read the book in order from the beginning to the end. The chapters are written in such a way that each one builds on content in the previous chapters. Chapters 1 through 4 in particular are best read in sequence, as it is in these chapters that I lay out the foundational concepts.

## Write It Out

For the exercises in this book, I encourage you to actually write everything down by hand instead of on a computer. Writing things on paper actually has an impressive array of benefits that will help in your process. Writing activates more parts of the brain than typing does, focusing and engaging the brain to digest information and learn from it, while helping the brain to develop and grasp new ideas and concepts.[1] While it strengthens the memory – it's easier to remember things that you've written down – writing also triggers deeper parts of the emotional brain. So make an effort to write it out to work it out.

### Dude, Where's the Writing Space?

You may be thinking "Okay, I'm supposed to write it out, but there are no lines for it in the book!" There's a reason for that.

As much as I love reading self-help books, I've never been a fan of the lines provided for doing the exercises. Between you and me, I find them somewhat intimidating, or more accurately, accusatory. Why? They highlight the fact that I'm more interested in thinking through the exercises and finding out the next bit of information than writing my thoughts down. Additionally, due to my reverence for books, I abhor writing in them.

Personally, I find lines confining. My preference is to write on blank paper, free of lines so that neither my ideas nor my thinking are constrained.

So instead of providing space to write in the book, I recommend that you use the companion *Banish Your Inner Critic* Journal, or get a dedicated notebook of the variety that you like best, and use that to do the exercises in.

## Give Yourself Time to Process

As a good friend of mine likes to say, in this book, we're going to do deep. You're probably going to hit some pockets of feelings and emotions that have not seen the light of day for some time. Make sure that after you've read the information and the exercises, you give yourself time to mull things over and see what comes up for you. There's no need to rush this process. Your Inner Critic has been there for a long, long time. Give yourself adequate time to transform it.

Last but not least, here is my creative counsel: final recommendations for getting the most out of this process.

1) Set your intention to start the process of silencing your Inner Critic

2) Understand that this is a long game — not a sprint.

3) In place of only celebrating accomplishment, give yourself credit for effort. In other words, don't wait to give yourself kudos until you have been able to do something "perfectly" or have arrived at some point of completion. Congratulate yourself on having started the process at all, and continue to congratulate yourself for sticking with it.

4) Be kind to yourself. Now's the time, you've beaten yourself up enough.

# Read and Revisit

This book is only as powerful as your application of the concepts contained here. Don't just read the book – really make an effort to put the foundational principles and exercises into practice. And bear in mind that sometimes we need to return to a book to really take full advantage of the teachings in it. As you change and develop, you will be ready for new information. Something that only partially resonated when you read it the first time may be exactly what you need for a breakthrough when you revisit it the second, third, or even fourth time.

# THE ORIGIN OF THE INNER THOUGHTS

The inner thoughts at the beginning of each chapter are not fabricated. Rather, they are from attendees to my Banish Your Inner Critic keynote and creativity workshops from 2015 to 2016. I lead an exercise that I got from my friend and colleague Jessie Shternshus: I ask everyone to write down one fear that they have around creativity, crumple the paper into a ball, and then throw it across the room. Then I have everyone pick up a paper ball that lands near them and share what was written there out loud. I've gathered these "snowballs" to use as examples of actual fears gathered anonymously from professionals just like you. The "snowballs" come from attendees at conferences like Adobe Max: The Creativity Conference, HOW Interactive, the British Columbia Chapter of the American Marketing Association, MinneWebCon, UX Lisbon, UX Australia, Delight Conference and others.

# DISCLAIMERS

This book is not intended to be a substitute for the advice or care of a trained mental health professional, so readers should consult with one regarding any serious matters relating to your mental health or concerning serious mental health conditions. The information contained within this book is strictly for educational purposes. If you wish to apply these ideas, you are taking full responsibility for your choices, actions, and results.

For the anecdotes at the beginning of the chapters, the names and identifying details have been altered or changed complete to protect the privacy of the individuals. Actual names and details were used only with each individual's permission and blessing.

Last but not least, know in advance that "earworms" – pieces of music that get stuck in your mind that are incredibly difficult to dislodge – may be caused by certain chapter, section, or subsection titles in this book. The only known antidote for a pervasive earworm is to replace it with another. I apologize in advance. If it makes you feel any better, I had the song "Emotions" by Samantha Sang and the Bee Gees running through my head the entire time I was writing Chapter 1 – and that subtitle didn't even make the final cut.

*I fear...*

*my work won't be good enough.*

**1**

# CHAPTER 1 | WHY BANISH THE INNER CRITIC?

**This chapter examines:**

*Creativity and Creative Flow*

*Inner Critic Origins*

*Creativity v. the Inner Critic*

*The Need to Reclaim Creativity*

*A Call to Action*

*"What is this self inside us, this silent observer,*
*Severe and speechless critic, who can terrorise us*
*And urge us on to futile activity,*
*And in the end, judge us still more severely*
*For the errors into which his own reproaches drove us?"*

— **T.S. Eliot**, *The Elder Statesman*

# OUR INTRINSIC CREATIVITY

The idea first comes to you unbidden. A glimmer on the edge of your perception, it's hazy, not fully formed, its edges fuzzy and indistinct. "Where did that come from?" you wonder briefly. But once you put your full attention on the idea, the longer you focus, the more clear and distinct it becomes. You begin to feel a welling within: a push from your gut and a quickening of your heart.

You *have* to capture it, this idea. You grab a piece of paper and jot down notes or do a quick sketch. Or maybe you record a quick voice memo on your phone. But the idea won't leave you alone, and returns to you with increased insistence and clarity. Your brain starts to explode with related ideas as you start to connect the dots. Your imagination takes over, visualizing how to execute this concept that has stolen your attention.

Nothing – no mental barrier of self-doubt or questioning – comes between you and your creative work. Nothing in you says "no" or "I don't know." Instead, everything in you says "yes" as you begin the process of making your idea manifest. And the more the details fall into place like puzzle pieces coming together, the more "yes" you feel. A rush of energy flows through you, compelling and motivating you to prioritize your brainchild. Interest, curiosity, and fascination take over.

Hours fly by as you are engrossed in your project. In the midst of making, you feel clear, super-focused, and confident. Once you've finally acted upon your idea, you feel a sense of completion and satisfaction.

While it is not the same for every single creative endeavor, this is the essence of the experience. Most people coming out of the throes of creating will tell you, face aglow and eyes still shining, that the experience, on the whole, was amazing. Regardless of whether you were designing an interface for an app, getting down ideas for your startup, writing a blog post, developing software, cooking a six-course gourmet dinner, or choreographing a performance – the process going on in your head and the sensations you were having were universal.

In fact, in my keynotes and workshops, one of my favorite pieces of audience participation is when I ask the attendees about what creative flow feels like for them. The responses – regardless of the audience location or demographics – are remarkably similar. Here are the words that come up time and time again:

Timeless • Connected • Happy • Good • Strong • Clear • Focused • Confident • Alive • Vibrant • Energized • Everything flows • Euphoric • Trance-like • Enjoyable • Empowered • Capable

When we are creative, we are blissfully "in the zone," engaged in soul-satisfying making and producing. In his book *Creativity*, Mihaly Csikszentmihalyi, the pioneering researcher who first identified the state of flow, says, "when we are involved in creativity, we feel that we are living more fully than during the rest of life." Yes! Creativity makes us feel fully alive.

Before you fall back on any limited ideas around what creativity is, allow me to dispel a few myths. You don't have to be a visual artist, writer, or musician to be creative. You don't have to be eccentric, neurotic, tortured, or starving. Creativity isn't solely the domain of a group of "special" people whom you'll never be a part of.

We are born creative. Creativity is about seeing possibilities. It's a spark, a stirring, an impetus: a powerful force that compels us to create and bring an idea to life.

This power is in everybody. We all have the desire to create something out of nothing, be it a recipe, a poem, or a business. Creativity isn't what you produce or the medium you use to produce it.

What's more, we each have our own unique form of creativity, so don't be fooled into believing that just because what you are great at creating isn't "art" that it's not valid. In fact, if you are an engineer, scientist, or anyone else of an analytic bent, and you believe yourself to be in the category of "people who aren't creative," you're wrong. Instead, you are one of the most creative and imaginative kinds of people on the planet.

I'm here to tell you that you are creative. Yes, YOU.

Creativity is the essence of our being and a part of our DNA. Indeed, neuroscience shows that we are literally wired for it.

## Your Brain on Creativity

Everyone has the capacity to experience the "optimal state of consciousness where we both feel and perform our best."[1] One of the great paradoxes of creative flow, however, is that you can't force it; you can only create the proper environment for accessing it. The conditions needed to get into a flow state are a confluence of uninterrupted time to concentrate, clear goals, the correct ratio of challenge to skill, and immediate feedback from our actions.[2] Then the magic happens.

Once we get into flow, time perception becomes altered. Hours seem like minutes, and/or minutes seem like hours. We feel a euphoric sense of control and personal power, but paradoxically lose our sense of self. Performance of all kinds is heightened tremendously – creative performance in particular. But it gets even better: the effects of flow go beyond the immediate moment. Harvard researcher Teresa Amabile discovered that people continue to feel creative the day after.[3] I call this "the flow afterglow." As we increasingly achieve creative flow, we train our brains to be even more creative.

The good news is that if you don't think of yourself as creative or trust your creativity, you can now relax. Being creative is built into the way our brains are designed to work. On a cellular level during the flow state, serotonin and dopamine, which are the pleasure-inducing brain chemicals or neurotransmitters, wash over our brains. Another neurotransmitter, endorphin, improves focus – helping to shut out distractions. This increases our ability to make new mental connections, further enhancing performance. Anandamide, a neurotransmitter whose name is derived from the Sanskrit word for bliss, enters the scene. In addition to encouraging the brain to practice lateral thinking[4] and to release even more dopamine, anandamide helps generate pleasure and motivation

Speaking of the brain, creativity does not happen because the "imaginative" right brain takes over the "analytical" left brain. In fact, scientists consider the concept of creativity being seated in the right side of the brain as archaic.[5]

The most exciting finding about creativity in the brain is this: researchers now consider creativity to be based in the part of the brain responsible for planning, self-evaluation, and self-censorship.[6] The dorsolateral prefrontal cortex is where the majority of higher cognitive functions of working memory, mental imagery, and willed action (specifically self-monitoring and impulse control) lives. In other words, this is the part of the brain that interprets situations, envisions consequences, and then adapts behavior accordingly. Contrary to what you might think, the goal is not for this area to be active. Rather, creative magic happens when the dorsolateral prefrontal cortex powers down and stays quiet. Simply put, creativity comes from relaxing self-evaluation and self-judgment – and the self-criticism and self-doubt that result from them.

Therein lies the rub.

## Creativity, Interrupted

Children are terrific examples of unfettered creativity; they effortlessly create worlds with their imagination. As a child, you did this too. When we were younger, we trusted the creative spark that lives within us, and we easily played with ideas and let them out into the world. Imagination was our boon companion, and creativity, our best friend.

Over time, our once close relationship with our creativity becomes strained. Instead of exercising our ability to bring forth something new and positive into the world, we begin to practice creativity's evil twin, destructivity: using our imagination in ways that sabotage our creative efforts. Why? Because a new player crops up, wedging itself between us and our once best buddy of creativity. Posing as a sworn protector, this interloper begins to whisper doubts in our ear after every letdown, every unexpected criticism, and every perceived failure.

Where we used to trust in the flow of inspiration and ideas from our creativity, we now begin to second-guess these messages through the filter of this new interpreter. We start to fall prey to the incessant internal critical voice that tells us that we don't know enough, that we might look stupid and be criticized, that our ideas aren't original, that we aren't working hard enough – and that we have to do, be, and produce more in order to be accepted. We fall victim to our anxiety that we'll be found out as a fraud, that our work has to be executed perfectly to be recognized and valued, that we will fail at the challenges we take on, or that we can't keep up with the skills and technologies that we need for our work. It's no wonder we crack under the weight of the belief that we aren't enough.

What happened to the unselfconscious state of flowing creativity that we used to enter so easily? What happened to the life-in-Technicolor experiences that left us with a sense of wonder at what we produced and excitement at doing more in the future?

My friend, your enjoyable creative process and access to your creative power have been usurped by internal critical thoughts rooted in old fears and mistaken beliefs. May I introduce to you: the Inner Critic.

# MEET THE INNER CRITIC

While we are born creative, we are *not* born self-critical. Strong self-reflection is necessary to help a child evaluate her or his behavior in order to make good choices. However, self-judgment and self-criticism replaces self-reflection, and it then grows unchecked during adolescence, through adulthood, and to the ends of our lives into a force that blocks us from reaching our creative potential. Excessive self-criticism can become the predominant influence in our lives, erecting obstructions to opportunities and holding us back from stepping into our creative greatness. What is this particular form of unchecked self-criticism? This psychological construct is known as the Inner Critic.

Born from experiences internalized early in life, the Inner Critic is an amalgamation of every critical thing we've ever heard (or thought we heard) from people of influence. In their attempts to push us to conform to the norms of society, parents, older family members or caretakers, teachers, coaches, siblings, peers, and friends are a fount of criticism-filled messages. In our impressionable state, we internalize these criticisms. We model them, viewing ourselves from a place of criticism and judgment. We may even unconsciously emulate the negative beliefs that the people closest to us hold about themselves.

Thus, messages from our childhood like, "you will never be successful" or "your ideas are no good" embed themselves into our psyches. As we get older, these criticisms and judgments become so deeply ingrained that we no longer can recognize them as messages that originated from outside of our own minds. We then believe these critical messages to be our own truths, forming the warp and weft of the fabric of how we relate to ourselves.

Although the Inner Critic is also known as the inner critical voice[7], you may not detect its presence by actually hearing a voice. The Inner Critic can be sneaky, working to avoid detection by trying to appear as your native thoughts. So familiar as to be invisible, your Inner Critic reflex may be so automatic that you may not even register the thoughts. If you do not detect its presence, you'll most likely recognize the Inner Critic through the habitual negative self-talk that directly influences your behavior.

What drives the Inner Critic? The desire to protect ourselves.

Our emotional minds developed the Inner Critic as a protection strategy against situations in which we could be judged, rejected, or criticized. In its determination to keep these potential future threats at bay, the Inner Critic defends our well-being and social safety the moment we have a sense of losing either. I think of the Inner Critic as a proactive mental threat-to-self system.

But all of this still doesn't answer the question of what's the true source of the Inner Critic. What do our inner critical thoughts have in common at their core? One word: Fear.

If you're feeling anxious, guilty, or ashamed around your creativity, it's likely a result of the Inner Critic's handiwork. When we are deep in the woods of our inner critical thoughts, in essence, we are experiencing fear. Having these feelings disrupts relaxed and ordered thinking, and in its place, we experience what Csikszentmihalyi calls "disordered attention." In this state, we turn our attention inward and focus on the negative, destroying our ability to pursue positive external goals or even accomplish the task at hand. The more we are in this state of mind, the more our capacity for enjoyment plummets as it become more difficult to learn anything new. Instead, we rehash old information, wandering the forest of our fears with no means to problem-solve our way out of it.

## CREATIVITY VS. THE INNER CRITIC

Earlier, we learned that the prefrontal cortex, the part of the brain that judges, criticizes, and rules self-inhibition, falls silent when we go into creative flow. *This is the seat of the Inner Critic.* Research shows that not only does a quiet Inner Critic facilitate creative flow, but creative flow conversely keeps the Inner Critic quiet. Creativity and the Inner Critic, then, are inextricably connected. But they are binary: they cannot coexist. If your Inner Critic is in control, then accessing your creativity will be elusive at best and impossible at worst.

Yes, you've had success with creative projects, and yes, you may have been fairly satisfied with what you produced after the fact. However, if you had an overly active Inner Critic during the process, the fact that you were able to produce was *despite* its overbearing presence rather than because of its allegedly beneficial input. Instead of feeling protected, you had to slog through a quagmire of anxiety. Is this really how you want to create?

Any self-judgment, self-criticism, or doubts about your abilities will obliterate creative flow, ripping you from your creative high to cast you back on the ground while you grapple with your fears. Your prefrontal cortex, which was previously favorably inactive, fires back up with a litany of allegedly rational reasons to go into self-protection mode. All while this transpires, the door to your creative power slams shut and you cannot fully realize your vision. The Inner Critic is the enemy of creativity, productivity, and sanity.

In contrast, when we are in creative flow, we feel the full potential of our personal creative power, an enhanced and strengthened sense of self. People who experience creative flow regularly report feeling focused and creative, engaged and motivated, active and connected, and strong and in control. This place of empowerment is our true creative home.

Feeling fully creative like this is what we want and need. But so many of us cut ourselves off from this power, by judging ideas before they have a chance to develop, attempting to attain unreachable standards, creating barriers for ourselves, keeping our imaginations under wraps, or denying that we are creative at all. But we can do better. We can do more with this powerful force.

If you think of creating as an unpleasant and agonizing process – then you're not thinking about actual creating. Instead, you're recalling the sensation of the Inner Critic triggering your fears and supplanting the process. *It's the Inner Critic that makes creating painful.* Your critical thoughts are the main blockade to your creativity. They thwart the fluid process of ideas moving from your internal subconscious universe to your conscious mind to access and make tangible.

In succumbing to the voice of doubt, we relinquish our creative power to the Inner Critic. According to Csikszentmihalyi, the struggle for wrestling control from the Inner Critic is no less than the battle for the self. Make no mistake: the struggle is real.

Here is the simple truth:

*To be creative, you have to silence the Inner Critic.*

Banishing the Inner Critic is what we need to do to reclaim our creative power.

# RECLAIMING CREATIVITY

First, the bad news: we each have an Inner Critic, and try as we might, we can neither run away from our Inner Critic nor completely destroy it. The Inner Critic is a part of our psyche and being human.

Don't throw up your hands in despair! Despite all of the psychological power that it holds, the Inner Critic is really a way of thinking – a series of thoughts. Even more simply put, it is electrical impulses in the brain. Neurons firing. Chemicals being released and recognized by receptors in the brain. Just as we can learn to control our breathing, we can learn to have a better handle on these processes in our brains to be more in control of our thoughts, beliefs, and consequent actions.

Now here's the good news: if we can learn to switch off (or at the very least, tone down) the self-evaluation, self-judgment and criticism, and self-doubt, then we can activate and light up the areas in the brain associated with self-expression. We can create the space and lay the foundations for getting into our creative flow.

Remember that child full of wonder and unfettered creativity at the beginning of the chapter? That's you deep inside. Also inside is the self that embodies all of the inherent potential you were born with and that will always be there: the capacities you've realized and those that you have yet to actualize. I like to think of this as your true self, your Creative Self. It existed before the layers of societal expectation were heaped upon your shoulders, and it will stand triumphant once you shake off the shoulds, musts, and oughts. This part of you is what you started with: completely connected to your own flow of ideas, with a perspective on the world which only you have, and an experiential filter that comprises your own unique creativity.

This inherent Creative Self is key. It is what fills people with awe when witnessing an inspired musical performance or a gifted athlete. This complete absence of friction, self-doubt, and self-judgment entrances and inspires us. It's beautiful. Their complete expression of the Creative Self gives us something to aspire to ourselves.

Did you know that there is no word in the Tibetan language for creativity or being creative? The closest translation is "natural."[7] In other words, if you want to be more creative, you have to be more natural, more of yourself. However, the Inner Critic tells us that only if we're hard on ourselves can we become the people we're meant to be. This is a lie. The people who we are meant to be are exactly who we are. We're meant to become more of ourselves – not cookie cutter copies of those around us.

Your Creative Self is where your creative power lies, the source of your brilliance. This is your powerful self; it is your brain clicking into gear and activating the wonderfully complex network that is hardwired not only into your brain but your soul. The Creative Self trusts itself, knows its strengths, and delights in pushing its boundaries. The Creative Self is far stronger, far more knowledgeable, and infinitely more capable than the Inner Critic.[8] We need to reduce the Inner Critic's interference so the Creative Self can do what it does best: creating.

The Inner Critic is like static, while the Creative Self is the station you're trying to tune in to. We do have a choice: we don't have to listen to the static. By giving the Inner Critic less of our bandwidth, we access, express, and cultivate our creativity; we take back our creative power. From this place of reclaimed creative power, we can go after even bigger challenges.

Reclaiming creativity is an act of courage: choosing to act in the face of the fear that the Inner Critic generates, and making a conscious choice to think differently in order to access your Creative Self.

How do we reach this Creative Self? Trying to fix the affliction of the Inner Critic with its own tools is not going to work. You can't bully, threaten, or coerce the Inner Critic. It wrote the handbook and knows all of the tricks. No, we have to use a totally different approach to banish the Inner Critic.

With training, the mind can replace distorted patterns of thinking. To release the Inner Critic's hold on our creative thinking and access to our creativity, we're going to set out to learn new approaches, practices, and tools. In the coming chapters, we'll discover much-needed antidotes to the Inner Critic's pernicious guises of the fear of judgment and criticism, being highly self-critical, feeling deficient, having a habit of comparison, and denying creativity.

Are you ready? Let's retrain our minds so that we can banish the Inner Critic, access our Creative Selves, and reclaim our creative power.

*I feel safer being small*

# CHAPTER 2 | TAKE BACK YOUR CREATIVE POWER

**This chapter examines:**

*Neuroplasticity*

*Attention and Focus*

*Meta-Cognitive Learning*

*Mindfulness*

*Self-Compassion*

*Identifying the Inner Critical Voice*

*Guises of the Inner Critic*

*Inner Critic Questionnaire*

*"Resistance has no strength of its own. Every ounce of juice it possesses comes from us. We feed it with power by our fear of it. Master that fear and conquer Resistance."*

– **Steven Pressfield,** *The War of Art*

Feeling the flow of ideas rushing forth from inside of you to interface with the world is an amazing sensation. What is not such an amazing sensation, however, is when this outpouring is met with judgment and criticism. In the absence of a strong sense of self, it's easy to feel like you need to do something to try to prevent the threat of criticism in the future.

As the self-appointed protector of your sense of self, the Inner Critic strikes a deal. "Tell you what," it says, "You listen to my guidance, and I'll keep you safe. In exchange, all you need to do is hand over the creative part of yourself to me."

You're skeptical. "But...how will I access my creativity?"

"Oh, you can still get to it – you'll totally have visiting rights," says the Inner Critic. "You just have to go through me, that's all. You'll feel better and I'll get to do my job. It's a win-win situation."

You're still not entirely convinced, but you don't know what else to do. Reluctantly, you relinquish your Creative Self, your best buddy and keeper of your creative power, to the care of the Inner Critic.

As time goes on, however, it's clear that you got a bum deal. The only time you can get through to see your Creative Self is when the Inner Critic is relaxed, distracted, or asleep. And because it's so dedicated to its job, you rarely see your creativity anymore. In fact, it's been so long since you've seen your Creative Self that you're not even sure you'd recognize it.

The so-called "protective" guidance of the Inner Critic is misleading, based on incomplete or inaccurate information, or just plain wrong.

Instead of feeling protected and safe, you feel more vulnerable to the prospect of external criticisms and less confident of yourself and your abilities. What's more, the Inner Critic lacks both bedside manner and compassion, so its messages are often hurtful – and now they come from inside your head instead of from other people.

But even worse than being hurtful, the Inner Critic's messages have poisoned you, leaving you mesmerized and confused, causing you to wander around in a daze of self-criticism, self-judgment, and self-doubt. You've become so disoriented by the spurious messages of the Inner Critic that you don't realize you've gone astray, wandering farther and farther away from your Creative Self and creative power. Now you're lost and don't quite remember how to get back to where the Inner Critic is keeping your Creative Self. Under the influence of the Inner Critic, you've forgotten that your Creative Self and your creative power actually haven't gone anywhere. They are both still home.

You were duped. Things aren't better with the Inner Critic in charge. The Inner Critic's guidance isn't helping. The messages aren't even original – they're all based on what other people have said to you. What's worse, the Inner Critic is not protecting your Creative Self; instead the over-zealous guarding causes it to starve.

When you made the deal, what you didn't know is this: the reason the Inner Critic is keeping your Creative Self so tightly under wraps is that it is aware of one of paradoxes of creativity – that expressing creativity is an expression of power, and because it is so powerful, it's also a threat.

The expression of creativity opens worlds of possibilities and activates probable futures. Within this is the potential of becoming more visible, and therefore being open to the threat of criticism. Such vulnerability triggers the fear of losing our sense of belonging and safety in the world. The Inner Critic is keenly aware of this. Its goal is to prevent this eventuality at all costs. Unfortunately, because creativity is something that gets stronger and expands the more we use it, your Creative Self now slowly languishes.

Allowing your Inner Critic to continue barring your access to your creativity is a grave injustice; the Inner Critic doesn't really know what to do with your power, it just fears the potential ramifications of it. But you do know. You're the one who knows what to do with your creative power: how to channel it, leverage it, and expand upon it. You know what you are drawn to create, what comes effortlessly to you and through you. You know that your capacity to be creative will only increase the more you use it.

You realize that you don't need your Inner Critic to protect your Creative Self. You can choose to learn new ways to bolster your sense of self to protect against external criticisms and judgments.

It's time to break the deal.

It's time to take back what is rightfully yours.

It's time to regain your close relationship with your Creative Self.

It's time to take back your creative power.

## TO RECLAIM, WE MUST REBUILD

*"I want to reclaim who I am."*

– **Elizabeth Edwards,** *author and attorney*

You're motivated. You're ready for a change. You're weary of the overly active inner critical voice that disrupts your focus and prevents your talents from shining. You're ready to stop letting toxic self-criticism drive your inner self into oblivion, ready to begin doing things differently. You want to be more of who you are and to reach your potential.

You're ready to return to your Creative Self and reclaim your creativity. But how? How do we start taking back power from our Inner Critic so we can do the creative work we're capable of? By banishing the Inner Critic.

You may be frustrated because past approaches to trying to deal with your Inner Critic haven't felt effective. But there's a reason why they didn't. Attempting to silence the Inner Critic solely with affirmations and other feel-good pablum doesn't work. The habitual nature of well-ensconced inner critical thoughts makes them remarkably stubborn and difficult to displace.

To reclaim our creativity, we must rebuild. We must rebuild the mind frame in which we are so accustomed to the Inner Critic's messages that we have become complacent and feel helpless at the prospect of changing our own minds, believing "this is just the way I am."

Then we need to rebuild the very structure and circuitry that generates our self-critical thoughts and encourage these parts of our brains to fade in the face of different thoughts coming from newly developed structures and networks. The thinking and emotional circuits of our brains are far more alterable than we think. Profound mental changes can come from training the brain to think, and therefore work, differently.

The Inner Critic uses the tendencies of the brain and the tools of the mind to fulfill its role as protector. To take back our creative power, we will do the same.

Banishing the Inner Critic is all about building a new mind frame. Literally.

# RECOGNIZE THE POWER OF THINKING DIFFERENTLY

*"Think Different."*

— **Apple Inc.**

Many of us have built up a lifelong habit of being hard on ourselves: beating ourselves up for alleged mistakes or missteps, preemptively judging ourselves, and worse. When confronted with adverse situations or an unloved personal trait, our brains fall into a groove of self-chastisement, a knee-jerk reaction of self-berating. If you've had experience with mastering a sport, an instrument, or a language (spoken, written, or programming), then you know that repetition is what makes a skill stick to the point that you no longer have to think to execute it. It becomes a reflex. We can think of the Inner Critic as a mastered reflex: a habitual response strengthened by years of practice.

To take back the reins of power from the Inner Critic of our mind, emotions, and actions, we need to learn to have better control over what we think on a regular basis. The path to banishing our Inner Critic starts by changing our thoughts. I'm sure that this sounds overly simplistic. But when you understand the ever-changing nature of our brains, you'll see how effective changing our thoughts truly is.

## Take Advantage of the Brain's Plasticity

*"The brain is a far more open system than we ever imagined, and nature has gone very far to help us perceive and take in the world around us. It has given us a brain that survives in a changing world by changing itself."*

— **Norman Doidge,** *The Brain That Changes Itself: Stories of Personal Triumph from the Frontiers of Brain Science*

Although we developed our self-critical patterns of thinking when we were young, and as a result, they are well-entrenched, their habitual nature works to our advantage. We can break and replace obsolete thought patterns with new, more supportive ones. Before you dismiss this as empty encouragement toward "the power of positive thinking," understand that the process works because of neuroscience. Specifically, we'll leverage the quality of our brains known as neuroplasticity: the ability to create new connections between nerve cells in response to change.

For years, the accepted model was that the nerve structure of the adult brain was fixed and locked in place. But more recent findings show that this stance is completely inaccurate. Instead of settling into a static mass of rigid neurons in adulthood, our brains are highly adaptable and, in fact, undergo continuous change during our lives. We can thank neuroplasticity for our ability to learn new facts, develop new skills, and adapt to new conditions.[1]

What we think about most gets the most space in our brains. Thought circuits and neuronal networks are constantly being created and dismantled. Mental focus and concentration push various regions of the brain to expand, while low activity in other areas signals their disuse. The more activity that a brain function, thought process, or skill gets, the more neural real estate it is allotted. Alternately, certain brain cells mark unused circuits and eventually prune them away for the expansion of those pathways crackling with activity.[2]
In a very real and concrete way, the thoughts that comprise our everyday thinking sculpt and mold our brains.[3]

What you think about is determined by what you pay attention to. The information that our brains and minds take in and make use of depends on how new and interesting it is, how strong a signal it has, or how much attention we give it. It's attention that decides what our senses take in. Without attention, experiences don't register in the mind and may not even be stored in memory. Brain imaging shows that when we pay attention to something, not only are the neurons involved activated, but neural activity in other areas is suppressed as a result.[4] Such activation and suppression effectively strengthens one network of neurons over another. In fact, attention is so central to neuroplasticity that in her book *Train Your Mind, Change Your Brain,* author Sharon Begley suggests that training your attention can be considered "the gateway to plasticity."[5]

The problem is that when the Inner Critic makes an appearance, the resulting self-critical thoughts steal our attention and thus our brainpower away from what's in front of us. Our focus shifts away from what is happening in the present to our fear-tinged memories of previous disappointments or our anxieties of a negative future.

To think differently, attention is key. In his book, *The Inner Game of Work,* W. Timothy Gallwey eloquently describes how the combination of attention and focus is a natural barrier to the Inner Critic. He says, "...when we are giving full attention, self-interference is neutralized. In the fullness of focus, there is no room for [the Inner Critic's] fears or doubts."[6] Our internal equilibrium is a direct result of our ability to maintain focus on thoughts that nourish and sustain our positive sense of self. When our Inner Critic reflex kicks in and distracts us from what we're doing, redirecting our focus by thinking different thoughts is what "distracts" us back to our purpose.

## Rehabilitate Your Thoughts

*"When we direct our thoughts properly, we can control our emotions."*
— **W. Clement Stone,** *author, businessman and philanthropist*

Our brains' plastic nature extends to emotions as well. For the purposes of silencing the Inner Critic, this is the mother lode of neuroplasticity. By altering connections between the thinking brain and the emotional brain, research shows that thoughts have the power to transform our emotions, behavior, and mind frames.[7] In fact, the findings from various studies of employing new ways to look at, deal with, and generate thoughts to treat imbalanced mental states caused by distorted thinking have been the stuff that shifts paradigms.

These studies employed mental training based on cognitive therapy, mindfulness training, or a combination of both, which are all forms of meta-cognitive learning. Meta-cognitive learning is the deceptively simple yet powerful practice of learning from observing one's mind and thoughts. What they found is this:

- What and how a person thinks about things can mean the difference between staying depressed or returning to a more positive mind frame with reduced incidence of relapse.[8]

- What and how a person thinks about things can mean the difference between feeling at the mercy of obsessive-compulsive disorder or feeling in control of it.[9]

Using a meta-cognitive approach to apply new methods to deal with self-critical thoughts helps people reverse deep feelings of anxiety, shame, and the tendency to self-attack.[10] Therapies based on meta-cognitive learning target the thinking brain, but they are also highly effective at rebalancing distressed mental states.

Further results from these studies indicate that with the proper structure, our aspiration to banish the Inner Critic is more than attainable – it's likely. Consciously thinking about our thoughts in a different way not only alters the very circuits those thoughts run on,[11] but also reshapes how we process information,[12] and creates a long-term impact on our thinking patterns and brain pathways.[13]

Our minds are so much more powerful than we realize. In our quest to quiet the inner voice of heightened self-criticism, our thoughts can heal.

Through observing our mind and thoughts, we can learn to identify distressing emotional responses and unhelpful thinking about the self and the world. By using a framework for reappraising thoughts that previously have been emotional hooks or triggers, we can relate differently to negative thoughts, feelings, and memories.[14] As we begin to challenge inaccurate thinking and modify beliefs, we can transform unwanted moods and behavior patterns for the better. Our brains can learn how to function differently, and we can break our Inner Critic "reflex."

# Build A Whole New Mind Frame

*"The greatest weapon against stress is our ability to choose one thought over another."*

— **William James,** *psychologist and philosopher*

If you feel like your vociferous Inner Critic has continuously thoroughly thrown you off balance mentally and emotionally, that's because it has. The brain is very good at building a neural structure from negative experiences,[15] which means that the Inner Critic gets stronger from the repetition of toxic thoughts. This weakens our mental foundation. By repeating the Inner Critic's mistaken beliefs, we're inadvertently training our minds to grow ever more self-critical. If we're not open to changing our thoughts, we will continue to harm ourselves with this habitual hurtful thinking.

Fortunately, we've just discovered unequivocally that the brain can change. From your own experience, you know that when you've built skills to a level of mastery, but then you discontinue their use, those skills deteriorate. For example, you took piano lessons for seven years as a child, but it's been so many years that you can no longer read music. It's been ages since you've played tennis, so you've lost your power serve. The Spanish that you spoke so well during your year in Buenos Aires twenty-five years ago has become embarrassingly rusty. When skills lie fallow, they become more difficult to employ with ease.

The fact that the Inner Critic is a result of habitual thinking like a skill or a reflex works to our advantage. We have the power to transform it and take away the source of its strength: the continuation of self-critical thoughts. It's not the average daily thoughts that have the power to encourage robust mental health, however. It's thinking differently by challenging unhelpful habitual thought-patterns and replacing them with new and improved ones that restore the mind to balance. And the exciting part is that this is not hopeful speculation or supposition; this is proven by science. The effects of intentional, mindful effort on brain function, errant neurochemistry, and even the very structure of the brain itself can be observed through neuroimaging.[16]

With the knowledge of neuroplasticity and our capacity to positively affect and transform the emotional brain, in terms of diminishing the strength of the Inner Critic and its hold on our thoughts and emotions, the field of what's possible just opened up exponentially in front of us. In *Train Your Mind, Change Your Brain*, Begley puts it beautifully: "We are not stuck with the brain we were born with but have the capacity to willfully direct which functions will flower and which will wither, which moral capacities emerge and which do not, which emotions flourish and which ones are stilled."[17] This, my friend, is a whole new ballgame. The opportunity to completely transform our Inner Critic dynamic is within our reach if we choose to pursue it.

But guess what? You already have chosen. By reading this book, you have already started upon the journey back to your Creative Self through banishing your Inner Critic.

The choice to focus upon different thoughts is at the very core of this process. For the noxious thoughts that the Inner Critic produces, a mind that questions, challenges, and chooses new thoughts to focus on is the antidote. By thinking new thoughts, the mind can make its own medicine. By intentionally changing our thoughts, we practice "top-down plasticity"[18] which literally changes our brains.

Through thinking new thoughts, the mind can make its own medicine. To begin healing the affliction of an overactive Inner Critic that bars us from our creative selves, our minds are not only going to produce medicine, but also rebuild our creative health, one new thought at a time. With time and practice, our new mind frame will turn the Inner Critic's once insistent roar down to the level of a whisper.

How will we do this? We'll rewire our brains from the inside out through administering a Creative Dose.

# GIVE YOURSELF A CREATIVE DOSE

*"It is not enough that you have a refined sense why and when you become anxious: you must then do something."*

— **Eric Maisel,** *Mastering Creative Anxiety*

From this point forward, the habit of letting your Inner Critic disrupt your confidence and block you from the fullness of your creative capacities is over.

Through practicing certain kinds of mental training, our mind is capable of healing itself. Thus, much in the same way that medicine helps the body heal, the exercises in this book are named "Creative Doses." The Creative Doses help us to create the medicine that is the antidote to the messages of the Inner Critic: new thoughts. Their purpose is to place you in a more clear-thinking and realistic mindset, helping you see the distorted attitudes of your Inner Critic more clearly and stop identifying with them. The exercises are designed to help refortify your sense of self – your Creative Self in particular. And much like medicine, the underlying concepts, practices, and tools of the Creative Doses have a cumulative effect: the more you use and apply them, the more effective they will become. We will also see ourselves and the path we need to take to get back to our creative power more clearly.

You may be thinking, "Think new thoughts?! If it were that easy, I would have done it already!" I hear you. Here's the thing: most of us have not had all of the information or structure we needed to do that. Random, unfocused efforts produce random, unpredictable results. You may have been doing the equivalent of trying to throw darts while lacking both an actual dart and a bull's-eye.

With the Creative Doses, however, we will embark upon a process of deliberate change based on the meeting point of neuroscience and psychology. Following in the footsteps of the studies using metacognitive learning, our process focuses on increasing awareness of our thoughts and emotions and shifting our attention to those that are more positive and supportive. Over time, this practice will effectively build new circuits of self-confidence, giving the well-worn self-critical thinking paths less activity and helping them to fade from disuse.

Despite sounding aggressive, this process of banishing the Inner Critic is actually a kinder, gentler approach. Force is not what's needed. The Inner Critic has strong-arm tactics of manipulation through strong negative emotions down to a science. Fighting the Inner Critic doesn't work, nor does criticizing or judging it. Resisting the Inner Critic doesn't work either – I'm sure you're familiar with the adage, "what you resist, persists." No, if any of those tactics worked well, they would have worked by now. What *will* work is to institute the kind of thinking that is the polar opposite of how the Inner Critic operates. To start creating profound and meaningful change, we are going to become aware of the Inner Critic's thoughts and the feelings that accompany those thoughts. We will look at them impartially, practice self-kindness, show ourselves compassion, and then choose to think and feel something different.

The absolute very first step is to not beat yourself up for having inner critical thoughts. There's nothing wrong with you for having an Inner Critic! It's part of the human condition. Remember, the Inner Critic is a mental protection response that we all have. None of us asked for those situations in which some scathing criticism came out of nowhere. None of us consciously opted to take on the opinions, fears, and mistaken beliefs of the people we looked up to. If you had learned differently, then naturally, you would do differently. Seriously, don't beat yourself up. There's no need to be self-critical about being self-critical. And besides, those days are about to become a thing of the past.

The next step is to acknowledge that you may be nervous about this process. The idea of changing this way of thinking that you've had for so long may make you apprehensive. You may be thinking, "Aren't the self-critical messages what keep me motivated and able to achieve? Doesn't the modified behavior that self-critical thoughts encourage prevent the threat of future criticism from coming to me?" Here's the thing: The longer we listen to the messages, the more we forget who we are and the importance of what we have given up. The more we forget our home, and the farther we wander from our best friend and source of personal power. We lose touch with just how creative we truly are.

I will say this many times throughout this book: we're not our inner critical thoughts. We are so, so much more. Inner critical thoughts hold us back from the prospect of fully realizing our greatness, our ability to feed our souls and contribute to the greater good.

Through the Creative Doses, we'll cultivate a talent for noticing when inner critical thoughts appear or when our behavior is indicative of self-judgment, criticism, or doubt. We'll become gifted in our new capacity to recognize and then soothe feelings of distress when they appear. The ability to choose one thought over another will become our superpower. We will become experts at giving ourselves the very thing that the Inner Critic been trying to create for us all of this time – a sense of safety and reassurance – through applying two powerful tools.

Allow me to introduce you to the practices that are the bedrock of this process and that are at the heart of our journey of transformation: mindfulness and self-compassion. Let's learn what makes these two approaches so incredibly effective in our efforts to banish the Inner Critic, and then practice them with our first Creative Doses.

## Become Full of Mind

*"The gift of mindfulness, then, is that by accepting the present moment you are better able to shape your future moments with wisdom and clarity."*

— **Kristin Neff,** *Self-Compassion: Stop Beating Yourself Up and Leave Insecurity Behind*

Let's be real: having a full-blown Inner Critic episode can be pretty awful. You feel vulnerable and unsure of yourself. (Even if it's just under the surface, it's still there.) Despite feeling as though a giant hole is about to suck you down to one of the nine levels of the Inferno, outwardly you not only need to appear as if nothing is wrong, but you're also somehow still supposed to produce. Yikes!

The Inner Critic encourages something that Kristin Neff, the author of the book *Self Compassion* calls "over-identification," which is "being so carried away by our personal drama that we can't clearly see what is occurring in the present moment."[19] In the midst of over-identifying, it's nearly impossible to realize that your self-critical thoughts are not an accurate reflection of reality. We're so used to being caught up in our ingrained self-critical stories the Inner Critic is telling us that we can't see they are just that: stories.

But without a tool to use or practice to put into place, gaining perspective is easier said than done. We need an approach that acts as a counterbalance, a methodology that will get us out of our internally focused self-critical thought loop, providing the mental distance to not only see the situation and ourselves clearly, but also perspective so that we can make better choices about where to direct our attention and place our focus. And in particular, we need a way to respond more evenly to the times our Inner Critic rears up and self-critical thoughts paralyze us, leaving us feeling vulnerable and defensive. Enter mindfulness.

What is mindfulness? It's the basic human ability to be fully present, aware of where we are and what we're doing, while not being overly reactive to or overwhelmed by what's going on around us. It's a form of meta-awareness: being aware of being aware. Imagine standing outside of your own mind, observing your thoughts and feeling as if they were happening to someone else. You're fully aware but impartial, and therefore not caught up in the story that your mind (or Inner Critic) is spinning about the situation. This is being mindful.

In terms of disrupting our inner critical thoughts, mindfulness is an ideal tool. When we are mindful, we clearly see and accept what is happening in the present moment without reacting with judgment, reflection, or internal commentary.[20] Mindfulness gives us the opportunity to respond rather than just react, and we can move to a place of more balanced and clear thinking. From this place of more balanced and clear thinking, we can acknowledge self-critical thoughts objectively. What's more, regularly practicing mindfulness positively transforms the emotional mind by establishing emotional balance[21] and raising our baseline level of happiness.[22]

Because mindfulness is about attention and focus, it plays well with neuroplasticity. Being mindfully aware of the Inner Critic helps us focus our attention on other thoughts. Then intentionally redirecting attention and focus will decrease the activity of our self-critical thought circuits, so they will eventually be pruned away, eventually altering our brain circuitry for the better. To start banishing the Inner Critic, mindfulness fits our needs perfectly.

Typically, when we want to change something, we think that it involves force and effort. Your inclination may be to try to alter your behavior by actively working to "change" your self-critical thoughts: to tell yourself, "Stop thinking that way!" and then reprimand yourself when you think those thoughts again anyway. Sound familiar? Thankfully, mindfulness is the opposite of that.

The best thing about starting to practice mindfulness is that it's not about making yourself do something. It is more about acceptance and shifting focus. In a lot of ways, it's about giving yourself permission to just sit and look at things without having to think about, process, analyze, react, or respond to them. Doesn't that sound like a refreshing change? It's like giving your brain a vacation!

In using mindfulness to see the Inner Critic's messages as an outcome of it trying to protect you, you can begin to be more impartial. Even more importantly, you begin to instill the practice of not reacting to self-critical thoughts by instead realizing that these thoughts are merely a habitual reaction to a stimulus. Ultimately, you don't have to believe what your Inner Critic is spouting, which gives its messages less weight and validity.

Here's the best part: mindfulness is something we all naturally already possess! However, it's more readily available when we practice it on a daily basis, and gets stronger by exercising it regularly. As it is one of the core practices of our work, let's start building our "mindfulness muscles" right now.

 ## CREATIVE DOSE: Mindful Thought Acceptance

*Purpose: To learn to accept thoughts instead of reacting to them*

Instead of believing everything that passes through your mind, practice observing your thoughts instead. Here are three methods for using mindfulness to become more impartial and less reactive to the thinking reflex that is the Inner Critic.

### Part 1: Mindful Thought Disbelief

Thoughts, emotions, and perceptions aren't necessarily reality. Choosing to believe thoughts is what gives them power, even though it frequently doesn't feel that way. Remember thoughts aren't facts. There's a fantastic bumper sticker that reads, "Don't believe everything you think."

Rather than trying to force yourself to think positively, do this:

*Accept that your mind will produce negative thoughts, which you don't have to believe.*

When you've done that, your mental follow-up to inner critical thoughts could be "Thoughts are not facts" or "I can watch this thought without having to respond to it."[23]

By creating the extra buffer of the awareness of choice, we maintain better control of where we focus our mental energies, and therefore, what we think and consequently, believe.

### Part 2: Acknowledge and Observe

Instead of trying to ignore, fight, suppress, or otherwise control your thoughts and feelings, use mindfulness and look at them as if you were looking at the thoughts and feelings of another person outside of yourself.

Ask yourself these questions:

- Would you react the same way to your own thoughts and feelings?

- Would you judge those thoughts or feelings or be more objective about them?

Acknowledge your thoughts and feelings, but instead of getting wrapped up in them, look upon them with calm interest.

And then, with the same level of detachment, watch as they pass on and others take their place.

## Part 3: The Inner Critic is a Brain Event

Research shows that when patients viewed disordered thinking as "events of the mind" rather than as truth, a different region of the brain fired up, which reduced the risk of relapse.[24] We will do the same with inner critical thoughts: we will think of them as "brain events" rather than the truth about ourselves or a situation.

This impartiality avoids igniting the circuitry associated with self-critical thoughts. It allows us to see situations and ourselves within them more clearly, providing much-needed perspective and insight. By thinking differently about our inner critical thoughts, and seeing them less as the truth about us and more of a habitual protective reflex of the mind, we can then begin to dismiss these thoughts as products of an over-active network or as circuitry that is misfiring, and again, we choose not to respond or react to them.

When your Inner Critic comes up, instead of getting wrapped up in the thoughts of self-judgment, self-criticism or self-doubt, you can think this to yourself:

"Oh, my brain is doing that Inner Critic thing again."

"My Inner Critic circuit is running again."

Then shift your attention back to what you are doing.

This simple practice will prevent you from activating the emotions that were the typical response to these thoughts. By doing this, you can divert the whole thought cascade that used to happen would be diverted.

By thinking differently about the thoughts that previously caused you no end of angst and consternation, you will effectively suppress activity in the part of your brain that regularly generates those self-critical thoughts.

## Awaken Your Compassionate Self

*"Self-compassion can melt away your Inner Critic."*

— **Sandra Bienkowski,** *writer*

In place of self-criticism, we need to actively begin to practice the opposite: self-compassion. Self-compassion is taking our natural capacity for sympathetic concern for others and turning it toward ourselves; particularly during moments of feeling inadequate, disappointed, and suffering. Self-compassion is realizing that self-criticism is the enemy and then acting to reverse its deleterious effects. Research has shown self-compassion to be "a key antidote" to toxic self-criticism.[25] In fact, it is probably the most powerful tool in our toolbox to reverse a tendency to self-criticize.

If you've been in the practice of regularly using harsh self-talk as a motivator, you may be concerned that amping up your levels of self-kindness and compassion will make you lose your "edge," leaving you a lazy and unmotivated slacker. Despite our ability to spend a weekend (or several) binge-watching Netflix, humans aren't inclined to idleness. In fact, our natural tendency is to be engaged and to work. In her book, *Reality is Broken,* author Jane McGonigal says that humans prefer challenge to boredom and that "we prefer productivity to dissipation."[26] Ironically, self-criticism can actually hold us back from reaching our goals;[27] instead, reassuring ourselves through self-kindness and self-compassion motivates us to attain them.

Self-compassion is a critical element in our ability to properly care for ourselves emotionally. Writer Sandra Bienkowski puts it this way:

"Living without self-compassion is like driving a car you never take in for regular maintenance. Eventually your car won't work right and it breaks down."[28] As a tool and practice for maintaining our emotional equilibrium, it has an impressive list of benefits. When we're feeling inadequate, self-compassion helps us to feel more secure and accepted by activating our innate care-giving system and encouraging the release of oxytocin.[29] It decreases insecurity, self-consciousness, and the tendency to compare ourselves with others, and increases confidence through building our belief that we are worthy and capable.[30] It lessens depression and anxiety,[31] and as a result, gives you back energy formerly spent being down on yourself. It can foster emotional resilience and mental toughness and shore up inner strength and courage. Self–compassion helps to increases levels of calm and even joy.

Still not sold? Self-compassion also strongly correlates with achieving mastery in your field and optimal performance.[32] Additional benefits of building up your level of self-compassion are that you will have higher standards for yourself, work harder through enhanced motivation, and take more responsibility for your actions, and you will have more "grit."

But here's the coup de grace: practicing self-compassion helps us to unblock and express creativity, which enables us to access higher levels of creative thinking and creative originality.[33] Self-compassion enables us to nurture our creativity instead of stifle it.

Yes to *all* of this! This dizzying array of the benefits of self-compassion is precisely what we need when our Inner Critic has worn us down.

Self-compassion has two parts: the first is making a conscious effort to stop self-judgment. The second is to actively comfort ourselves, the same as we would a friend in need. To see how the mechanism of self-compassion works, do this: Think about how you would feel toward and treat a dear friend – especially if your friend came to you seeking support during a difficult time in life. What feelings would you extend toward your friend? What would you tell your friend? What kind of language would you use to comfort your friend? Envision this whole scenario playing out in your head. Now take note of and mentally record those feelings and messages. This is your self-compassion template: how you will now treat and talk to yourself in place of self-criticism. You will now treat yourself with the same kindness and care with which you would treat a friend.

How do we put self-compassion into practice? In practicing the positive self-to-self relating of self-compassion, our goals are to become sensitive to our distress, understand the roots of our distress, have empathy for ourselves, and finally view ourselves and our situations without judgment.[34] It's self-compassion that we will use to develop empathy for the distress we've experienced due to the Inner Critic.

The Inner Critic is a purveyor of emotionally damaging messages. Having an overzealous Inner Critic doesn't feel good – in fact, it hurts. You and I know that there's nothing enjoyable about being in the throes of an Inner Critic episode. The first step in beginning to break the Inner Critic reflex through self-compassion is to acknowledge how hurtful it has been all of these years. The constant barrage of negative self-talk and self-criticism wears away at our sense of self and confidence. The original core directive of the Inner Critic was to protect, but the true consequence of its limiting messages is the slow and steady disintegration of our being.

The second step is to upgrade our self-talk. The primary way to put self-compassion into action and start being kinder to ourselves is through changing our self-talk from being critical to being supportive. The trick is to use sympathetic rather than chastising language when we talk to ourselves. Then we reframe our inner dialogue so that we express empathy for ourselves and our circumstances. Through this two-step approach we can begin to silence the Inner Critic.

Self-compassion and mindfulness make a great team: mindfulness is actually one of the keys to self-compassion. Mindfulness gives us the space to treat ourselves with kindness. When we improve our mindfulness skills, we automatically improve our ability to be self-compassionate.

When it comes to banishing the Inner Critic, the combination of mindfulness and self-compassion pack a one-two punch as far as quieting self-critical thoughts, which is why the two are the foundation of our process. Mindfulness increases awareness, enabling us to begin to dismiss the thoughts that thwart our creativity. Then through self-compassion, we can replace these hurtful thoughts with supportive ones.

Self-compassion paves the way to self-acceptance. Ironically, it is in fully accepting ourselves as we are that we open the space for change in our lives. We will transform the dynamic of the Inner Critic by replacing the threat of toxic self-criticism through generating feelings of warmth and compassion. Instead of continuing the habit of beating ourselves up, we will comfort ourselves instead, reassuring ourselves in the face of profound self-doubt. Finally, instead of discounting our creativity and thereby blocking it, we will start to respect and nurture our powerful creative selves and create the space to let for our creativity to flow.

When you start building up your compassion muscles, you'll see that they've always been there at the ready to direct concern not only toward others, but also toward yourself.

 ## Creative Dose: Self-Esteem vs. Self-Indulgence vs. Self-Compassion

*Purpose: To better understand how self-compassion is different*

What are the differences between self-esteem, self-indulgence, and self-compassion?

- **Self-Esteem** is about feeling good about yourself in relationship to others. In the face of pain, self-esteem would have you feel better because you convince yourself that you are still doing better than other people. Negative outcomes of high self-esteem are ignoring or denying stress, pains, and disappointments, and putting others down.

- **Self-Indulgence** is about catering to your whims without true regard for your well-being. In the face of pain and discomfort, self-indulgence would have you distract yourself away from your discomfort or numb it without acknowledging it.

- **Self-Compassion** is about feeling good about yourself and caring for your well-being. In the face of pain, self-compassion has you give yourself empathy, nurturing, and kindness. While self-pity says, "feel sorry for me," self-compassion remembers that everyone suffers, offering comfort in response to suffering.[35]

 ## Creative Dose: The Voice of Support

*Purpose: To begin to cultivate compassion for yourself*

After years of being hard on yourself, you can attest to the fact that with criticism, instead of gaining a sense of comfort and safety, deep down inside, you end up feeling just the opposite.

When we feel kindness, understanding, acceptance, and support from others, it activates our soothing innate caregiving response, and our systems are infused with oxytocin, the hormone of bonding. As a result, our feelings of trust, calm, connectedness, and safety also increase.

Not only that, but when we feel accepted by others, our ability to generate warmth and compassion for ourselves increases as well. Practicing self-compassion eases the sense of threat produced by the Inner Critic and helps create a feeling of being protected.[36] It follows that if we feel a sense of acceptance by others, then we can better generate compassion for ourselves.

I think of this as "compassion by association." We're going to use a technique called a compassionate reframe[37] to trigger this mechanism of using the feeling of compassion to proffer self-compassion. This exercise is adapted from the "Perfect Nurturer" approach developed by Deborah Lee.[38]

**Part 1: Use the Self-Compassion Template**

When you feel yourself starting to think inner critical thoughts, take a moment to close your eyes.

Become aware of your Inner Critic's thoughts.

Then shift attention to your breathing to get grounded in your body and in the present moment.

Then using the self-compassion template described earlier, focus on putting yourself in a kind and empathetic mind frame.

**Part 2: The Embodiment of Warm Support**

Close your eyes again. Think of a person who will be your creativity cheerleader. It could be anyone: a supportive family member, a religious or historical figure, or even a beloved fictional character.

From this point on, this person will represent your ultimate ideal of caring, support, and encouragement. This person radiates the qualities of strength, wisdom, and acceptance without judgment. Imagine that this person wants the absolute best for you and does not wish to see any hurt or harm come to you.

To fully envision this person who is the embodiment of warm support, employ all of your senses to firmly embed the image and feel of this person in your head.

- What does this person look like?

- How is this person dressed?

- What does his or her voice sound like?

- How do you feel when this person gives you kind messages of support?

- Is your support person accompanied by a pleasant smell like baking bread, freshly cut grass, orange blossoms, or the sea?

- Focus on your cheerleader having an attitude of caring for you and extending feelings of warmth towards you. It may help to recollect feelings of warmth you've experienced from others in the past and then draw upon that sensation.

When you are in the midst of mentally beating yourself up for some perceived misstep, invoke your Creativity Cheerleader. Ask yourself, "What would my cheerleader say to me right now?"

Imagine your cheerleader telling you exactly what you need to hear in that moment.

- What does your Creativity Cheerleader say to you?

- How do his or her words and actions make you feel?

Hold the feeling of being supported in your mind to have it anchor itself in your being.

### Part 3: Your Future Creatively Confident Self

In addition to (or instead of) your warm support coming from someone else, you can have it come from yourself. But it's not the you from the present – it's the you from the future who is completely confident about owning her or his creativity.

That's right: your future creatively confident self can be your Creativity Cheerleader to coach you through your Inner Critic angst.

If you need help, think about what you needed to hear when you were in the throes of an Inner Critic attack in the past.

What kind of advice and guidance would you have wanted to hear back then?

- Knowing what you know now, what would you tell your past self?

Now in the present, your badass creative self has come from the future to show you some love and give you some support.

- What kind of wise advice and guidance does your future self offer?

- How does your future self encourage you to be kind to yourself?

No matter who you choose as your creativity cheerleader, to start to build and exercise your self-compassion muscles, keep this voice of guidance and support in mind as you dive into this process.

# GLEAN YOUR INNER CRITIC AFFLICTIONS

*"GUIL: I'm afflicted.*
*ROS: I see.*
*GUIL: Glean what afflicts me."*

— **Tom Stoppard**, *Rosencrantz and Guildenstern are Dead*

Now that we are more familiar with the practices that provide a common thread throughout the work that we are doing, we're well-equipped to set out on the road to change and empowerment.

Our first order of business is to understand the workings of the Inner Critic. It's been doing its job for so long that you may be numb to its presence. But it's there, trust me.

These exercises are designed to help you get a better handle on how your Inner Critic shows up in your life and affects you, and some new ways to start dealing with it.

Ready? Let's do this.

# Recognize Your Inner Critical Voice

*"It's one thing to lie to ourselves. It's another thing to believe it."*
— **Steven Pressfield,** *The War of Art*

The Inner Critic is so strongly convinced of its position that it uses incendiary language to make its point. In fact, this is one of the easiest ways to detect the Inner Critic. Whenever you think in absolutes or hyperbole like, "I'll never get better at this" or "I'm always behind schedule" you can be sure that you're witnessing the Inner Critic's handiwork.

One key practice of meditation is acknowledging thoughts that come up and then ignoring them to focus your attention elsewhere. When you create distance between you and your self-critical thoughts, you'll begin to notice that they are often temporary. One will bubble up into your consciousness, then be replaced by another one, and so on. The only way a thought sticks is when you pay attention to it.

Here's the great thing about employing a more mindful approach to your Inner Critic: you start seeing its comments as just thoughts. You stop seeing whatever your Inner Critic presents as immediate calls to action, accurate, or even true. You'll find that some thoughts are worth paying attention to and some are not. Guess which the ones the Inner Critic generates are? It's a whole new world.

Until you build your awareness of your habitual inner critical thoughts, however, it may help to poke a stick at them to bring them out into the open.

## Creative Dose: The Critical Voices in Your Head

*Purpose: To start to unearth your inner critical thoughts*

You know you have an active Inner Critic, but you've gotten so used to its diatribes that it barely registers with you anymore, right? To bring your inner critical voice back into your consciousness, we're going to use Mad Libs to imitate your Inner Critic.

Fill in the following sentences with the first words that come to you. Write as many variations of each sentence as you can before moving on to the next one. Or you can run through the list multiple times, answering each question differently.

I can't _____ because _____.

I'm not _____ enough.

I'm afraid that I'm _____ because I _____.

I never _____ because I always _____.

I'm afraid that I'll _____ because I _____.

I can't _____ because I'm not as _____ as others.

If I _____ then people will _____.

I shouldn't _____ because I haven't _____.

I _____because my ideas _____.

I'm too _____.

Did you discover some thoughts and beliefs that you didn't know were there? Nice work! Now you are better equipped to start the process of refuting or dismissing them. You may want to do these Mad Libs every couple of months to see if you can bring to light any new mistaken beliefs that have been lying just beneath the surface of your conscious mind.

Here's a bonus question for you:

My biggest fear around my creativity is

_____

_____

_____

Spend time on this question. Is it patently true? Is it circumstantially true? Make a commitment to start challenging this fear.

Remember, we're now using mindfulness to observe our thoughts, so don't believe everything you think.

## Give It A Name

As you are well aware, trying not to think about something never works. The term for this phenomenon is "thought stopping."[39] It's ineffective because it forces you to pay attention to the very thought that you're trying so desperately to avoid. Similarly, attempting to act like your Inner Critic doesn't exist and isn't wreaking havoc in your consciousness when you are having an "episode" is like denying that you're trying to walk with a broken leg. It's painful and unnecessary. Being in denial about something doesn't change the facts. Most of the time, the most helpful thing to do is to call a spade a spade, because then you can take positive action.

If you've never read the young adult science fiction classic *A Wind in the Door* by Madeleine L'Engle, I highly recommend it. In the book, the main character Meg finds that she has a subtle, yet potent superpower: she is able to Name things, and that doing so gives them identity, shape, and substance. I encourage you to channel this power toward recognizing when your Inner Critic makes an appearance, and then putting a name to it.

Make an effort to keep in mind that there's your Inner Critic, and then there's You. You are so much bigger and grander than your Inner Critic. The fact that you can even recognize that there are different parts of yourself at play speaks to the part of your consciousness that is a higher-level observer, who impartially views all that you do, say, and think. Profound, but true.

On a psychological level, this practice creates mental distance between You and the self-critical thoughts. Thinking about your thoughts differently keeps those Inner Critic circuits from firing, which is the key to begin changing them.

Applying the practice of naming your Inner Critic will accomplish several things. First, it increases your awareness of what feels like a threat to the self and your automatic response to it. Second, naming it creates the needed mental distance between you and your inner critical voice. Third, it opens up the space to extend compassion to the part of your psyche that feels attacked and needs comforting.

## Creative Dose: Identify It and Name It

*Purpose: To become more conscious of the Inner Critic's presence*

The sensations may start slowly, creeping over your awareness. You start feeling anxious, your head gets that familiar sense of pressure, and you start making snarky remarks to yourself about your behavior or global disparaging comments about who you are as a person. It's happened so many times before, but now you see it clearly: you're having an Inner Critic attack.

## Part 1: Call It

When you realize you are beginning to feel an impending Inner Critic attack, the best thing you can do stop it is to name it. That's right, name it.

Say something like the following out loud (if you're around people, you can think it in your head):

"My Inner Critic is rearing its head."

"I'm having an Inner Critic attack right now."

"Oh look: my Inner Critic is here." (*waves*)

Anything that helps you realize that the overwrought internal protector is attempting to take over your thinking is useful.

Respond to noticing the appearance of your Inner Critic dispassionately, as if you are remarking upon the grass being green or the sky being blue. The goal is to begin disconnecting from emotions while noticing that inner critical thoughts are coming up.

## Part 2: Give Your Inner Critic a Name

Have fun with it: give your Inner Critic an actual name and a personality.

Give your Inner Critic a name, and when it shows up, you can be like, "Hey Bart."

Continue having fun with this and give your Inner Critic a personality and affect as well. For example, you can imagine your Inner Critic talking with a silly voice and being overly dramatic about everything.

When you've made your Inner Critic less of a prominent presence in your mind, return your attention to the task at hand.

### Part 3: Give Your Inner Critic a Back story

If we're going to personalize the Inner Critic, we might as well go for it, right?

Your Inner Critic came from somewhere, aren't you curious to know from where and why?

Envision in your mind's eye who your Inner Critic is and what it's all about.

Then sit down and write it out your Inner Critic's origin story. You can use this framework to get started:

Hello, I'm your Inner Critic and my name is _____.
I was born in _____, because _____
_____...

Keep adding to the story until you feel complete with it.

What did you discover about your Inner Critic that you didn't know before?

## Learn the Guises of the Inner Critic

The rest of this book is devoted to exploring the different forms of how the Inner Critic shows up with regard to creativity. What you'll discover is that the Inner Critic is a shape-shifter, assuming various guises to most effectively push you to avoid future threats to the self.

At keynotes and in workshops, I often lead an exercise I call an indoor "snowball fight." In this exercise, audience members write down the answer the question "What is your biggest fear around creativity?" on a blank piece of paper and then throw their balled-up paper at each other. These "snowballs" have become the best unlikely research tool. After gathering and compiling the responses over several months, I noticed similarities, trends, and frequently verbatim responses. It is from this information that I've determined the forms of the Inner Critic that affect creative people the most.

Some of the forms of the Inner Critic I've identified are common psychology terms. For those that aren't, I've created monikers for them.

## Creative Dose: The Many Faces of The Inner Critic

*Purpose: To recognize the various guises of the Inner Critic*

Read through this list of the various forms of the Inner Critic and put a check by each one that strikes a chord with you.

- ❑ **Judgment Dread:** You have a paralyzing fear of having your ideas and work be judged and criticized by others. You hold yourself and your ideas back and are loathe to put yourself out there creatively. You feel crushed by feedback and criticism. For fear of being judged, you lack self-trust.

- ❑ **High Self-Criticism:** Little or nothing that you do creatively is right, good, or acceptable. You are overly critical of your ideas and frequent dismiss them. You're rarely pleased with your work and consequently discount your efforts.

- ❑ **Deficiency Anxiety:** You feel that you are somehow intrinsically lacking or inadequate at your core, and that you, your ideas, and your creations aren't good enough.

- ❏ **Proficiency Anxiety:** You're afraid of not knowing enough, not being good at what you do, or not being able to keep up with acquiring new knowledge and skills.

- ❏ **Originality Anxiety:** You believe everything you create must be new, unique, and cutting-edge, and if it is not, that it doesn't have any merit or value.

- ❏ **Comparison Syndrome:** You feel inadequate and therefore can't see your unique brilliance. You experience despair from envy of others' success, feeling like a failure in comparison.

- ❏ **Creativity Denial:** You're in full-on denial about having any creativity or being creative at all. By holding on to this belief, you make it true, blocking the generation of creative ideas. This behavior starts a self-perpetuating cycle in which you are less able to come up with original ideas. It's a self-imposed state of creativity paralysis.

- ❏ **Overwhelm Obstruction:** You are so focused on the stuff you feel you "have" to do that you don't have the bandwidth to divert to creative thinking. Being creatively inspired seems like a pipe dream and something for other people. Doing anything creative is yet another thing to do on the long list of things that are already on your plate.

- ❏ **Creativity Misgivings:** You sometimes think of yourself as creative, but you don't trust your creativity at all – you see your creativity as fleeting, unreliable, and capricious. You live in perpetual fear that your creativity will dry up and that your capacity to come up with any more ideas will disappear.

# Know Thy Inner Critic

The previous exercises have helped us build awareness as to when our Inner Critic shows up. Now you can more clearly identify your inner critical thoughts when they come up and call out your Inner Critic when it tries to take over your thinking (and you may have even given it a name). You're starting to calmly observe inner critical thoughts instead of reacting to them, and you've become more familiar with the various forms of the Inner Critic.

Now it's time to go deep.

For our minds to start making the medicine of new thoughts, we need to know exactly what we're treating.

To start banishing your Inner Critic in earnest, you need to go beyond merely knowing about the different forms of the Inner Critic – you need to know which form plagues *you* the most.

## Creative Dose: Identify Your Inner Critic Achilles' Heel

*Purpose: To determine which aspects of the Inner Critic are most relevant to you*

Like the Greek mythological hero Achilles, we all have a particular area where our Inner Critic is the most vocal, doing its best to trigger fear and inhibit our behavior to keep us safe. I think of this as our Inner Critic Achilles' heel.

To see which versions of the Inner Critic are most relevant to you, complete the Inner Critic Achilles' Heel Questionnaire. Which of the phrases closely describe thoughts you've had or have regularly?

**Inner Critic Achilles' Heel Questionnaire**

| CHAPTER | NAME | QUESTION | TRUE | FALSE |
|---------|------|----------|------|-------|
| 3 | Judgment Dread | I enjoy sharing my ideas to get feedback. | ⊖ | ⊕ |
| | | I obsess about any criticism I get, replaying it in my head. | ⊕✓ | ⊖ |
| | | I constantly judge how I'm creative. | ⊕ | ⊕✓ |
| 4 | High Self-Criticism | I'm rarely satisfied with my own work. | ⊕ | ⊕✓ |
| | | When I see that somebody else has a better idea, I drop mine. | ⊕ | ⊖✓ |
| | | My work always looks better to me after I've been away from it for a while. | ⊕✓ | ⊕ |
| 5 | Deficiency Anxiety | I don't feel that I've accomplished enough in my career. | ⊕✓ | ⊖ |
| | | I have a lot of creative talent, even if I don't always show it. | ⊕✓ | ⊕ |
| | | I'm nothing like the other creative people I know. | ⊕ | ✓⊖ |
| 5 | Proficiency Anxiety | I keep all of my technical skills sharp and keep abreast of trends. | ⊖ | ⊕✓ |
| | | I'm slow at coming up with new ideas | ⊕ | ⊖✓ |
| | | Collaboration is for people who don't know enough to do it all themselves. | ⊕ | ⊕✓ |

| CHAPTER | NAME | QUESTION | TRUE | FALSE |
|---------|------|----------|------|-------|
| 5 | Originality Anxiety | I don't like working on something unless it's my idea. | ⊘ | ⊘ ✓ |
| | | I find the ideas I come up with interesting and compelling. | ⊘ ✓ | ⊘ |
| | | I'm just a copycat. | ⊘ | ⊘ ✓ |
| 6 | Comparison Syndrome | When my friends are successful I find my own progress lacking. | ⊘ | ⊘ ✓ |
| | | I'm more focused on my own goals than what other peopleare doing. | ⊘ ✓ | ⊘ |
| | | Everybody seems to come up with better ideas than me. | ⊘ | ⊘ ✓ |
| 6 | Comparison Syndrome | When my friends are successful I find my own progress lacking. | ⊘ | ⊘ ✓ |
| | | I'm more focused on my own goals than what other people are doing. | ⊘ ✓ | ⊘ |
| | | Everybody seems to come up with better ideas than me. | ⊘ | ⊘ ✓ |
| 7 | Creativity Denial | I'm more analytical than creative. | ⊘ | ⊘ ✓ |
| | | I totally trust in my ability to come up with new ideas. | ⊘ ✓ | ⊘ |
| | | People who tell me I'm creative are just being nice | ⊘ | ⊘ ✓ |

| CHAPTER | NAME | QUESTION | TRUE | FALSE |
|---------|------|----------|------|-------|
| 7 | Overwhelm Obstruction | Being creative takes a long time. | ⊘ (checked) | ⊖ |
| | | I often have so many ideas I don't know where to begin | ⊘ (checked) | ⊖ |
| | | I enjoy taking the time to be creative. | ⊖ (checked) | ⊘ |
| 7 | Creativity Misgivings | I must feel creative and inspired in order to create. | ⊘ | ⊖ (checked) |
| | | I trust my ability to come up with a lot of ideas when I'm working. | ⊖ (checked) | ⊘ |
| | | I'm nervous that at some point my creativity will run out. | ⊘ | ⊖ (checked) |

For every answer where you checked a circle with a vertical line, the score is 1. For every answer where you checked a circle with a horizontal line, the score is -1. The highest number you can get for a triad is 3, and the lowest is -3.

A negative score means you tested strong for the issues covered in that chapter. A positive score means you did not.

Each upcoming chapter in the book is devoted to a particular guise of the Inner Critic. We'll learn different ways to address each one, with targeted information followed by exercises designed to immediately put the concepts into practice.

For which forms of the Inner Critic did you score the highest negative or positive ? If you like, go directly to that chapter so that you can get the low-down on that form of the Inner Critic and start getting to work on quieting it immediately.

Or you can go ahead and read the book in the order it's written and discover what you can do for the other guises as well.

# IT ALL BEGINS WITH THE FIRST STEP

*"There is nothing you can't achieve with time, attention, and effort."*

— **James Shelton,** *former Deputy Secretary, U.S. Department of Education*

One of the most reliable ways to feel strong, confident, and powerful is to access and express creativity. Through the process of banishing our Inner Critic and reclaiming our creative power, we pave the way for the awe-inspiring unselfconsciousness that we admire in musicians, athletes, and other performers to shine through us. We will learn to distinguish between the voices of the Inner Critic and of the Creative Self. And ultimately, we will fulfill our soul's longing to become more of who we are, let our ideas out into the world, and make it better by doing so.

I said it earlier, but it bears repeating: reclaiming creativity is an act of courage. Before, we may have balked in the face of our fears that the Inner Critic amplified. But now that we are fortified with the combination of the knowledge that our brain is actually our ally and with potent tools for transformation, we are more than ready to meet head-on whatever comes up in this process of getting back to our creative selves.

Our challenge: Remove mental obstacles in order to tap into our creative power.

Our goal: Unleash our suppressed creative potential and return to our Creative Self.

Our tools: Neuroplasticity, harnessing attention and focus, mindfulness, self-compassion, and the Creative Doses.

It's time to begin the work of silencing the voice of self-doubt and unleashing your creativity. With time, attention, and effort, you'll see a marked change in your creative life.

The people who seem to effervesce ideas and effortlessly unleash their creativity know where their power lies and have found their way home. The remainder of this book contains the road map back to your Creative Self, so now we will embark upon a journey to do the same.

Ready? Let the banishing begin!

# REJECTION

**3**

## CHAPTER 3 | "PEOPLE WILL THINK MY WORK IS DUMB"
## *- JUDGMENT DREAD*

**This chapter examines:**

*Attachment*

*Belonging*

*Negativity Bias and Fear Conditioning*

*Fear of Rejection*

*Cognitive Distortions*

*Confirmation Bias*

*Awfulizing*

*Positive Optimism*

*Embracing Uniqueness*

*Self-Acceptance*

*Learning From Criticism*

*Building Self-Trust*

*Choosing to Contribute*

*"You can either be judged because you created something or ignored because you left your greatness inside of you."*

— **James Clear,** *author and entrepreneur*

When I started playing basketball in middle school, by my own assessment, I wasn't very good. And to my mind, that was a huge problem for an African-American girl who measured 5 feet 11 inc hes tall. As an adult, I'm now 6 foot 1 (185 cm), and my height is no longer an issue, but from the ages of 13 to 14 it caused me a great deal of angst.

Practice was great and I loved it. I enjoyed learning the plays, building my skills, and getting stronger. Furthermore, my team had a number of truly gifted athletes, evidenced by two consecutive seasons of being close to undefeated. One of them was my lifelong friend Anita, who was also naturally tall like me. Anita was a fantastic player and was one of the stars of the team. I didn't feel I could hold a candle to her basketball abilities.

The games were another story altogether. I didn't play in the games. More specifically, I *wouldn't* play in the games.

At the prospect of an upcoming game, my sense of dread would slowly start to build within me.  Whether at home or away games, my modus operandi was always the same. Dutifully, I went through the motions of putting on my uniform and doing the pre-game warm-up, doing my best to ignore my increasing anxiety. However, immediately after the team huddle, I would attempt to make myself as invisible as possible. I became a master at determining the exact location on the bench that ensured the maximum amount of invisibility: not the last person on the end (too easy to see!), but rather two or three girls in, so that I could try to disappear in between them.

Unfortunately, my hoped-for invisibility was never as long-lasting as I wished. At some point during every game, my coach Ms. Conine would lean down and call me. "Denise!" she'd say, beckoning me to her. Instead of jumping up with enthusiasm, I was engulfed in panic. My stomach would tighten with anxiety. I would beg, plead, and cajole her not to put me in: "I'm not ready, Ms. Conine! Let's wait until later. Put me in at the end of the game instead – I'll be ready then." Much of the time it worked, but occasionally she would be immune to my pleadings. Admitting defeat, I would grudgingly give my jersey number to the folks at the referee stand to be put in the game.

Why was I so desperate to avoid playing in the basketball games? To put it bluntly, I was a very tall black girl. I was convinced beyond a shadow of a doubt that everyone watching the games expected me to be an amazing player, and despite my efforts in practice, I was sure that I wasn't that player. What's more, while I had slender arms and legs, I was "chunky" around the middle. At one point during that time, in an attempt to motivate me to slim down, my well-intentioned cousin Linda drew a quick sketch of an plump oval with two long lines coming out of the bottom and two shorter lines coming out of each side and a smaller oval on top. She pushed it across the kitchen table to me. "This is what you look like," she said. So in addition to being afraid of being judged for my lack of prowess in basketball, I was also terrified of being seen by masses of people who I believed would invariably judge my slightly overweight body as awkward and wrong, with no possibility of ever becoming attractive. Despite fervent encouragement from my coach, I would not go onto the game floor. To me, it felt akin to setting myself up to be attacked by hundreds of unseen yet mighty assailants.

Looking back now, I can see how incredibly virulent my own Inner Critic was, paralyzing me into inaction to protect me from the prospect of being judged and criticized. By not playing in the games, I held myself back from building skill by learning from playing against people who were better than I was, but also from having fun. The irony is that had I gone ahead and played in the games, I would have been able to develop even sooner into the strong athlete that I eventually became. Because it wasn't other people who were judging me, it was really me who was judging my own self. In doing so, I created my own kind of setback.

I'm sure you've had an equivalent experience in your own life, and can totally relate to how the intensity of the fear of judgment and criticism can prevent us from expanding our range of skills and reaching our potential.

## ARE THEY JUDGING ME? THEY'RE JUDGING ME, AREN'T THEY?

Are you blocking yourself from sharing your ideas and allowing your true Creative Self to shine through because of fear of being judged and criticized? See if any of these points mirror your thoughts and feelings.

Do you hold yourself back due to a deep-seated fear of what others think of you or your work and how they will judge you? Does a high fear of rejection keep you from sharing your ideas and being fully who you are?

- ❑ "I'm afraid that people will think my work is dumb and laugh at what I produce."

- ❑ "I fear that people won't like what I make, will think it is bad, and then think less of me."

- ❑ "I'm afraid that somebody is going to tear into my writing and tell me that I'm all wrong and stupid."

- ❑ "I'm afraid of REJECTION."

Do you fear that your ideas are so "out there" that no one will really get them, and because of that, no one will support them (or you)?

- ❑ "I'm afraid others will see my ideas as being too crazy to be plausible."

- ❑ "I'm afraid that no one will get my meaning."

- ❑ "I'm afraid that it will be hard to get others on board with my ideas, and that no one will support them."

# DREADING JUDGMENT

*"All humans want/need to feel loved and accepted, because in our evolved past our very survival may have depended on it."*
**— The Compassionate Mind Foundation**

It's a normal workday, but for some reason, today you can't seem to get past your fear that your client won't like anything you produce. Or you're incredibly apprehensive about the prospect that your manager will be disappointed in your work. Or you practically have an anxiety attack envisioning someone, anyone, negatively judging your creations. You're trying to get into the creative zone, but you're frustrated because your thinking process has totally shut down. What's wrong? Actually, this is not at all surprising: the fear of being judged and criticized is a huge block to creativity, and self-conscious thinking quite specifically blocks getting into creative flow.[1]

Unfortunately, we see these scenarios far too often on a professional level. For fear of being judged and criticized, we stick to safe solutions and suggestions. We edit the essence of ourselves out of our work to make it more acceptable and palatable for the masses. We may become inflexible and rebel by shutting down any input that could be helpful.

But this form of the Inner Critic, which I call Judgment Dread, has even farther-reaching ramifications for us on a personal level. Fear of judgment and criticism causes us to become perpetually anxious about what others may be thinking about us. As a result, we stay locked in old patterns of behavior that don't serve us. We keep ourselves average, avoiding taking risks or trying anything new, and we stagnate emotionally. We suppress ourselves and hold ourselves back, curbing our actions and shutting down possibilities for our future. But is this how we want to live? Absolutely not!

If you judge and criticize yourself occasionally, don't beat yourself up for it. Everyone does it to some degree, and it is part of being a human in human society. However, if the fear of being judged and criticized has become a predominant part of how you see the world, how you operate within it, and how you relate to yourself, it's a problem. The fears and the self-consciousness that result from being afraid of being judged and criticized shut down the potential for a satisfying life, creative or otherwise. If you have a strong fear of being judged or having your work judged, learning how to manage Judgment Dread is crucial to letting your creativity flow again.

With the previous chapter's focus on neuroscience being an integral part of starting our process of reclaiming creativity, it's easy to forget that there are psychological elements to the origins of the Inner Critic as well. In the first chapter, I suggested that the Inner Critic was a "proactive mental threat-to-self system." Based on the various psychological tools and tendencies of thought that the Inner Critic assembles to meet its primary directive of protection, the term "system" is apt.

A system is a set of interrelated and interconnected elements that together form a complex whole and that continually influence each other to maintain the system's existence and to achieve its goals. The Inner Critic deftly employs a combination of our primal need to attach and belong, the brain's tendency to scan for and catalogue threats, distorted thinking, and our tendency to seek confirmation of our beliefs and convictions. This special blend of mental inclinations is what gives the Inner Critic its proclivity for hypervigilance in the name of trying to protect the self. In the face of threats – both real and imagined – this very finely tuned Inner Critic "system" goes into high alert mode.

But it's the use of a few of the more primal aspects of our mind that explains why the Inner Critic becomes such an influential force in our psychological makeup. The fear of being judged and criticized stems from the drive to ensure that our basic needs are met and that we'll be able to create the next generation. In other words: survival.

## UNDERSTAND THE NEED TO BELONG

*"We are evolved to strive for a sense of belonging, acceptance and respect in the minds of others because over millions of years these have been highly conducive to our survival and prosperity."*

Compassionate Mind Foundation

When determining what our essential needs are, we need look no further than psychologist Abraham Maslow's Hierarchy of Needs. The first tier is related to the physiological necessities that we can't live without: air, water, and food. When we can sustain our bodies, we need to achieve a sense of safety, protecting ourselves from the elements and other creatures with shelter and clothing. The next level of importance is the need to belong a group to fulfill the need to reproduce and carry on the next generation, known as "belongingness." But with regard to the Inner Critic, it's even simpler than this progression. Without meeting the human emotional need to affiliate with and be accepted by a group, getting the first two levels of needs met – physical survival and safety – is extraordinarily difficult. How do we get to belongingness? We become attached.

Attachment – an emotional bond with another person – evolved as a solution to threats to safety in the environment. Attachment helped with an infant staying close to the parents, which improved the child's chances for survival and staying alive to adulthood.

In terms of care for offspring, the purpose of protecting them was to ensure that they would live to reproduce. However, protection not only meant keeping the child out of harm's way in the natural environment, but also within the social world of humans. Survival, for both caretakers and children alike, depended on being liked by the group. Caretakers are responsible for making sure that children understand the norms of the social group and follow social expectations to avoid negative sentiment from others. To encourage socially acceptable behavior and to maintain good social standing, caretakers used intense language in the form of criticism, triggering strong emotions that ensured that the messages would stick. We're incredibly dependent upon the positive feelings of others towards us, as good feelings from others towards us generate a sense of safety. As a result, much of our everyday thinking is related to creating positive feelings and impressions in the minds of others.[2]

In many ways, attachment and belongingness can be seen as the source of the development of the Inner Critic, but it's identifying with internalized negative messages from others that gives the Inner Critic its shape and identity.

How people perceive us is of such high importance that we are prone to take on the values and belief systems of those around us, further increasing our sense of belongingness and safety. Herein lies the trap, however. We don't merely take on their values. We also take on and internalize their messages to us about ourselves, both positive and negative. It is the internalization and mimicking of the strong criticisms we've heard to modify our behavior for social acceptance that creates the Inner Critic.

But the need to belong doesn't stop there. For our now attached and belonging selves, maintaining good standing with the group is the top priority. To protect us, the Inner Critic amps up its surveillance and actively scans for the threat of a loss of good feelings from the group in the form of rejection.

## Know Negativity Bias and the Nature of Fear

*"We are something of a tragic species because our minds are easily taken over by ancient brain systems that give rise to fears, passions, and desires for...self-protection."*

— **Dr. Paul Gilbert,** *founder of Compassion Focused Therapy*

Even though he proved Mr. Jones wrong, Eliott can still recall with vivid detail the moment when his high school guidance counselor told him that he didn't think he was college material. He can almost hear the shouts of the students in the gym next door, smell the slightly damp odor of the small, windowless office, feel the rough texture of the plastic chair under his moist palms that he had sandwiched underneath his thighs to contain his sense of shock as his hopes for the future evaporated in front of his eyes.

Interestingly, Eliott doesn't remember the same level of detail from another event that same week. His shop teacher complimented him on the oar that he had honed from salvaged wood. Through college, he constantly battled the feeling that with his working class background he didn't really belong in university. But he worked through his misgivings to get his MFA, with a specialty in found object sculpture.

The first experience, but not the second, embedded itself so thoroughly into Eliott's memory because of the brain's tendency to focus on the negative. Evolutionary psychologists refer to this as "negativity bias." Rick Hanson, author of *Wired for Happiness* and *Buddha's Brain* is fond of saying "the brain is like Velcro for negative experiences and Teflon for positive ones."[3]

According to Hanson, for a positive experience to transfer to our long-term memory, we have to put effort toward holding the experience in our minds. In stark contrast, when a negative experience does happen – particularly early in our lives – the brain lights up like a like a sports arena scoreboard. Then fear conditioning, an evolutionary self-defense mechanism that enables us to acquire and store information about de facto or potentially harmful circumstances, kicks in. The mind embeds the experience into long-term memory, easily accessible for future need and indelibly marked in our minds. We tend to overlook the positive in our lives, and focus on the negative as if our lives depended upon it – because back hundreds of thousands of years ago, it did.

In the natural environment, negative information typically signifies a threat. Imagine yourself as a hunter-gatherer, out exploring a new area for food. Ahead of you, just off to the right, you notice a slight movement in the bush, and then a brightly colored snake emerges and slithers across the path. A while later, a lovely winged butterfly flits in front of you. Which do you think your brain will catalogue and then remind you of the next time you are in that location and how do you think you'll act? Because the snake is considered a threat, it is far more important than the ephemeral beauty of a butterfly to a brain bent on survival. If you returned to that spot, you'd be on the lookout for snakes and would exercise caution or even be afraid. You probably would not, however, look for butterflies.

These days, most of us don't have to worry about de facto snakes in the grass. But living in the modern world and dealing with people means we are strongly influenced by the need to belong. As social beings, we are most alert to threats that come from those with whom we are closest. Through the ancient circuitry of negativity bias, our brains nonetheless find the emotional equivalent of "snakes" and react to them: when looking at and evaluating ourselves as well as others, we tend to weigh negative facts more heavily than positive ones.[4] Then fear conditioning facilitates our ability to remember criticism and judgment far more easily than we do praise.

To be able to protect us in an effective way, we need to upgrade the ancient circuitry running the Inner Critic "system" with the latest update on our present lives and our present emotional needs. To facilitate this upgrade, we'll employ the more recently evolved part of our brains and utilize the new habit of mindfulness that we are starting to build. Hanson elaborates our goal in a recent online article: "...a mind that sees real threats more clearly, acts more effectively in dealing with them, and is less rattled or distracted by exaggerated, manageable, or false alarms."[5] Being more aware of what your brain and mind do when sensing a potential threat in the form of being judged and receiving criticism will encourage the development of a calmer part of the mind.

With this new information and guidance, our brains can start to respond only to true threats instead of potentially fabricated ones.

 ## Creative Dose: F.E.A.R.

*Purpose: To challenge the fears that underlie fears of being judged*

The purpose of fear is to protect us from danger in the form of a perceived loss of safety or personal security or a threat of physical pain. In order to not feel fear, people work to avoid threats. The problem is that a strong tendency towards negativity makes us see threats everywhere, and instead of dealing with them, we go into avoidance.

Indeed, the acronym F.E.A.R. is sometimes described as meaning F*ck Everything and Run. Let's be honest, this is actually pretty accurate – this is what we often do when faced with a situation that scares us, intimidates us, or holds the potential of our being judged or criticized. We've all done it at some point in our lives. We've abandoned a project because we felt overwhelmed or out of our league. We've let a strong potential business prospect languish into nothingness. Or we've preemptively shot down every idea we have for fear that others will think it's stupid. The popular expression "I can't EVEN" is a strong indicator of a trend for us to turn away from anything that seems to be too much. The problem is much like the 1970s horror movie *When a Stranger Calls*.[6] The threat is not coming from the outside world, it's coming from inside of our own heads – and try as we might, we can't run away from ourselves.

There is a great quote from the movie *After Earth*[7] which I feel is a great tool for helping us to put fear into perspective. The character Cypher Raige says this: "Fear is not real. It is a product of the thoughts you create. Do not misunderstand me. Danger is very real. But fear is a choice."

The better-known description for F.E.A.R. is False Evidence Appearing Real. In contrast, this way of looking at fear is empowering. Combined with the wisdom of Cypher's quote, we have a powerful tool for becoming more aware of our reactions and beginning the process of reframing them. Through mastering our fears, we can begin to conquer the Inner Critic, and in particular, our fear of being judged and criticized.

The next time you are feeling afraid of something like showing your work to others to get feedback or even a big client presentation, take a mental step back from the situation and really assess it.

Ask yourself this question:

- Is there actual immediate *danger*? In other words, will your safety be compromised, will you be hurt physically, or is your security at risk?

If not, then realize that your fear is coming from **thoughts** you are generating about events *that have not happened yet*.

Therefore, instead of feeling fear, you can start to feel hope, because you are in a position to affect what will happen in the future. If you feel like you are in a hopeless situation, it's the perfect time to get help from friends or professionals.

Let's take "False Evidence Appearing Real" to the next level with an even more positive spin on F.E.A.R.: Face Everything And Rise. By facing the fears that exist solely in your head, like the fear of being judged and criticized, you create the opportunity to move yourself to a completely different place, triumphing over the limiting thoughts of the Inner Critic.

Don't be tricked into believing there is a threat when one truly does not exist. You have options: you don't have to sit in fear.

# Reconcile the Fear of Rejection

*"Evolution has programmed us to feel rejection in our guts. This is how the tribe enforced obedience, by wielding the threat of expulsion. Fear of rejection isn't just psychological, it's biological."*

— **Steven Pressfield**, *The War of Art*

Because of his father's international career, Matthew grew up on multiple continents. Conceived in Africa, born in Australia, and then flown back to Africa at the age of 6 weeks, he lived in Gabon until the age of 2. Although his childhood memories from that time are hazy, he clearly remembers his nanny, whom he adored. She would sing and dance all day with Matthew on her hip, practically treating him as her own son. When Matthew started talking, unsurprisingly, it was in Swahili. And when music came along in his life, dancing with his nanny not only gave him a deep sense of complex rhythms, but also the ability to perfectly imitate any dance step someone was doing.

Dismayed that their son was completely out of touch with the culture of his heritage, his parents moved the family back to Australia. They bought a property on the edge of the outback in Western Australia that was lovely and sprawling, but the natural environment had its dangers, including snakes. To keep Matthew safe, his father instructed him to sing as he walked in the bush to alert the snakes to his presence. Matthew spent countless contented hours wandering through the bush and singing his heart out.

When he got a little older, he started attending a private all-boys school, and teachers discovered his talent. They asked him to perform at assemblies in front of the whole school, which Matthew would throw himself into wholeheartedly. All was well until one day after school on the bus home, when a group of boys attacked him. Tying his hair to a pole on the bus, they beat him up while teasing him about singing and dancing. This went on for months. Each day when he got home, he was a mess physically, but he was in even worse shape mentally. He vowed to never perform again – it was far, far too dangerous.

Throughout his teens and early adulthood, a rage simmered, emerging as abuse to those close to him. His behavior was driven by fear and no longer by joy. Matthew finally decided to look at his fears of expressing his creativity in the way that was most natural for him and heal this wounded part of his soul. He started dabbling in improv, which led to him to sing again and to begin performing poetry to audiences all over the world. Doing Kung Fu helped him to gravitate back to dancing. Now Matthew is a creative powerhouse who is a published author, owns two creative businesses that have been succeeding for over a decade, has spoken at TED and several other of the world's premier thought-leadership conferences, and coaches individuals to awaken their innate creativity.

Thankfully, most of us had not had such a physically violent experience to deter us from expressing our creativity, but when we feel judged by or receive strong criticism from others, it can feel incredibly threatening nonetheless. Why? Because of contempt.

People are shown contempt when they are not only disliked, but also deemed less than, worthless, and undeserving of respect. When people are shown contempt, their position in the group is in the most jeopardy, because contempt leads to a person being considered the "other," then considered not to be valuable, and ultimately outcast from the society. To the older parts of our brains, contempt equals rejection, and thus difficulty surviving. Contempt is the antithesis of belonging.

Contempt is communicated overtly by verbal insults, name-calling, and physical violence. However, it is frequently conveyed more subtly nonverbally, especially through tone of voice.[8] Thanks to negativity bias combined with our deep need to belong, our brains are subconsciously on constant lookout for threat in the form of contempt, and we learn to read people incredibly quickly, also known as thin-slicing.[8] That's right: whether we know it or not, subliminally we are tuned into every micro-expression, every subtle gesture and change in body language, every intake of breath and other subtle verbal communication cues. Back in the day, lacking awareness of these cues made our chances for survival very slim, so we developed and finely honed these skills to maintain our good standing with the group.

When positive feelings toward us seem on the decline or no longer exist, we feel vulnerable and threatened – and rightly so. In the older part of our brains, the prospect of rejection is equated so strongly with perishing that it immediately triggers a fear response. The problem is that this primordial drive to avoid contempt is still alive and well in modern times.

Much like Matthew vowing to never perform again, at some point in our lives, we've avoided putting ourselves into situations where we will potentially be judged and criticized to avoid this form of rejection. In the name of protection, the Inner Critic takes all of the criticisms and comments that we've heard over the course of our lives, internalizes them, and uses them to try to modify our behavior to avoid rejection. We learn to relate to ourselves as others have related to us[9] – we start to self-judge. Given this, Judgment Dread's effect of shutting down our creative efforts makes total sense. Since being unvalued by the group is such an innate fear, this form of the Inner Critic is set on obstructing our creativity, works really hard to hold us back from sharing our ideas, and further pushes us to become our own worst judges and our own harshest critics.

Fortunately, our access to the "tribe" these days is in many ways better than ever. With the ease of communication and the advent of being able to travel practically anywhere in the world, the concept of "the group" or our "tribe" is greatly expanded. Even if we don't fit with our family, town or city, country, culture, or religion of origin, many of us now have the freedom to set out into the world and find the people with whom we do fit: people who will accept us, who will fulfill the need to belong that is an inherent part of our being human, and who will also help to support our creativity.

Raising our awareness of our deep-seated need to belong and avoidance of rejection will transform it from both overtly and subtly influencing our behavior. We can't control people's tone of voice, but we also read a lot from expressions. Let's take conscious control of the need to feel validation from others by reading it on their faces. Instead of letting our search for the threat of contempt run in the background, we can hack our brain's tendency to thin-slice and instead create a situation in which we see the face of validation and confirmation when we need it.

## Creative Dose: A Face of Approval

*Purpose: To trigger a sense of safety in the brain*

Charles Schwab has said "I have yet to find the man, however exalted his station, who did not do better work and put forth greater effort under a spirit of approval than under a spirit of criticism." It turns out that these are not just empty words. One study showed that people are better able to cope with setbacks and challenges when they were primed with an approving face of a professor.[10] Our brains respond immediately and positively to reading approval on the faces of those we respect. This is great news – it means that with support we can leverage the brain's propensity to do better as a way to mitigate rejection. Imagine the face of someone you care about who has been consistently supportive of you during your whole life. Imagine that you have a photo of the person smiling at you with an air of, "You've got this!"

You can also use an actual photo if you have one. Another powerful option is to draw a picture of this person, if you're so moved. As you're drawing it, infuse the experience of feeling supported into the process of creating the image, which will further strengthen your mental and emotional association when you look at the picture.

Post the photo or picture where you do your creative work if you can. If any fears of rejection come up while you are attempting to create, take several moments to either envision that person's face in your mind's eye, or to gaze at the photo and imagine the person's approval of you and confidence in your capabilities.

You can also use this tool whenever you experience any kind of setback. For example, you didn't make the improv team tryouts, they chose another candidate for the job you really wanted, or your book proposal got rejected – again. See your face of approval and know that you're going to be all right.

# SEE REALITY MORE CLEARLY

*"You take the blue pill — the story ends, you wake up in your bed and believe whatever you want to believe. You take the red pill — you stay in Wonderland, and I show you how deep the rabbit hole goes. Remember: all I'm offering is the truth. Nothing more."*

— **Morpheus,** *a character in the movie The Matrix*

We've already seen how negativity bias influences our perceptions and makes us more sensitive to judgment and criticism. But the Inner Critic's way of operating is also influenced by two other forms of our inclination to depart from rational thinking and good judgment, otherwise known as cognitive biases. Cognitive biases are like filters on the real world that create an alternate reality of sorts, a distorted perception of what's real and the realm of what's possible for us. There are actually multiple versions of reality; it just depends on which is influencing us and coloring our thoughts.

The thoughts generated by the Inner Critic appear to be rational, based in fact, and therefore unquestionably true, but that's their danger. The deceptively logical nature of the Inner Critic persuades us to follow its restrictive rules without even being aware of it. But the messages of the Inner Critic and the thinking that it encourages – particularly with regard to the fear of being judged and criticized – often couldn't be further from the truth. Instead of seeing situations as they are, we start to see them as we fear they could be. Much like looking at an object through water, although you're seeing the item, you're not seeing its clear, true shape.

When you realize that part of the Inner Critic's modus operandi is to create an alternate version of reality using distorted thinking, you have a choice of which reality you will decide to live in. Much like in *The Matrix*, after you take the red pill and start seeing how strongly cognitive biases have colored your thinking, you'll never be able to go back to your old perceptions of what is real and what isn't. Like Neo, you'll see that you actually have a choice of which reality to believe is real. Let's look at how you can choose the red pill of living your life according to what is factually true and then infusing it with optimism, rather than taking the blue pill of continuing to see life through cognitive biases that generate negativity.

## Recognize Cognitive Distortions

*"Reality? Your 'reality,' sir, is lies and balderdash, and I'm delighted to say that I have no grasp of it whatsoever."*

**—Baron Munchausen,** *a character in the movie The Adventures of Baron Munchausen*

The mind is very clever. So clever, in fact, that it can convince itself that things are true even when they are not.

Our brains interpret and assign meaning to situations all of the time without us even realizing it. But the interpretation is frequently done with limited information and scant facts. So our fear-conditioned negatively-biased imaginative brains fill in our gaps in knowledge, and more often than not skew our thinking and push us to negatively misinterpret situations. This form of thinking is known as cognitive distortion.

Cognitive distortions are a lens through which we perceive reality to be different than it actually is. We start to see the self and the world through what I think of as "Inner Critic-colored glasses." where cognitive distortions are the frames, one lens is negativity bias, and the other lens is confirmation bias, which we'll learn about soon.

Despite cognitive distortions being largely inaccurate, they are a regular part of our thinking, and are so automatic that they're virtually unnoticeable without concentrated effort to detect them.

When you do identify the cognitive distortions, you can see within them other people's criticisms at their source. Our Inner Critic, true to form as our dedicated protector, takes critical comments as base material and sculpts them into truisms.

The problem with cognitive distortions is that this thinking is seductive. We can't tell that we are seeing reality through a warped lens. We are convinced that our perception of this reality is accurate and true and are completely oblivious to the fact that we've actually put a personal spin on things.

Everyone experiences cognitive distortions to some extent. The problem occurs when we believe this warped version is the sole option for what's real.

With an increased awareness of cognitive distortions, you'll start to see that multiple versions of reality exist – it all depends on which you are allowing to influence and color your thoughts. You'll also see that you have the power to choose which version of reality you pay attention to.

## *Know Your Cognitive Distortions*

Although some sources list ten cognitive distortions, others list up to fifty. This list includes those that are most relevant to the Inner Critic.

While reading, play close attention to see whether any of these altered versions of thinking sound familiar to you. How many have stuck with you, become internalized, and become highly influential in of how you see yourself and the world?

1) **Mental Filter** (also called selective abstraction or tunnel vision) / **Magnification and Minimization** (also called the binocular trick). You find ample evidence to support negative beliefs, but filter out any positive counterexamples. You put all of your focus on the one negative thing that went wrong in a situation, and filter out everything else that went right by overlooking

it. Or you exaggerate the importance of the negative events, situations, actions, or qualities, and you minimize the significance of the positive ones.

Example: "They hated my workshop! 35 of the 40 attendees gave me 5 stars, but 2 people gave me only 2 stars."

2) **Overgeneralization.** You make a broad, sweeping negative conclusion from a single isolated occurrence and then apply it to all instances of its kind, making a truism from it.

Example: "They rejected my talk proposal. I'll never be a speaker!"

3) **Jumping to Conclusions.** You negatively interpret the meaning of a situation without any actual evidence or facts to support your conclusion.

Example: When your boss gives you a less than perfect performance evaluation, you think, "I'm never going to get promoted; my boss probably plans to fire me."

4) **Mind Reading.** You determine that the thoughts of others toward you are unfavorable despite lacking sufficient evidence, considering other more likely possibilities, or even checking it out.

Example: "He's thinking that I don't know the first thing about this project."

5) **Fortune Telling or Catastrophizing.** You predict that circumstances will turn out poorly, and then are convinced that your prediction is fact despite lacking supportive evidence. You only see the worst possible outcome of a situation and expect the worst-case scenario to happen without considering other more likely outcomes.

Example: "You didn't call me when you got home – I thought you had gotten into an accident and were hurt!"

6) **Emotional Reasoning**. You turn feelings into facts and assume that the way you feel emotionally is a reflection of reality, and ignore evidence to the contrary. In other words, you believe that because you feel it, it must be true.

Example: "I feel frightened right now. That must mean I'm in real physical danger."

7) **All or Nothing Thinking** (also called black and white, polarized, or dichotomous thinking). You look at situations in black and white categories instead of along a continuum. You think in absolutes and frequently use terms such as *always, never, every,* and *forever*.

Example: "If I'm not a complete success, I'm a total failure."

8) **Should Statements** (also called imperatives). You use *shoulds* and *should nots* as your main source of motivation, holding yourself to a precise and strict list of acceptable behavior. You mentally chastise yourself if you don't conform, because you've overestimated how dire the repercussions would be if you don't. Other terms used are *must* and *ought*.

Example: "By now, I should be a more successful designer than I am."

9) **Disqualifying/Diminishing the Positive**. You discount or ignore positive experiences, situations, attributes, and qualities, and recognize and emphasize only the negative.
Example: "I earned more money than I ever have last year, but I had to pay so much in taxes. I'm still not successful."

10) **Personalization**. You assume responsibility for negative events and circumstances that are outside of your control, blaming

yourself unnecessarily for situations without considering more plausible explanations for the root causes. Or you believe that others are behaving negatively because of you.

Example: "If I hadn't let you go rollerblading, you wouldn't have broken your leg."

11) **Labeling and Mislabeling.** You generalize and make labels of negative characterizations of yourself and others based on perceived shortcomings and a limited set of behaviors, without considering facts indicating otherwise. And then you set yourself up to embody the label. This is an extreme form of overgeneralization.

Example: "I'm a loser."

Anything sound familiar? It should. Cognitive distortions are like the mouthpiece of the Inner Critic, a primary vehicle through which the Inner Critic communicates some of the core messages. Cognitive Distortions poison the way in which we relate to ourselves, how and what we communicate with our selves, further solidifying our mistaken beliefs.

With this understanding, we can choose to see situations and ourselves as they truly are, without seeing everything through the thoughts and perceptions created by our Inner Critic-colored glasses. Let's remove these cognitively distorted spectacles and crush them underfoot by becoming more aware of the nature of our thoughts and beliefs and then challenging them.

## Creative Dose: Surprise Journal

*Purpose: To challenge instilled self-critical beliefs about life in general and your creativity in particular*

The Inner Critic tends to be a bit of a know-it-all, of the "been there, done that; know exactly what's going to happen" bent. One thing to do to begin to dismantle the authority of the Inner Critic and the distorted thinking it proffers is to start keeping a record of instances when it was flat-out wrong. What better way to do that than to notice every time your expectations of being judged are disproven and you're taken by surprise?

To challenge the cognitive distortions used by Inner Critic through the element of surprise, start keeping a Surprise Journal[11] to help you notice and note times when your cognitive distortions were shown to be exactly that: inaccurate thinking, and myths you created from it.

## Step 1: Note

During the course of a week, strive to note at least fifteen instances in which you experienced surprise about thoughts that you had believed to be patently true. Notice also any moments when you experienced confusion or your negative expectations were not met and when an outcome was more positive than you had anticipated.

You can use this structure to capture your instances of where your beliefs were challenged:

Previous belief:_____

My surprise!_____

## Step 2: Inquire

For each moment of surprise, ask yourself these questions:

- Why was this instance surprising?
- What does why and how I was surprised tell me about myself?

You can use this structure to capture your surprises and insights from them:

Surprise: _____

Why surprised? _____

My insight: _____

## Step 3: Relate

Take the same process and apply it to your creativity.
Note when your creativity surprised you, for example, an idea
that came out of nowhere, how you ended up solving a problem or
troubleshooting, or a new skill you picked up and started to apply. Ask
yourself the same questions as in the Inquire section.

You can use this structure to capture your surprises and insights about
your creativity:

Creative instance: _____

Why surprised? _____

My insight: _____

What did you learn about your creativity and your creative process?
Did the process help you see the kinds of cognitive distortions
that have been clouding your self-perceptions and challenge your
assumptions about your creativity?

# Seek Positive Confirmation

*"The problem with worry is that we attract the very thing we are trying
to avoid. We live a self-fulfilling prophecy. Life keeps its agreement
with us through our beliefs, because whatever we think about, we
bring about. Life is like a mirror. It reflects back whatever image we
present to it."*

**— Dr. Robert Anthony,** *author*

A college friend of mine, Phillip, had a habit of being incredibly
sensitive to people judging and second-guessing him. And you know
what? *It happened all of the time.* Despite his success with putting
himself through school, managing a disability, and working with

limited resources, when he tried to get support for his endeavors, people still seemed to question his abilities. I couldn't understand for the life of me why he had to fight the battles that he did, because I could clearly see all of his talents and abilities, his hard work ethic, and his ability to effortlessly generate business ideas. After a point, he began to *expect* that people would judge him and discount his capabilities. Phillip's expectations of being judged went on to color his perception of himself. This self-perception influenced his behavior and demeanor and consequently set the stage for how he interacted with people – and how they responded to him. He saw the potential for rejection in the form of judgment and criticism everywhere, and he found it. It became a self-fulfilling prophecy.

When we are afraid of being judged, almost everything said to us seems like a condemnation of some sort. We're constantly on the lookout for a comment, a facial expression, a tone of voice that proves to us just what we suspected: that this person or those people are judging us. With the Inner Critic in the driver's seat, we find these dreaded negative assessments all too easily due to another inclination of the brain: confirmation bias.

Confirmation bias is the tendency of the brain to seek out evidence to confirm deeply held beliefs or hypotheses while dismissing or ignoring any evidence that doesn't support them. Under the influence of confirmation bias, ambiguous information is interpreted to support the held belief or hypothesis, situations are remembered selectively (particularly emotionally charged situations), and mistaken beliefs are acted upon as though they are true. It's important to bear in mind that confirmation bias is nonpartisan: such bias can apply to either the negative or the positive. The problem is that we usually use it to confirm our fears instead of our hopes.

We see what we expect to see. When it comes to having Judgment Dread, not only do we look for evidence that people are judging us, but then the confirmation of our fears about how we're not okay negatively impacts how we see ourselves. When we don't feel seen and supported, and thus feel rejected, we end up internalizing people's judgments and strong criticisms as a truth about us. In his book *The Inner Game of Work*, author Tim Galwey provides a spot-on description of this phenomenon: "...if I identify with a concept such as 'I am not good enough,' I will probably start looking at my feelings and behaviors through the lens of that concept. I will also interpret how others view me through that same lens. And I will no doubt be able to find ample 'evidence' to support my basic negative self-image. The negative concept is now fortified and will be used to find more supportive evidence." [12] Just like in Phillip's case above, it's a self-fulfilling prophecy.

Negative confirmation bias is one of the many tools the Inner Critic uses to ensure that we will modify our behavior to avoid any potential future hurt. But avoiding hurt is rarely what comes of it. This version of cognitive bias warps our perceptions of the world around us into one different from what actually is, enticing our brains into an un-fun house of mirrors that reflect our amplified fears back to us. When Judgment Dread is at the helm of your consciousness, then so much of what you see and think will be from a self-judging standpoint. Who needs other people to be judgmental and critical when we can do it ourselves with such venom? Not only do we judge ourselves, but we also begin to inhibit behavior and hold ourselves back. We confirm people's unfavorable judgments by stifling our potential. We completely miss kudos. We dismiss or deflect compliments. Praise barely registers with us. And support is overlooked. We live within the confines of a limited and distorted truth, mistakenly believing that in this cage of our own making we'll be safe. We lose a sense of how vast and wide the field of potentiality is for us, and what is truly possible.

Thankfully, confirmation bias doesn't only work for creating a negative self-fulfilling prophecy; it can also work for the positive as well. What a relief! You can use your powers of focus to activate the process of shifting your brain to a different place by searching for confirmations of positive thoughts and beliefs. Instead of looking for judgment and finding it, you can gently encourage your brain to look for appreciation and respect. Rather than living in a place of constant preparation for being pummeled by harsh criticism, you can shift your focus to seek confirmation of kudos and praise. Rather than walking around in a perpetual state of feeling that no one believes in you, you can be on the hunt for support. And because of the nature of cognitive bias, you will start to find all of these.

Take confirmation and use it as a force for good, to seek out positivity rather than negativity. Doing so will shift your perception away from life as a series of one judgment after another.

Through this shift, you'll transform your perceptions of yourself as well.

## Creative Dose: Swipe File of Support

*Purpose: To have evidence that you are appreciated to counter a fear of being criticized*

In advertising, there is a practice of keeping something called a "swipe file." Advertising professionals "swipe" examples of great marketing copy or advertising slogans and put them into a file to call upon for ideas and inspiration later.

For those moments when your sense of being liked and appreciated by others is flagging and your fear of being judged or even rejected starts to take over, or even if you just need a little boost of encouragement, you should have your own swipe file of kudos and compliments you've received for your work, creative or otherwise.[13] The goal is to keep all of these items to remind yourself that people appreciate the work that you're doing. But even more than that, I believe that a "kudos file" can also help placate the part of our brain that is on constant alert for the prospect of being rejected from the group. It can help us settle into the knowledge that we are supported and cared for, and therefore, that we are safe.

So, taking a cue from advertisers, I encourage you to start keeping a swipe file of love.

Gather up every positive physical note, thank-you letter, or other kinds of praise into a folder that you keep handy. For digital items, you should save emails and favorite Tweets, and take screenshots of comments and responses from the various social media platforms. Aggregate all of these and save them into a folder aptly named "Kudos File" – or whatever name rings true for you. Continue to save everything and anything that indicates people's expression of how talented and wonderful you are.

When you feel that you need to make sure you're okay and you do good work and positively affect people's lives to boot, check your kudos file.

*Bonus Action:* Spread the love by contributing to someone else's kudos file!

Whenever you feel moved, send an unsolicited email (or even better, an actual card) of thanks and gratitude to family, friends, colleagues, clients, and consultants to let them know how much you appreciate them and their work.[14] Not only will the other person feel fantastic, but you will feel pretty fabulous as well.

# Stop Awfulizing

*"Never give a negative thought an inch or it will take a mile."*

— **Matshona Dhliwayo,** *author*

The Inner Critic practically makes an art form out of spinning wild tales of potential doom in alternate futures. Through the habit of imagining worst-case scenarios in our heads, then replaying them, and then amplifying them, we take negativity bias to an extreme form known as "awfulizing." If the prospect of putting your creative ideas "out there" makes you a little apprehensive, that's normal and understandable. However, if you find yourself spending energy getting worked up about what *would have* happened if, for example, your boss hadn't liked your ideas (naturally, it means that you would have been fired, then would have lost your apartment because you couldn't pay the rent, and then you would become homeless), then you know you have stepped into awfulizing territory.

Unfortunately, there are consequences to creating stories of what would have happened – you shouldn't dismiss them as a product of your imagination running wild. Merely thinking about events as terrible actually hampers one's ability to cope with real-life situations.[15] In the long run, the tendency to awfulize hurts us far more than it helps.

We can choose to stop the madness. Instead of getting caught up in awfulized versions of a dystopic future, we can be mindful of that they are only stories spun by our Inner Critic. We can then encourage our wonderfully imaginative minds to produce new stories that put us in a more realistic, yet positive mindframe.

### Creative Dose: "And then..."

*Purpose: To practice realistic optimism to counter awfulizing*

To counter negativity bias in the form of awfulizing, Tony Schwartz, CEO of The Energy Project, encourages practicing realistic optimism instead.[16] With realistic optimism, for any given situation you imagine and tell the most hopeful story possible. This is not the time for fantasy, however. Rather, you base your optimistic projection on the facts without either embellishing them or minimizing them.

Think of something that you are afraid of regarding your work or your creativity being judged or criticized that is making you anxious and may even be paralyzing you from any forward movement. Maybe you're giving your first talk at a conference, you have an art opening, or you are writing an article for a prestigious website.

First, on a piece of paper or in a journal, write down and answer the question:

- What am I afraid will happen?

Next, write down a response to this question:

- What could happen?

However, instead of going into a place where your anxious thoughts push you to awfulize the situation, actively apply realistic optimism. Tell yourself the story of what could possibly happen using "and then..." to devise an alternative that is positive instead of the feared outcome. Build upon this new realistically optimistic story by making each of your "and then..." additions more positive until you feel better and your fear diminishes.

Use this framework:

and then _____ ,

and then _____ ,

and then _____ ...

For example, maybe you're afraid of opening up an Etsy store for the letterpress greeting cards that you've been making in your spare time. You're afraid that no one will buy them, your creative efforts won't be recognized and appreciated, and it will be a wasted effort. However, what *could* happen is that because you submitted them as a new product, the cards could be featured on a popular design website. And then the increased visibility could drive more traffic to your store. And then that increased visibility could garner interviews on design podcasts for you. And then... And then...

You get the idea.

This is also a great exercise to do with a partner! Ping pong "and then's" back and forth to see what optimistic futures you can envision together.

Regardless of the situation, you're going to be thinking something about it. A tendency to awfulize sends your thoughts into a downward spiral into negativity. However, applying the same thinking mechanism, you can deliberately point your thoughts and the stories you create in the opposite direction, up into positivity.

# PRACTICE RADICAL RATIFICATION

*"Critics are not the enemy – the battle is in our own head."*
— **Steven Pressfield**, *The War of Art*

The way to stop living in fear of being judged and criticized is to start practicing radical ratification, which is all about deeply validating ourselves. Instead of proactively judging ourselves in order to beat others to it, we are going to accept who we are regardless of what other people think. Instead of seeking approval from others, we will approve of and support ourselves. People learn how to treat us from us. It's time to for us to shore up our levels of self-respect so that we are less vulnerable to others' capricious views of us.

So often, the true problem with criticism is not that it happens at all or what the people say, but in how we deal with it. We put up our mental hand and block it, we tense up for the anticipated blow of the critical words and don't hear them, or we take criticisms to heart and absorb their toxicity into both our emotional and physical bodies, causing stress and illness. We alter our lives and shut doors to the future that our souls desire.

Our lives have the potential to be so much grander, so much more vivid, fulfilling, and satisfying than the fears of threat, limitation, and lack that others project upon us.

Instead of judging ourselves, we need to trust in our abilities, embrace our uniqueness, and fully accept who we are and how we are creative.

Instead of letting external criticism fortify our internal fears, we need to reframe criticism and see it as a tool for growth and building self-trust. Not only there are gems to be had from the content of criticism, but the input can be a way for us to bolster our sense of what we know is right in our gut.

Contrary to what anyone may believe, it's never too late to get the support, approval, and permission that we've always wanted but never received enough. It's just that now, we will let it bubble up from an internal source instead of searching for it outside of ourselves the world over.

Let's look how we can shake off the mental shackles that we have weighed ourselves down with and get to a place where we're trusting in our capabilities and are more emotionally resilient. When we change our relationship with judgment and criticism, we can start to let our greatness out into the world.

## Stop Hiding in Plain Sight

*"Courage starts with showing up and letting ourselves be seen."*

— **Brené Brown,** *author, scholar and public speaker*

Remember my story of playing basketball and my desperate attempt to hide in plain sight? It's very hard to miss a 6-foot tall woman, and in many places in the world, it's even harder to miss a 6-foot tall African-American woman! I couldn't hide if I wanted to. It was only when I embraced my height and my athletic build that I started coming into my own as a teenager. In my adult life, making a conscious choice to be seen for who I am transformed my body, helping me let go of the last 50 of the 100 pounds I wanted to release, enabled me to create a new life in a new city on the other side of the country from where I had lived for almost 18 years, and further motivated me to pursue my dream of becoming an author and a speaker.

If you wrestle with the fear of standing out or of being too unique or avant-garde for fear of being judged, here's my recommendation: dig down and find the courage to embrace it. Own it. Flaunt it even.

And then, revel in the opportunities that open up when you stop working so hard to fit your round peg of a self into a square hole.

 ## Creative Dose: Your Uniqueness Advantage

*Purpose: To discover how being unique is an asset*

Meryl Streep, award-winning actress, beautifully states how powerful accepting your uniqueness is. She says, "...everyone thinks there is a perfect way to be...but your difference, your thing that is unique to you, is the most valuable thing you have. The weird thing about you is the thing that makes people remember you....Whatever is weird about you maybe is your strength."[17]

Here are three steps to begin capitalizing on your uniqueness and making what's different about you work for you.

## Step 1: Make a Vow

In his book, *Mastering Creative Anxiety*, Eric Maisel asserts that we must master the anxiety of individuality, and he provides a vow that you must make to yourself: "I must be myself. That will provoke anxiety, and I will deal with it."[18]

Promise yourself that you will start to release the expectations of others and begin to unearth and reveal the real you. Promise yourself that you will strive to be no one other than yourself. If you're still unclear as to who exactly that is, promise that you'll fully commit yourself to a journey of discovery.

As a matter of fact, sit down right now and make this vow yourself. Seriously. Here's a structure for you to use:

As of this day _____ of the year _____, I hereby vow to

_____

_____

_____

If you want to get really official with it, you can print out a proclamation of commitment to self[1] and use that instead.

Congratulations! You've made a wonderful commitment to yourself and your creative future.

## Step 2: Reframe It

Use these questions to reframe uniqueness:

- How does being unique work to your advantage? List all of the ways that being unique helps, not hurts, you.

---

[1] You can download your Commitment to Self Vow here: creativedo.se/commitment-to-self-vow

Being unique helps me by

_____

- How does being exactly who you are make things easier for you?

List all of the things that would improve in your life if you stopped trying to suppress who you are.

In being who I am, my life would be better because

_____

_____

_____

Remember: your uniqueness is your strength. Your experiences, perspectives, and knowledge are something that no other single person on earth has. Your work is to take the uniqueness that is you and put it to good use in your life and in the world.

## Accept Who You Are

*"Stop expecting others to show you love, acceptance, commitment, and respect when you don't even show that to yourself."*

**—Steve Maraboli,** *author*

A few months ago, I tuned in to the language that I used to describe my own creativity and I was shocked: I realized that I had been judging myself my entire life for the way in which I am creative. (And no, the irony of the fact that I travel around encouraging people to embrace and express their creativity is not lost on me.) I'll tell you what happened.

One of my crafty outlets is making handmade herbal soap from scratch. When I first started making it back in 1998, I got tired of having people ask me what was in it, so I created labels for the different scents. Then I designed a logo. Then I refined the packaging to look really polished so I could sell it. This behavior is not unusual for me – in fact, it is my modus operandi.

If I make something, you can best be sure that I will also develop the branding for it and design some sort of packaging. However, when talking to a friend about a recent soapmaking endeavor I did to make unique thank-you gifts for clients, I heard myself saying "Yeah, I'm just going to make some soap this weekend, and then I need to find the right gift boxes for it. I'm just ridiculous that way..." Whoa, wait. I'm "ridiculous" for my desire to make a beautiful, polished, finished product? But then I noticed that I used the same kind of language when talking about the earrings that I make. And when I used to make handmade stationery sets about 15 years ago, I used the same kind of disparaging and dismissive language. The judgment that pervaded my tone when talking about my creations to others was both surprising and saddening.

I truly love the things I make. I find them absolutely lovely, which is one of the reasons I make them. But my own Inner Critic had taken on the role of judging myself before anyone else could. I judged myself because crafts are somehow considered not "real" art as fine arts are. I judged myself because "I take things too far" by making them polished and professional. And get this: despite my line of work, I even judged myself for having the desire to want to make things with my hands rather than always creating more cerebral output like writing or visual design. In that moment of calling my creative expression "ridiculous," I saw how I had never *fully* accepted who I am: a person who loves creating **products**.

And as soon as I realized this, it was like a light went on for me, and something in my brain clicked into place. YA-USSSS! *I create products!* I started to see how everything I did already was a reflection of my product-making mind: my keynotes, my workshops with their branded printed workbooks and email follow-up series, my desire to make card sets to stimulate creativity, and the multitude of other ideas I have. I'm happy to say that this realization has set the stage for how I intend to structure my business from this point forward.

Look at how you are judging yourself: who you are, what you naturally love to do, and your interests, penchants, and passions. Are you keeping moments of pure creative enjoyment at bay? Are you blocking your creativity because it doesn't fit with how you feel it "should" be to be legitimate? Are you holding yourself back from achieving greatness by judging yourself? Are you limiting your options because you believe that you should be some way other than how and who you are?

By accepting yourself and your creativity as it is and where it is (instead of judging it and saying it's not moving fast enough, your ideas are not original, and such), you give it the opportunity to grow and develop. Creativity is like a plant, it needs the proper environment to grow and flourish. Being in a place of judging your creativity is like wanting to grow a tall tree, but instead constantly snipping away at the young plant and making it a bonsai. If you continue to do so, your creativity will never grow to be what it could be. Instead it will remain tightly constrained and controlled, in a completely different form than it would be in its natural state.

One of the most important components of diffusing self-judgment before it spirals out of control is to notice where you are right now. Accept who you are now, and see what gifts you have. The more you focus on appreciating yourself, the less attention you'll be able to devote to harshly judging yourself or the prospect of being judged by others.

## Creative Dose: Embrace Your Shake

*Purpose: To accept and work with who you are and the talents you have*

There is an incredibly inspiring TED talk by the artist Phil Hansen.[20] Phil is a fine artist who was obsessed with pointillism. He would spend hours making artwork from conglomerations of small points of color to create full tableaus. Doing such work requires an immense amount of precision and thus physical control. However, Phil started to notice that he was developing a shake in his hands, which was problematic to his chosen art medium. Over time, his shake became more and more pronounced until he couldn't hold a writing instrument still at all. Devastated and thinking his art career over, he lapsed into a deep depression and relinquished his art. He decided to visit a neurologist to see if there was any hope of a cure. His doctor had grave news: Phil had permanent nerve damage and he wouldn't be able to continue doing the art he loved. But then his doctor said something that changed everything for him: "Why don't you embrace the shake?" Phil immediately rushed home to take advantage of making art with his shaky hand. This epiphany led to an exploration of different forms of his artistic expression and an explosion of his creativity. The video is well worth the watch!

Now that you've made a vow to commit to yourself and are getting in touch with how your uniqueness works for you, the next step is to be like Phil, and to embrace your "shake," whatever that may be.

## Step 1: Identify

Think of qualities within you that you have dismissed, disparaged, or felt were somehow a weakness.

- How are these qualities, inclinations, and skills actually strengths?

- What would your career, business, and life be like if you fully accepted them?

## Step 2: Leverage

Start to envision how you will leverage these new-found strengths.

- How will you make these strengths work for you?

- What are some ways can you play within them?

- How will you start to infuse these strengths into your work or even restructure your work to fit them?

Let go of the idea that you somehow need to be another person or a different way to be okay. Stop trying to be anything other than exactly who you are. Accept exactly who you are and what you have to work with. Start working within this paradigm and see how this new perspective pushes your creativity. Whatever you have judged within yourself and thought was a liability, discover how you can exploit it. When you start to see it as one of your strengths, you can begin to celebrate your unique version of creativity.

# Live Better Through Criticism

*"The trouble with most of us is that we'd rather be ruined by praise than saved by criticism."*

— **Norman Vincent Peale,** *author*

Years ago I met a guy who was a waiter at one of my favorite breakfast eateries. He was tall, quirky, and hilarious. Although he was a waiter in his day job, he aspired to be on radio and had a late-night show at a local independent radio station. I was quite taken by him and wanted to get to know him better. We had several enjoyable conversations by phone, and when we finally met up, it felt like a date. I thought all was going well – until I called him one day not long after to share a great experience I'd had the night before. Super happy to be talking with him and enthused about the experience itself, I eagerly shared the details, my thoughts, and my feelings about it.

When I done, he was silent. "Hey, are you there?" I asked. And then it came. "You just went on and on!" he exclaimed. "I couldn't get a word in edgewise. It was like 'The Denise Show' – like all you wanted was an audience." I was absolutely stunned. I thought we had built a rapport and were becoming friends. I thought that because of this, he would be interested in hearing about my life and getting to know me better, as I wanted to get to know him. Clearly somewhere in there I had read the situation and him incorrectly.

Suffice to say, that was our last conversation. But for a very long time afterward, his words stuck with me, irritating my subconscious like a small stiff hair trapped beneath my clothing, scratching at my skin. I asked myself: Am I so self-centered as to be insensitive to my listener? Do I really go on and on when I talk? Do I act like it's "The Denise Show" when I'm telling a story? For quite some time, I became hypervigilant about how much I was talking during conversations, careful not to say too much for fear of another similar reprimand.

The fascinating thing about his criticism is that there was actually more than a kernel of truth to it, but instead of it being about my weaknesses, it was insight into my talents and strengths.

A couple of years after that incident, I taught my first soap-making workshop – a pivotal experience that showed me that I loved to teach. Doing those workshops led me to start teaching web design and development courses at a community college. And through going to my first ever web design conference, I discovered that I wanted to be a speaker. Now, approximately 20 years after I received that criticism, I am a professional speaker. It is my job to get on a stage and talk for upwards of an hour, and regardless of the event, during the time of my talk, it essentially is "The Denise Show." And for the record, I absolutely *love* what I do – it is an utterly perfect fit to my personality and skills.

The upshot? One person's criticism can be another person's insight in disguise.

Look for the positive truth in criticisms and learn from them. If we tense up, block, or react negatively to the information given, we can't hear potentially valuable information clearly, take it in, or make use of it. Start to see criticisms as a way to grow, to make yourself better, and most importantly, learn about yourself. Transform your relationship with criticism and use it as a tool to improve yourself and your life.

## Creative Dose: Curious and Open

*Purpose: To have a toolbox of ways to stay open to criticism*

We can adopt a practice of becoming curious and staying open in the face of criticism so that we may learn from it.

Here are some power tips for learning to take in criticism well and use it to get better at whatever you are doing:

1) **Breathe.** Get yourself grounded and make an effort to stay relaxed so that you don't end up blocking the information through being tense, anxious, or defensive.

2) **Detach.** Make an effort to detach whatever criticism you get from your self-worth. Even when it seems that a person is criticizing who you are as a person, there's a good chance that what they are really criticizing is your behavior.

3) **Listen actively.** One of the best ways to do so is to write everything down.[21] This will help you detach from your emotions and put you more into a listening mode. Ask questions to clarify points, and make notes of items to double-check or focus on when you review your notes. Taking notes gives you the advantage of having time and space away from the feedback later, which will enable you to revisit the input and process it over time.

4) **Get specifics.** What specifically does the person think you need to improve? What are her or his thoughts and suggestions on how you can do so?

5) **Find the relevant.** Take criticisms with a grain of salt. Use your powers of discernment to keep what is relevant and ignore the rest.

6) **Invite.** Actively solicit constructive criticism or ask for it – and be appreciative of their suggestions.

7) **Discover.** Set your intention to discover new perspectives and ideas that you may not have considered. This actually works to counter any confirmation bias you may have that you weren't aware of.

8) **Be curious.** Approach the criticisms with curiosity. Look for what was the most interesting thing the person said. It could be been that they revealed a major insight through that point.

9) **Grow.** The criticism can help to shine light on issues that you still need to resolve within yourself: fears, doubts, and insecurities. Be open to finding an emotional sore spot that the input motivates you to start healing.

10) **Save time and learn.** Changing how you react to criticism is actually a time-saver: if you really take in the information and learn from it, you will save yourself making the same mistakes and having to try to learn the lessons in the future.[22] And don't we all want to save time so that we can spend it on the enjoyable parts of life – like creating?

Knowing that there may be at least one gem, if not more, of valuable information contained within criticism, how will you change the way you respond to it?

# Stay True to Yourself

*"I silence my inner critics exactly the same way I silence my real-life critics: By saying to them very quietly, but very firmly, 'If you don't like what I'm doing, go write your own f\*\*king book.' "*

— **Elizabeth Gilbert,** *author*

There are times when your ideas are so creative and leading edge that people are critical of them because they simply don't have the capacity to see your vision. In his book, *Ignore Everybody*,[23] artist and entrepreneur Hugh McLeod shares this gem of advice: "Ignore everybody. The more original your idea is, the less good advice other people will be able to give you." All too often, people will weigh in on matters about which they have absolutely no clue.

Staying true to ourselves, no matter what, is key. How people perceive you actually has little to do with you: judgment says more about the one judging than the one being judged. Often criticism and judgment are nothing more than someone projecting their insecurities, fear, and negativity onto you. Although judgments and criticisms may feel as limiting and suffocating as the squeeze of a boa constrictor, know that you have the power to extricate yourself from the hold of uninformed comments.

We can show the people who don't see our vision or us clearly some compassion. I have a Welsh friend who uses an expression that amuses me to no end: "Well, bless their little cotton socks!" he often says (which is often shortened to "bless their cottons!"). When we encounter external judgment, we can remember that someone else's opinion is not our problem, and take the higher road by wishing that person well, and then wishing them on their way.

In the grand scheme of things, how others see you isn't important. How you see yourself, however, is everything. Regardless of whatever criticism or judgment comes your way, having a base of a strong sense of self will help you weather the storm of anything that people may say about your work. In an online article, relationship expert Dr. Margaret Paul puts it beautifully: "High self-worth or low self-worth is the result of how we treat ourselves – not about what others think of us."[24]

Build your sense of self by prioritizing yourself. Don't let others define you – live by your own values. Get to know your own strengths and limitations, viewing them without judgment, but simply as facts about who you are. And finally, continue to learn to operate from your center by trusting your self more, cultivating a deep belief in what you are doing.

We can work on tuning into that small clear voice inside – our Creative Self – that tells us what is our own truth. And we can begin to act accordingly by standing up for ourselves, championing our ideas, and getting out of a place of fear, uncertainty, and doubt. We can start to learn to communicate our ideas and projects better to garner the support that we want and need.

In essence, we start taking back our creative power and living a life that is authentic to the Self.

 ## Creative Dose: More Clear, More Empowered

*Purpose: To put external criticisms into perspective*

Here are some suggestions to stay grounded in the face of unhelpful criticism.

### Option 1: A Drop In the Ocean

Whenever you receive criticism, whether it's well-intentioned, constructive, malicious, or just plain irrelevant, put it into perspective.

Imagine the criticism as a drop of dense black ink and see it falling into the ocean. Watch as the drop mixes with the surrounding water and gets lighter and lighter until it is indistinguishable.

You'll find that this helps wash the criticism away from your mind so you can focus your brain on continuing to generate big ideas.

**Option 2: Preferred Treatment**

If someone criticizes you harshly, you can stand up for yourself and teach them how you'd prefer to be treated.

To a harsh or poorly thought through and delivered criticism, you can respond with something like, "Your points are completely valid and I appreciate you sharing them with me. However, I would take them far better if you changed your tone of voice."

Take back your power. Establish how people will treat you, not the other way around.

# Choose to Contribute

*"Criticism is something you can easily avoid by saying nothing, doing nothing, and being nothing."*
— **Aristotle**

I have a confession: I have had quite a few moments when I have been afraid of being judged for this book. However, one morning earlier this week while washing dishes, I had a realization: in the grand scheme of things, it simply doesn't matter whether folks judge it or not. Of course I would love for this book to be a profound experience for everyone who reads it. I would love for people to love it. However, while the objective of writing this book is to help people, it is also about developing my own personal creative process.

In the inception stage, creativity is really about the relationship that you have with yourself and what you are bringing forth. It's about letting out what's inside of you. And in the moment of creation, what you are making doesn't have anything to do with other people. It's about you and your work. In those moments that you spend bringing your creation into the world, no one else matters.

You already know this, but it bears stating nonetheless: no matter what it is you do or create, there will always be someone out in the world for whom it is not a good fit. You simply can't please everyone – and you shouldn't strive to. When you find the people with whom your work strongly resonates, you will have discovered the treasure trove of your "tribe."

As creatives (if you have not yet accepted that you are creative by default, don't protest any longer – just accept it), we often feel that a rejection of our ideas, skills, or what we produce with our talent, is a rejection of us as people. But it's not. The criticism is not about who you are as a person, but something that came through you. We identify strongly with what we produce – it feels like an extension of ourselves. But when we take a more mindful approach, we can realize that what we produce is not us at all, but rather an object or concept, which much as children do, takes on an identity and life of its own after it leaves us. It touches the lives of people. You could even think of your creation as having its own individual relationship with these people, which you aren't really a party to anymore.

Ultimately, you create for both yourself and for others, but they are two different parts of the whole process. We create to contribute to our own growth and self-actualization and ostensibly for others' as well. At some point with your creative work, you have to make a choice: is it more important for you to protect the Self from judgment and keep what you have inside, or to contribute and enrich your own life as well as others'? In my mind, the answer is always that it is more important to make a positive contribution to your Self and to the world.

Decide that it is more important to contribute something to the world than it is to protect yourself, and let those big, beautiful ideas inside of you come out.

## Creative Dose: Focus on the Work

*Purpose: To manage anxiety about potential criticism of your work*

If you are feeling anxious about what people might say about your work or your creations, what will help is to focus on the work itself, and not your feelings of anxiety about it.

### Step 1: Feel Fascination

Focus on truly interfacing with what you are making: become deeply interested in it and seek to discover all that you can about it. It's a lot of like being in love, when learning more about your beloved is a fascinating journey, and you're always eager to find out more.

Commit yourself to discovering these things:

- What is the soul of this idea or project?

- What does this project aspire to be?

- What makes this idea or project tick?

What other aspects can you discover about your idea or project?

### Step 2: Feel Honored

Another perspective you can take is that idea that an idea or project chooses you, and not the other way around. Look at the initial spark of insight and then the compulsion to see an idea through to completion as existing because that idea chose you, out of all of the people on this planet, to come through into the world and become tangible.

When I use this perspective to think about what I'm creating or working on, I not only feel incredibly flattered, but I feel a sense of honor at being the one chosen to help to make "my" idea manifest.

Ask yourself:

- What is the best way for you to respect and honor the spirit of the idea that has chosen you to be its vehicle for coming into the world?

- What does the idea want you to do to truly communicate all of what it is?

### Option 3: Feel Hopeful

You can also think about the potential good that whatever you're creating will do. It may affect one person, it may affect thousands or more. Focus on creating results and helping others, and infuse your work with positive intentions and your vision of its usefulness. This will help you focus on the road ahead instead of the walls of anxiety next to you.[25] Take several moments and ponder:

- Who are the people that you would like to touch with your idea?

- How will what you're making improve the lives of others?

All of the options incorporate a bit of a mindful approach. By shifting your focus away from some nebulous and most likely unfounded fear of being judged, you will effectively distract yourself back to what is directly in front of you and what you are bringing forth.

# WE'VE ONLY JUST BEGUN

You have to hand it to the Inner Critic, it works really hard to try to keep us safe using a wide arsenal of brain processes and psychological tendencies. You would think that constantly being on the lookout for threats would exhaust the Inner Critic, but it is tenacious and tireless in its pursuit of keeping us safe – bless its cotton socks!

Creativity is the ability to come up with ideas by trusting yourself, allowing, and then getting out of the way. Creativity is also having the courage to act on your ideas. To get to that wonderful un-self-conscious place where we can let our ideas flow, we need to make a commitment to challenge our Judgment Dread. We can't control what people say to us or how they perceive our work, or for that matter, us as people. But we can get a better handle on our own perceptions and how to best deal with whatever does come to us.

Our work, however, is not yet done – we've only just begun. As you learned in the previous chapter, the Inner Critic has a variety of guises that it uses in the name of protection. And because fear of judgment and criticism are so closely related, you won't be surprised to learn that once we start to judge ourselves, then becoming highly self-critical is not far behind.

*1) It-'ll be boring and suck*

# CHAPTER 4 | "NOTHING I DO IS ANY GOOD" – *HIGH SELF-CRITICISM*

**This chapter examines:**

*Origins of Inner Self-Talk*

*Expectations and Shame*

*Inner Critic v. Attacked Self*

*Rumination*

*Self-Distancing*

*Self-Censoring and Ideacide*

*Selective Hearing aka the Cocktail Party Effect*

*Non-Dominant Brain Hemisphere*

*Gestures, Thought, and Learning*

*Training the Inner Critic*

*"The part that we create from is far stronger and deeper than the part that needs healing. The part that we create from can't be touched by anything our parents did or society did."*

— **Steven Pressfield,** *The War of Art*

Growing up, Anneke loved science fiction and comic books. She was a huge fan of the X-Men, and looked forward to getting the newest edition every month at the local comic book store. Her talent for drawing and her reading interests naturally converged, and drawing pictures of fantastic female characters and superheroes became her favorite thing to do. She got great support from her mother, who would hang her pictures all over their small three-bedroom house. Other people, however, were a different story.

From the age of six to twelve, Anneke had the same teacher for art class: Mr. Stephens. A frustrated illustrator himself, Mr. Stephens was of the mind that drawing superheroes and illustrating comic books was an inappropriate aspiration for girls. Anneke's sketches were often met with a furrowed brow and string of thinly-veiled criticisms disguised as helpful feedback as a result.

However, a decisive event for Anneke happened at summer camp when she was twelve years old. During an arts and crafts session, she drew a super-mermaid with long hair, muscular arms, and a shell bikini-top. She was extremely pleased with it. As she was admiring her handiwork and was about to show it to her best friend sitting next to her, another girl came up behind her, looked over Anneke's shoulder at the drawing, and declared, "It looks like a frog." Anneke's first reaction was furious indignation. She played it tough and challenged the girl: "What?! What do you know? Can you even draw?" Inwardly however, Anneke was crestfallen. She thought to herself, "Maybe my artwork isn't any good. Maybe drawing superheroes is too crazy for a girl to do, just like my art teacher said."

Although she continued to draw after that, Anneke limited herself to the more "feminine" area of portraits. In high school, she moved into graphic design, and upon graduating, she took the safe route of going to school for commercial advertising design instead of following a curriculum in cartooning, comics, and illustration as her soul still yearned to do. In advertising school, most constructive criticisms from her instructors were heard as a repetition of the scathing commentary on her abilities that she had heard when she was younger. Anneke developed a habit of jumping in to point out the faults of her work before anyone else could. She was never happy with her work, regardless of the positive feedback that she did receive.

After school, Anneke took on a job as a designer at a national upscale travel and leisure magazine, and her pattern of self-criticism continued. She spent hours coming up with ideas for layouts that never made it past the trash can. While she was trying to create, her regular internal train of thought was "You can't do that; no one's going to go for that," and "Really?! Is that all you can come up with?" Anything that made it past her high wall of criticism was too bold and brash, the colors weren't quite right, the flow was off, or didn't have enough originality. Any comments from managers to guide her to see other options were met with the thought "See, Anneke? Your ideas suck."

Now in her early fifties and stuck in a cycle of profound self-criticism that has extended beyond her creative work into the rest of her life, Anneke has a wistful nostalgia for the life that she could have lived, wondering how it would have been had she pursued becoming a comic book artist like she dreamed instead of letting an unsolicited, mean-spirited comment from a practical stranger turn her away from it. Unfortunately, she feels it's too late in her life to pursue that course. To help her return to the happier creative self of her childhood, she sought my counsel.

When she relayed her stories to me, my heart went out her, but I had to stop her from beating up on herself about creativity. "Anneke, you're bludgeoning yourself!" I told her, "put the self-criticism hammer down and back away!" Fortunately, she found that amusing, and she took it to heart. Through our work together, she has come to see just how strongly she has internalized not only early criticisms and all that followed, but how strong her habit of chastising herself has become because of it. She has also recognized how much she truly missed creating her superheroines, and she has given herself permission to start drawing them again.

## PUT THE HAMMER DOWN

How aware are you of your own tendency to self-criticize? See if you can relate to any of these scenarios:

- ❑ You don't like anything you come up with. You lack objectivity and are hypercritical of all your ideas and your creations.

- ❑ You second-guess your ideas or your ability to make them happen.

- ❑ You make boring, safe decisions.

- ❑ You feel panic and anxiety at the prospect of creating for fear that you won't be able to do your idea justice.

The Inner Critic can be sneaky, appearing as rational thoughts. Do any of these sound familiar?

- ❑ "Everything I make is crap."

- ❑ "It will be boring and suck."

- ❑ "No one want to hear my ideas – they aren't interesting and are irrelevant. I just go on and on."

- ❑ "I'm wrong."

Does it feel like I'm reading your mind? It's because I've heard scores of people describe these thoughts. In Chapter 2, I mentioned that I lead an exercise in my creativity keynotes and workshops in which each person writes down one fear that he or she has around creativity, crumples the paper into a ball, and throws it across the room. Then everyone picks up the nearest paper ball and takes turns sharing, reading aloud what was written down. The amazing thing is the sheer number of thoughts that people have in common – in fact, the ones you just read came from these very people! So trust me, you're not alone.

## SELF-CRITICISM CONSTRAINS

*"There is nothing noble or righteous about self-criticism – let it go."*
— **Eric Maisel,** *Toxic Criticism*

It's truly sad that Anneke lost her sense of self and gave in to the criticism of her work. But it really wasn't about the comment that the girl at camp made, or her teacher for that matter. Their early critiques only reflected back her own self-doubts and fears that something was wrong with her drawing skill and what she wanted to draw to Anneke. Anneke had so thoroughly internalized those early criticisms and had repeated them to herself so much that they became the loudest part of her own internal dialogue about her creativity. And being the loudest part of her self-talk and ensuing self-perception, these criticisms and the beliefs they produced colored and guided all of her actions.

Anneke, like so many people, may feel that the way her career played out is "just life." Sometimes it's just life that we don't always get to do the work that we love or get our dream jobs. Some of us are just destined to show up and get our paychecks. And if we are able to do something even remotely creative, we're lucky, right? Wrong. It wasn't "just life" that killed her dreams, preventing Anneke from doing the creative work she was meant to do. It was the Inner Critic in the form of High Self-Criticism that banged the nails in the coffin of pursuing a life doing the kind of visual art she loved.

High Self-Criticism is the archenemy of creativity and the killer of ideas. It's High Self-Criticism that causes us to censor ourselves, pushing us to barricade any ideas from coming through us for fear of them being criticized. For the few ideas that do make it through, it's High Self-Criticism that makes us so critical that we squeeze what little bit of life was left out of these ideas, leaving them emaciated and colorless.

But high Self-Criticism is not only dangerous to our creativity, it hurts our well-being. Habitually thinking highly self-critical thoughts paralyzes us and keeps us stuck in unproductive ruts. Highly self-critical people are not only more prone to rumination and procrastination; they are also more likely to struggle with depression their whole lives. Being mired in High Self-Criticism makes us regularly criticize ourselves strongly, revisit things that we've done or said in the past, frequently put ourselves down, and feel that others are constantly reacting negatively to us.[1] Furthermore, high self-criticism is associated with fewer positive life events,[2] as high self-criticism dashes hopes and obliterates aspirations. Whether it comes from other people or we generate it ourselves and direct it inward, harsh criticism damages our self-confidence and can steer us completely off course, causing us to live lives that don't fit who we truly are.

Many of us are in a stupor from our high self-criticism. Self-criticism sits at the core of the Inner Critic's workings, giving rise to the self-doubt that underlies our fears that we aren't good enough, the anxiety that causes us to compare ourselves with others, and the inability to see ourselves clearly that compels us to deny that we are creative at all. High Self-Criticism dissolves the foundations of our creative self-esteem like acid.

But as the opening quote suggests, our inherent self – the Creative Self – is more resilient than the internalized criticisms that we've aggregated over the course of our lives. To move away from the censoring of our ideas and who we are in order to share both with the world, we need to break the habit of being highly self-critical. And because High Self-Criticism is such a cornerstone built into the mistaken beliefs that fuel all inner critical thinking, we will need to employ a wide range of approaches to dismantle the habit and the thinking patterns that support it at their source.

To get at these roots, we need look no further than how we learned to talk to ourselves and how our inner self-talk has contributed to High Self-Criticism. We'll find that managing our self-talk is the key to banishing the Inner Critic; it can mean the difference between emotional breakdown or personal breakthrough.

# ATTEND TO YOUR SELF-TALK

*"Almost nothing does more psychological damage than criticism."*
— **Eric Maisel,** *psychologist, creativity coach, and author*

Everyone engages in self-talk to some extent – some more than others. The current popular thought is that talking to yourself a lot means you're a genius. Whether this is true or not, talking out loud does help us solve problems, enabling us to run through different scenarios and alternative strategies. Talking to oneself makes the brain work more efficiently, helping to spark memory and better organize thoughts. In fact, experts consider self-talk to be a subset of thinking,[3] because self-talk helps us to stimulate and direct our actions, evaluate them, and then deliberately shape our behavior for the better.

Although we may not all talk to ourselves out loud, each of us engages in inner self-talk. Whether we are aware of it or not, we constantly produce an internal running commentary about ourselves and the world. Self-talk, then, is a key component to building self-perception. All is well when self-talk is positive or neutral, but when it becomes harsh and shaded with negativity, that's when we need to pay attention and take action.

Self-talk starts during the early childhood years. Children talk out loud as a way to better learn and make sense of the world. In her article "The Voice of Reason," writer Pamela Weintraub calls self-talk at this age "a kind of instruction manual, a self-generated road map to mastery,"[4] and suggests that the self-talk actually influences and affects the task at hand. As children, talking our way through a skill enables us to focus, improves learning and information assimilation, and imprints the problem-solving into our minds. At this age, self-talk actually informs and guides behavior. As the tasks increase in complexity, so does the quantity and quality of a child's self-talk. As we age and our mastery grows, our self-talk becomes internalized, but remains an important part of our ongoing internal dialogue.

However, self-talk is not done in a vacuum. Adults guide children's learning, helping them to build skills that they can then use on their own. As a result, self-talk becomes a "...social act, an embrace and reinterpretation of teachings picked up from knowledgeable elders,"[5] as children parrot back instructions through their little-kid filter. In other words, as children we not only talk ourselves through a task, but we mimic how the teaching adult talked us through the task's steps. This is where the process can go wrong.

As highly impressionable students, if a child is learning from an adult who is impatient, abrupt, or regularly punctuates instructions with angry outbursts or disparaging comments in response to the child's confusion at not knowing the next steps of a task or at making mistakes, the child will use the harsh language of the instructor as her or his template for self-talk. The internalized toxic criticisms then become incorporated into the child's own internal dialogue and self-talk. People then take this early childhood template of self-talk into adulthood. When you witness children admonishing themselves with comments like "why can't you figure this out?!" you're not only seeing them mimicking the criticisms that they received, you're witnessing the beginnings of the Inner Critic in the form of High Self-Criticism in action. High Self-Criticism is self-talk gone awry.

But it goes much deeper than merely a question of internal self-talk. When a person experiences a lot of harsh criticism early in life and is thus prone to highly critical self-talk, the original criticisms will subconsciously drive their behavior as an adult.

# Release Outdated Expectations and Shake Off Shame

*"Shame...is this web of unobtainable, conflicting, competing expectations about who we're supposed to be. And it's a straitjacket."*

— **Brené Brown,** *"Listening to Shame" TED talk*

Gladys feels she needs to "solve the problems of the world" – or at least solve the problems of the people in her world. She spends a lot of her time traveling from one family member to another to help out when they are in a jam, keep them company, and generally be supportive. But trying to be everything to everybody all the time is taking its toll on her. She's been feeling increasingly put-upon and taken for granted, which she is – mainly because giving of her time is such a large part of how she operates that people don't recognize and appreciate the huge amount of effort that she puts forth. Instead of giving Gladys a sense of satisfaction, these days her efforts are leaving her burned-out and emotionally exhausted.

Despite this, Gladys criticizes herself for the times when she can't do more for people and mentally scolds herself when she feels the need to take care of herself. She used to wonder why, until one day, a deeply buried memory bubbled to the surface. She was eight years old, and excited to go to the movies to see "Little Women." Her mother had promised to take her and a friend to the Saturday matinée. However, when Saturday arrived, something came up, and the movie plans were canceled. Gladys remembers bursting into tears. Feeling lied to and betrayed, she let go of being the accommodating child that she had always been and decided to stand up for herself for once. "You promised to take me!" she insisted to her mother. In response, her mother said something that cut her to her very core:

"Gladys," she said, "you're a very selfish little girl." Gladys now sees that for all of these years, she's been terrified of being seen as selfish again. Helping everyone is largely driven by her feeling of being a bad person and a disappointment, elicited by this early comment.

The criticism Gladys received from her mother is an example of the countless comments we each receive during childhood. Regardless of whether they were accurate, we've internalized these messages and they have been driving our self-perceptions and behavior ever since. Again, we can look to our negatively biased brains as one of the causes.

We make an implicit deal with our parents and caregivers: in exchange for their love, acceptance, and protection, we will be what and whom they need and want us to be.[6] It's through criticism that we receive the specifics of their expectations and the parameters of the behavior and conduct that they desire. It makes sense at a biological level why criticism is an effective corrective measure: humans, in fact all animals, "learn faster from pain than pleasure."[7] This has been deemed the "oops! response" by researchers at Vanderbilt University, in which the part of the brain that is in charge of the fight-or-flight facilitates learning from mistakes.[8]

Harsh criticisms from those whom we learn from and trust the most register instantly. Their words imprint directly upon the more primitive part of the brain, where emotional memories are stored. The experience of being criticized goes into implicit memory – the type of memory that helps us to remember things without thinking about them, and accordingly creates automatic reactions. Unfortunately, the more negative experiences a person has, the "darker" their implicit memory bank becomes[9] – and the more negative experiences unconsciously direct our behavior subconsciously.

This may be why psychologist and creativity coach Eric Maisel asserts that "almost nothing does more psychological damage than criticism."[10] We quickly learn to fear criticism and automatically work to avoid potentially stressful situations, particularly those where we could make mistakes. We become motivated by the desire to meet expectations and to live up to the standards established by our caregivers so as to avoid feeling the strong emotion that comes up when we fear that we have not lived up to expectations and thus have disappointed them: shame.

It's shame that we feel when we are threatened with or actually receive insult or ridicule, or experience humiliation, rejection, or even abandonment by others.[11] Getting shamed starts early in our childhoods, with strong comments accompanied by a look of disdain, such as, "I expected better from you," or "you know that's not right," or far worse coming from our caregivers to push us to do the right thing. This process is actually a part of our development. In the proper context, being shamed teaches us resilience and helps us to develop the ability to deal with feedback and criticism. Growing up, each of us, some more than others, experienced some form of shaming to guide us to modify our behavior.

The problem comes when shaming is not followed up with the messages of love and support that tell us that we're okay, that we're inherently good, and that our caregivers or instructors believe in us.

In the absence of encouraging messages to counterbalance shaming ones, we start to feel that we are nothing but our mistakes.[12] Being criticized makes us feel shame because we fear that we brought on the criticism – or even worse treatment – because we made some kind of gross error and didn't live up to the expectations of caregivers, a group, or a social context; or that maybe that there is something intrinsically wrong with us.

These fears trigger our fear of rejection, and as you'll recall from the previous chapter, because of our deep need to belong, we are particularly sensitive to any indications of rejection. As our ancient limbic fight-or-flight response is triggered both by tone of voice and angry faces,[13] criticism registers as potential for rejection and thus as a threat to self. In a similar way to what happens when we perceive ourselves to be judged by others, when we are criticized, the threat to the Inner Critic's self protection system kicks it into gear. To proactively prevent us from getting caught unawares by future external criticism and being rejected, the Inner Critic establishes expectations, issues commands, and even attempts to define and reshape our identities in order to alter or inhibit our actions.[14] How? The Inner Critic adjusts our internal self-talk to mimic the criticisms we've received. In other words, as a protection mechanism, we internalize criticisms and become self-critical.

Because of the intensity of the memory of past criticisms, much like a watchful parent, the Inner Critic doesn't trust the self to know how to behave without the intervention of its guidance. To keep us on our toes and alert to potential errors, the Inner Critic begins to proactively criticize the parts of the self that it fears won't be accepted by peers, authorities, and society in general. Following the leads of caregivers, the Inner Critic amasses all of the criticisms and negative comments that we've heard over the course of our lives and uses them to generate a steady stream of coercive shaming inner self-talk in an attempt to shield us from potential humiliation. Messages such as, "If you don't work harder / come up with better ideas / become wildly successful, no one will love you" become standard to push us to continually improve performance and strive to achieve to high, frequently unreasonable, standards that we have taken on from others. This is the essence of High Self-Criticism: self-shaming to get ourselves to behave in a way that meets high expectations in order to proactively protect ourselves.

The problem is that the Inner Critic is a little too good at what it does. Because we've so deeply internalized the criticisms from others and made them our own, we lose our awareness of them. Lacking a sense of our true nature and the fullness of our potential, we unknowingly try to force ourselves into the constraints of external expectations. Our internalized criticisms from others become the source of most of the "shoulds," "musts," and "oughts" that fuel these imperative cognitive distortions. As we grow older, these mistaken beliefs shape both how we see ourselves and what we're capable of, and they become an intrinsic part of who we believe we are. Furthermore, we can't see how much they are controlling our thinking and behavior. When we are highly self-critical, the Inner Critic underlies our motivations, and thus is largely in control of driving our actions. But here's the kicker: as children, we may "internalize and exaggerate the expectations of parents, peers, or society."[15] *Exaggerate* – what we have responded to and have been using for all of these years to define ourselves and guide our actions may not have even been accurate!

Constantly living with the fear of being criticized and the high self-criticism that comes from it is exhausting. We spend inordinate amounts of time and energy trying to please people and be who we think we're supposed to be to avoid the threat of criticism. We end up feeling constantly on our guard, anxious, and insecure about our performance, as well as constantly trying to avoid disappointment from some unseen source and the shame that accompanies it. As the Brené Brown quote indicated, shame is a straitjacket: inflexible and limiting. By trying to live up to other people's standards and their expectations of how we're supposed to be, we limit ourselves. We use *their* values as a guide and yardstick, instead of our own. One of the top regrets of the dying is not having had the courage to live a life that was true to themselves, instead of living the life that others expected of them.[16] A life driven by the desire to avoid shame by living up to the unreasonable expectations of others is no life at all: we end up feeling unfulfilled and resentful.

When we let High Self-Criticism rule us, we hold ourselves back and we don't pay heed to the desires and needs of our Creative Self. We need to start healing the deep well of shame that formed the Inner Critic. By doing so, we'll begin to go of the compulsion to avoid disapproval from others, begin to break our habit of being highly self-critical, and start living our lives based on our own values and aspirations. The first step is to get at the source of our self-critical thoughts and the inaccurate beliefs they've spawned in order to transform them.

## Creative Dose: Get At the Source

*Purpose: To become aware of your Inner Critic and start transforming mistaken beliefs*

In Chapter 2, we used Mad-Libs to suss out some of your most common inner critical thoughts. But have you ever wondered: where in the world did these thoughts come from? What messages did I receive to take these criticisms on and start thinking them myself?

To dismantle beliefs, first we need to become aware of them. Let's do some mental archeology and see if we can unearth the source of some of your self-criticisms and then diffuse their sting by reframing them.

## Part 1: Belief Awareness

Sit down with a journal or a piece of paper and answer the following questions.

- What are your top self-criticisms?

- What are the beliefs underlying these criticisms?

Write them down as a list.

Go down the list of these beliefs. For each one, ask yourself objectively:

- Is this belief categorically true?

See what you can find through this process. Then use the self-compassion template from Chapter 2 to comfort the part of yourself that unfairly received that harsh criticism.

## Part 2: Remember and Reframe

Choose one of the beliefs that has the most power or the biggest emotional charge on it. Sit quietly for several minutes and see whether you can recall when you acquired that belief. Try to remember the situation as it happened.

Next, remember the circumstances of the situation, where you were, who you were with, and what was said. Make an effort to concentrate on the details, not your feelings about the situation.

Keep expanding your recollections to add information that you may have found out about the circumstances and the person later on.

Did the person suffer from migraines? Were they in the process of getting a divorce? Did she hate her job? Was he really stressed out as a single parent?

Continue to add details like this until you begin to see other potential reasons why that person reacted in that manner and how that criticism may not have been about you at all.

You can use this framework:

What I realize now is that:_____

Did doing so shift the emotional charge of the memory?

What shifted for me?_____

How can I reframe this inaccurate thought, which became a belief and then a criticism, about myself?_____

---

# Come To Your Own Defense

*"Were we to meet this figure socially, this accusatory character, this internal critic, this unrelenting fault-finder, we would think there was something wrong with him. He would just be boring and cruel. We might think that something terrible had happened to him, that he was living in the aftermath, in the fallout, of some catastrophe. And we would be right."*

**— Adam Phillips,** *"Against Self-Criticism" essay*

Criticism triggers the Inner Critic threat-protection system the same way judgments do, but even more so. Our negatively biased brains are already on high alert scanning for danger, giving us high threat reactivity, and making us "easily hijacked by alarm."[16] When a criticism, insult, or put-down comes from an external source, it triggers the stress response, activating the threat system in the brain.[17] The amygdala – the oldest part of the brain, and the so-called "lizard brain" – is stimulated. We feel attacked. In response, our blood pressure goes up, and to easily activate the strength and energy needed to either confront or avoid the threat, our bodies are flooded with adrenaline and cortisol.[18] Simply put, criticism causes us to go into fight, flight, or freeze mode. We may lash out at the person, try to get away from the criticizer as quickly as possible, or we may end up sitting in stunned silence, unable to find the words for defense or rebuttal.

However, while this system evolved to address external threats and attacks, it is activated just as easily by emotional attacks from ourselves.[19] When criticism come from an internal source – when we self-criticize – the same mechanism is triggered. *Our brains respond in the same way as they do when the criticism comes from other people.*[20]

Whether the criticism is coming from the outside or inside of our own heads, our psyches feel threatened. In internalizing and mentally repeating strong criticisms and making them into self-criticism, the Inner Critic takes on the role of the criticizer. And because external criticisms feel like attacks, when we self-criticize, we are mentally attacking ourselves. You may think that the term *attacked* is strong. But when you consider that we respond the exact same way to internal self-criticisms as  to criticism and insults coming from others – that our amygdala is triggered and we go into threat response mode – the term *attack* is apt.

When the Inner Critic takes on the role of the external criticizer, we become of two minds and two selves. Don't think of this as a multiple personality disorder, like in the movie *Sybil* or the show the *United States of Tara*. Rather, when the Inner Critic is present, the psyche splits into multiple parts,[21] with one passing judgment upon and supplying criticisms to the other.[22]

This Inner Critic "attack" may take the form of mentally lambasting ourselves over perceived mistakes, personal failure, or rejection; becoming defensive and sabotaging our own efforts, or trying to distract ourselves and run away from dealing with areas that we could improve.[23] Because of this, I think of the two selves as the Inner Critic and the Attacked Self. The Inner Critic is the part of ourselves that is doing the criticizing. The Attacked Self is the equivalent of the inner child, and is the part of us that needs reassurance in the face of criticism, regardless of whether it's coming from people outside of ourselves or from our own minds.

The power dynamic is this: the Inner Critic essentially dominates the Attacked Self.[24] In the same way a caregiver-child relationship is that of dominant and subordinate,[25] the Inner Critic and the Attacked Self assume these roles too. And just as a parent or caregiver's reprimands were intended to keep us away from potential harm, the Inner Critic's severe directives compel us to hold ourselves back. The inhibited behavior that results from self-criticism shuts us down and keeps us from experiences that are seen to hold the prospect of threat. Unfortunately, instead of feeling safe and protected when the Inner Critic tries to protect us, we end up feeling *more* vulnerable and threatened.

The Inner Critic's objective of internalizing contempt was to help get us to belong more, but the harshness of our self-criticisms instead cause us to feel disconnected from others, isolated and alone, and potentially unworthy of belonging to the group.[26] The Inner Critic in the form of High Self-Criticism *causes* the very thing that it was trying to avoid!

It's no wonder self-criticism is such a creativity-killer. Knowing what we do about how the brain's self-evaluating part needs to be quiet for ideas to connect and come out of our heads, it's easy to see why High Self-Criticism – negative self-evaluation on steroids – is like an enormous dam that holds back ideas from flowing through. We literally can't be creative when we're being highly self-critical; our brains and systems are too busy looking for and armoring against danger and threat. It's also no small wonder that the Inner Critic feels so powerful and that at times we can feel so beaten down and controlled by it.[27] In this light, feeling overwhelmed by and on the defensive with our inner critical thoughts and disparaging self-talk — and as a result, completely, utterly unable to come up with new ideas or solutions — makes perfect sense.

When we are highly self-critical, our self-criticism initiates a process in which self-criticism begets more of the same, circling back to amplify itself and then spiraling out of control. It's an excruciating cycle. But we have the means to break it.

To reclaim our relinquished creativity, we are quite literally rebuilding our mind frames. In addition to leveraging neuroplasticity, we must rebuild the compromised foundations of our self-to-self relating. Thankfully, we are already developing the main tool that is the antidote to the venom of High Self-Criticism: self-compassion.

In addition to the array of benefits listed in Chapter 2, here's further confirmation of self-compassion's efficacy: a form of mental training based on meta-cognitive learning and self-compassion called Compassionate Mind Training (CMT) has been shown to help study participants significantly decrease their level of mental self-attacking. In this study, the participants' self-critical thoughts diminished in intensity and became less frequent and intrusive. The participants' ability to reassure themselves rose significantly, with self-soothing thoughts becoming more powerful and easier for them to access. They also reduced their fears of being judged by others, with a major reduction of feelings of inferiority in social comparison. Also, they experienced reduced feelings of isolation and aloneness.[28] These are precisely the outcomes that we are looking for to begin to shift out of our propensity to self-criticize.

We can make use of many of the practices employed in the study and directly apply self-compassion to shift the power dynamics of our two selves, give comfort to the Attacked Self and calm down our limbic systems, and subdue the Inner Critic so that the Attacked Self can relax and fade away – and allow the Creative Self to come to the fore.

Constantly being buffeted by messages from the Inner Critic wears down the younger, little-kid part of ourselves that just wants to be accepted and belong. To start creating profound and meaningful change, we have to give this part of ourselves the sense of safety that the Inner Critic has been working so hard to create for it.

To shift the power dynamics between the Inner Critic and the Attacked Self, we'll turn the tables on the Inner Critic. Again, we're going to tap into the caregiving system that we are built with. Instead of letting the Inner Critic beat up the kid part of ourselves, we are going to comfort ourselves. Through giving kind words to the self, we'll start to alleviate mental discomfort. As a result, we will transform the balance of the hormones our bodies produce and shift our emotions, moving us to a place of feeling increasingly more secure.

## Creative Dose: Compassion for the Selves

*Purpose: To show compassion to both the Attacked Self and the Inner Critic*

This exercise is adapted from the book *Self-Compassion* by Kristin Neff.[29]

### Step 1: Soothe the Attacked Self

Through generating feelings of warmth and compassion for the Attacked Self in place of toxic self-criticism, we can deflect the Inner Critic's attack.

Once you've become aware that your Inner Critic is being judgmental and critical, take a moment to think soothing thoughts to the part of yourself that feels attacked. Think in the same kind of language you would use to show compassion to and soothe a child or a loved one.

For example, if you find yourself thinking something like:

"I can't believe you missed that deadline! You're going to mess everything up for everyone on the team!"

You could soften it by telling yourself instead:

"I know you're working as hard as you can. Maybe you can find a way to simplify what you're doing to get it all completed."

You can give yourself comforting messages to counter the self-critical voice of the Inner Critic either by writing them down, thinking them, or saying them verbally.

What are some comforting messages that will work for you?

Comforting message:

_____

Comforting message:

_____

## Step 2: Soothe the Original Inner Critic

In a poignant quote from author Bryant H. McGill, he says, "...you reclaim your power by loving what you were once taught to hate." The Inner Critic can seem like this hugely powerful entity in our heads, but remember, the young part of ourselves was the seed of the Inner Critic.

Imagine this: a little kid playing dress up in oversized clothes, maybe as a police officer, a teacher, a librarian or other adult authority figure. This seed of our young selves merely tried to imitate what he or she thought behavior control looked like and how it was supposed to make you try to act. But it was as clueless as you were: both of you were children who didn't know any better.

When you think of the Inner Critic from this perspective, you can see that in many ways, it needs comforting and reassurance as well. When you find your Inner Critic getting active and forceful, some acknowledgement, calming words, and some guidelines for behavior may help to tone down its intensity.

For example, you may find yourself thinking something like this:

"You can't share this idea, everyone will think it's stupid."

Here's how you can respond this to your Inner Critic:

"I understand that you're trying to keep me safe from ridicule, but you actually don't know what people will think at all."

*Then you must follow with this very important request:*

"Please stop being so critical of what I do, it's really hurtful for me."

By kindly acknowledging the Inner Critic's concern, defusing its validity, and then responding to the Inner Critic with the knowledge that it's hurtful, you will be on the road to changing it from being an attacker to an ally.

## Stay In the Present

*"Humans have an intelligent brain that can literally be taken over by basic emotions."*

— **Dr. Paul Gilbert,** *founder of Compassion Focused Therapy*

Due to negativity bias, we already remember insults and criticisms more than we remember praise. Negativity bias also pulls the mind towards upsetting or negative thoughts rather than positive ones when it wanders. This tendency is normal when it is infrequent. But when we repeat these negative messages over and over in our heads because of High Self-Criticism, an entirely different process is at play. Interestingly, it's one of the things that we have in common with antelopes.

If we were antelopes, in the face of a threatening experience we would respond by temporarily kicking into reactive mode and bounding over the bush of the savannah to safety. However, as soon as the threat of danger had passed, we'd return to a state of calm known as responsive mode. But we are not antelopes, we are human. With a larger, more complex brain, our upgraded operating system not only includes a high-alert function that constantly scans for danger, but we also boast a larger memory capacity to store past incidents from which to learn. It's how we make use of this capacity to remember that is the practice that we share with antelopes. It's called ruminating.

Taken from the ability of antelope, cattle and other and other animals of its kind to chew food multiple times, psychologists use the term "ruminating" to refer to the practice of thinking thoughts associated with the symptoms, causes, and consequences of one's negative feelings over and over again in a recurring loop.

There are two versions of rumination:

1)  Thinking about events in the past.

2)  Worrying about events that could possibly happen in the future.

Much to our detriment, when we are highly self-critical, we have a tendency to draw upon our emotionally charged negative memories of being criticized far more often than is beneficial. The more we recycle the past and worry about things that are going to go wrong in the future, the stronger the ruminating circuit gets.[30]

In neuroscience, Hebb's Law is a well-known expression in the world of neural psychology which states: "neurons that fire together, wire together."[31] As we know from what we learned about neuroplasticity in Chapter 2, this brain function is fantastic when it comes to learning new skills or imprinting your mind with positive experiences. It's not so great, however, when we recycle painful memories, engage in highly critical self-talk, or get worked up about something we're afraid will happen in the future. Starting out as merely traces in the brain, the more these negative thoughts repeat, the more they create well-worn tracks in your neural circuits. This repetition creates a tendency to ruminate that will eventually turn into a rumination reflex.

Both depression and anxiety are the result of excess rumination, and with our special mental version of it, we humans constantly wrestle with both. Depression and anxiety are two sides of the same coin – both activate similar processes in the brain. One uses the imagination to replay memories and the feelings associated with them; the other employs the imagination to create possible negative scenarios and the emotions connected with those. With a particularly virulent Inner Critic, we can all too easily slip into a state of either or both.

Rumination uses up valuable mental resources: it diminishes concentration and reduces the performance of learned skills that have become automatic. More importantly, rumination is completely at odds with being creative. Research shows that creative thought "... recruits brain regions that are critical for daydreaming, imagining the future, remembering deeply personal memories, constructive internal reflection, meaning making, and social cognition."[32] That sounds remarkably similar to what we do when we ruminate. Furthermore, recycling memories and thoughts from the past actually "discourages active problem-solving, as people tend to stay fixated on the negative thoughts and emotions rather than put forth the effort to solve the underlying problem," keeping us blind to alternatives outside our narrowed perspective.[33] We can't do both: we can't come up with ideas while we are engaging the same network to recycle old thoughts and memories or create new negative ones. Ruminating steals away the brain capacity we need to envision workable solutions to the tasks and challenges directly in front of us – in other words, to exercise creativity.

Unsurprisingly, with their smaller brains and different memory capacity, antelopes do not suffer from beating themselves up over past mistakes or worrying about future ones. But we do, and we pay dearly for it on multiple levels. Self-critical ruminating initiates the cycle of constantly being on high alert to threat. Over time, the resulting high levels of cortisol perpetually running through our system deplete our reserves of the brain chemicals that help us experience pleasure.[34]

The mental toll of ruminating is equally distressing. Think of the mind/brain as a mental simulator that runs movies. These movies of past failures and potential futures are the equivalent of horror movies and leave a wake of highly self-critical and negativistic neural structure, which is part of the foundation upon which our sense of self and self-perception is built. This neural structure and the resultant way of thinking then begins to rule your behavior and color your perceptions. So, if you are beating yourself up about how you got nervous in the client presentation or that you're afraid that your work won't be good enough and you may be fired, it will negatively influence your future actions.

We have options. We don't have to keep reliving the criticisms and let them continue to affect us; we don't have to feed our self-attacking through self-criticism. We need to stay aware and vigilant to this habit. It only hurts us and put us in constant high alert, wearing down our minds and bodies. Everything that you've agonized about that happened in the past is no longer happening. The things you worry about? They haven't yet happened.

Recycling emotionally charged negative thoughts and memories can trap us in a holding pattern of depression and anxiety. Like I told Anneke, it's time to put the hammer down. Instead of rehashing the past or worrying about the future, you could be focused on the here and now, directing your powers of imagination toward the best way to move yourself forward into a future that you actually want.

## Creative Dose: The Anti-Rumination Hand Squeeze

*Purpose: To interrupt the rumination process and help you to refocus*

When you find yourself getting worked up over a thought that's blocking you from generating ideas, do this: Take a soft toy ball in your left hand and squeeze it for several minutes.

Studies show that rumination is associated with the left side of the brain, and that the activity of using your left hand to squeeze the toy ball stimulates the opposite side of the brain, breaking the rumination process by forcing activity to the opposite hemisphere.[35]

If you are left-handed and this exercise doesn't kick you out of ruminating, then try using your right hand instead.

## Creative Dose: S.H.I.F.T. to Three+3

*Purpose: To shift yourself out of ruminative self-criticism and into a place of self-appreciation*

In her book *The Happiness Project*, author Gretchen Rubin suggests that everyone should have a place in their minds that is sort of a safe space, an area of refuge, where there are only positive things: thoughts, memories, music, smells, and such. This is a place that we can escape to whenever we may be drawn to recalling and then ruminating upon negative thoughts, beliefs, or memories.[36] It turns out that this is sound advice; studies have shown that reliving positive memories reduces stress.[37]

However, when we're in limbic overload from negatively ruminating, before we can get to our happy place, we need a method to help us switch gears. Hopefully, you've started using the hand-squeeze technique to truncate the rumination process. Now, let's deliberately shift our brains into a different and more positive mindframe.

### Step 1: Determine Your Rumination Style

We all have negativity bias and we all ruminate to some extent. However, if you have High Self-Criticism, there's a good chance that your rumination reflex is strong, and it may be hurting you.

Look below and see which version of rumination you lean towards:

❑ **Depressive:** Continuously revisiting, thinking about, and generating negative emotions relating to events in the past. This is the version of rumination that, in its extreme form, contributes to depression.

❑ **Anxious:** Thinking of and generating negative emotions about events that could possibly happen in the future. In its extreme form, this version of rumination contributes to anxiety.

Knowing this about yourself is the first step to raising your awareness of the tendency to ruminate, and will help you recognize it better when you fall into it.

### Step 2: S.H.I.F.T.

Shifting attention to stop the ruminating circuit from being self-critical about any perceived mistakes or errors is key.

Acronyms are a great mnemonic device, so I've created one to help with the process of grounding ourselves when we go into the mode of being overly self-critical. As I've mentioned, banishing the Inner Critic has nothing to do with strong-arming. It is more about using your awareness to make different choices, which over time will eventually change how your brain works. Here's an acronym to keep in mind to move from being in an self-critical state of mind to one that is kinder to the self and supportive of creativity: S.H.I.F.T.

So, when you feel your Inner Critic coming up, mentally say to your Inner Critic "thank you for your thoughts," and then S.H.I.F.T.:

**S**tay present, taking several deep breaths to get yourself grounded and back into your body.

**H**ave compassion by understanding that you're feeling scared and commiting to give yourself comforting messages.

**I**nvoke mindfulness by realizing that you are not your thoughts and that you have the power to observe them without reacting to them.

**F**ocus attention, choosing to place your attention on alternative thoughts.

**T**rust your Creative Self, knowing that the creative part of you exists and it will come out when you relax.

These are suggestions, but to really solidify this as a tool that works for you, feel free to come up your own versions of staying present, having compassion, invoking mindfulness, focusing attention, and trusting in your creative self .

Or even better, use your creativity to come up with your own S.H.I.F.T. words, or even your own acronym, to help break you out of ruminating and put yourself into a calmer mindframe.

**Step 3: Make Your Three+3**

Now that you're shifting out of rumination into a calmer state of mind, you need to replace self-critical thoughts with self-supportive ones. When you recognize yourself falling into the habit of self-criticizing, use the Three+3 technique. We're combining two powerful practices in one exercise.

First, we will replace negative self-criticism with positive statements. Despite what you may think, affirmations do work, but not in the way that they are typically promoted. Instead of being a mechanism of changing thought patterns from old to new, studies show that affirmations are really good at showing us the range of possibilities. They are in essence "cognitive expanders."[38] Affirmations help to soften the blow of negative thoughts and to dampen defensiveness. While self-criticism and the subconscious sense of threat that it generates narrow perspective on the self, affirmations bolster self-worth by widening our tunnel vision and helping us to see ourselves and our potential more clearly. When it comes to being highly self-critical, affirmations help give us a much-needed alternative perspective.

Second, we'll employ a self-talk technique in which you address yourself in the third person. This has been shown to help people to think more clearly, gain perspective, and improve performance. Talking to yourself in the third person switches on the cognitive part of the brain, turns off the fight-or-flight response, and returns us to a place of calm self-control.[39]

*Before you need it*, do this:

1) Think of three qualities that you truly appreciate about yourself and are grateful for. Are you kind to others, respectful of people's time, a good listener, able to distill information quickly, honest, trustworthy, a loyal friend? Choose the three qualities that you feel best about and memorize them. Practice them to yourself so that your list becomes completely automatic. That way when you need to bring it to mind, it's readily available.

2) Now create a list of qualities that you appreciate about your creativity and are grateful for. Do you find your creativity delightful, whimsical, profound, moving, truthful, insightful, warming, thought-provoking, multilayered? Think of words that positively describe how you feel about your creativity or how your creativity makes you feel. Choose the top three that make you feel best – that provide a sense of warmth and satisfaction. Again, practice this list to yourself until it becomes automatic.

You've now got your Three+3.

**Step 4: Play Your Three+3**

Anytime you recognize yourself going into a mode of self-criticism, put your Three+3 to work.

Say to yourself, either mentally or out loud,

"Sheila, you are kind, thoughtful, and honest."

"Your creativity is delightful, profound, and inspiring."

Important: Remember to speak to yourself in the third person instead of using "I." You will gain the most benefit this way!

Over time, this practice will actually help to diverge from the well-worn mental paths of self-criticism in your brain.

# GET PERSPECTIVE AND GAIN CONTROL

*"The most common way people give up their power is by thinking they don't have any."*

— **Alice Walker,** *author and poet*

By staying in a state of perpetually feeling like we're under attack from our own self-criticism, much of our energy reserves are drained by a limbic system that's in constant crisis. However, now that we've learned where the practice of being highly self-critical comes from and have strategies for getting to the roots of our mistaken beliefs and breaking the cycle of strengthening them by repetition, we begin to see that we are not powerless against this particularly damaging guise of the Inner Critic. We have the wherewithal to regain the reins of control over both our minds and emotions.

To continue transforming our dynamic so that we get ourselves out of reactive mode, and to calm ourselves down enough so that we can start doing the work that we came here to do, we need to amp up our efforts to think differently so that we may do differently. To discover who we truly are without the fear of punishment motivating our choices and behaviors, we need to learn how to create distance between ourselves and our self-critical thoughts. As we are working to fully assimilate this new practice, we will be much like children talking their way through learning a new task. Thus, self-talk will be our main tool for success. However, unlike when we were younger, we will actively update our inner self-talk by being aware of and in control of it. This time, we know we have power.

## Create A Healthy Mental Distance

*"Beautiful things happen in your life when you distance yourself from negativity."*

**— Anonymous**

Criticism from others brings to light the qualities that we fear are our shortcomings. In addition to triggering our threat system, the criticisms that we received when we were younger were so poignant in large part because they voiced our fears about ourselves.

Here is the number-one rule when it comes to High Self-Criticism: do not accept everything your Inner Critic says as the gospel.

While they may feel like your own thoughts, remember that your self-criticisms are born from other people's beliefs and perceptions that were superimposed upon you and that you took on. It's what and how you believed you were *supposed* to do, think, and be to be valued, protected, and feel safe in the world. *However, it doesn't mean that any of those criticisms are actually true.*

Whenever you remember this fact, then it is easier to identify the underlying beliefs that were the seeds of your current self-criticisms. We need to stay vigilant about not over-identifying with the messages of the

Inner Critic. The more aware we are of these thoughts, the more we'll realize that we no longer need to continue telling ourselves these lies.

Through the heightened awareness of our thoughts, we'll hear how we talk to ourselves more clearly. And because we are working to return to the Creative Self, if this self-talk does not support our creativity, then we will change it. One method used in psychology is called "self-distancing," which is to see yourself as another person, and correspondingly, use self-talk to mentally refer to yourself in the third person as "you" instead of in the first person of "I," or even use your first name. (Remember, you've already practiced this in the Three+3 exercise.) Just the simple switch of pronouns or addressing yourself in the third person has the potential to dramatically transform your ability to execute tasks with aplomb.

Various studies have revealed directed inner talk to be an incredibly effective tool to reshape the psyche for success. Ethan Koss, director of the Emotion & Self-Control Laboratory at the University of Michigan, has determined that self-talk is "a powerful instrument of consciousness" that enables the brain to reach optimal performance.[40] Self-distancing has the power to affect the fight-or-flight response, and helps quell emotional reactions that narrow our perception of our options. Self-distancing flips a switch in the part of the brain that controls thoughts and another that controls fear, creating a bit of mental magic.[41] The practice of using this different language allows us to observe our circumstances and emotions in an alert and interested manner, much like the state we would be in when going to a new place. Psychological distance enables us to lower rumination, thus helping us to think more clearly. With negative thoughts at a minimum, we exercise self-control, perform better, and are able to gain the perspective we need to plan for the future.[42]

Self-distancing through changing self-talk is a highly underutilized tool, but we are going to change that. It's important to keep in mind that all of our self-perceptions are really only mental constructs – they are thoughts about ourselves and not who we are in the grandest sense.[43] Both the self and the mind are ever-changing and fluid. Our current versions of ourselves are an outcome of our past, but in every moment lies the potential for us to mold ourselves into a different future self. Through changing our self-talk, we will do just that.

## Creative Dose: Self-Talk Reboot

*Purpose: To transform self-talk into a tool for empowerment*

We're going to revamp how we talk to ourselves. It's time to celebrate: the days of mean self-talk are numbered! No more letting ourselves be beaten down by telling ourselves harsh criticisms in the first person. To separate ourselves from our self-critical thoughts, we're going to use self-distancing, and mentally take a few steps back so that we can see ourselves more clearly and then guide ourselves to where we want to go.

Fortuitously, it turns out that self-distancing is a great tool for mindfulness, helping us to stay aware of what's happening around us and view ourselves with objectivity, much as we would regard a friend. Because of this detachment from our self-critical stories, we can better practice self-kindness and compassion as well.

There are three steps to this process: First, we will practice getting distance from the part of ourselves that is the Inner Critic. Next, we will encourage ourselves as if we were a different person. Third, we will get a template for how to talk ourselves out of self-critical jams when we need it.

### Step 1: From I to You

The part of you that is the highly self-critical Inner Critic is not *you*. You are more than your Inner Critic and self-berating. So let's get some distance by giving your Inner Critic a voice and helping you to start to see and feel the difference between you and your self-criticisms. This exercise was adapted from the article "The Critical Inner Voice that Causes Depression," by Lisa Firestone, PhD.[119]

When it comes up, tune into the voice of your self-criticism. In your journal or on a sheet of paper, write down these thoughts. However, in place of "I", use "You."

For example, your thought may be "None of my ideas are any good."

You would change that to "None of your ideas are any good."

Commit to do this exercise for a week. It will quickly raise your awareness of just how harsh your inner talk has been, and will also make you question whether your self-critical thoughts are truly your own perspective or a stance that you've inherited. Once you see how mean your negative self-talk is, you'll be motivated to change it to something more positive.

### Step 2: Third-Person Power

In one of Ethan Koss' studies, participants were told to try to encourage themselves before giving a presentation. Those who used their names to give themselves a pep talk like "You can do this, Marcus. You've totally got this," gave better talks, ruminated less, and felt less shame about their performance afterward. In contrast, those who tried to bolster their nervousness by using "I" felt less calm and less positive.[44]

When you're in the ideation and creative stage of a project, when you most need ideas to flow, give yourself periodic boosts by talking to yourself in the third person.

Here are some examples:

- "Roxanne, you are going to come up with something great!"

- "Jonathon, just sit down and let your ideas flow."

- "Rashida, you really do great work."

**Part 3: Talk Yourself Through It**

Talking to yourself as if you're another person moves the focus away from the self. We'll flip a switch in our heads that turns the self off and turns on objectivity by leveraging the power that language has over our brains. It turns out that the emotional parts of the brain don't respond well to the scolding we've been practicing when being highly self-critical – but it does great with same type of encouragement that we would give to a friend. The distance also helps us to apply the wisdom that we activate when we advise others.

When you are trying to do your creative work and have a particularly strong moment of high self-criticism that threatens to paralyze you from moving forward, you can talk to yourself in the same way an objective advisor, mentor, or coach would.

Let's try this exercise, adapted from the article "The Voice of Reason," by Pamela Weintraub.[43]

Say that you agreed to give a talk at the last minute and you only had one day to prepare for it. You're unsure of what you've developed, and as a result, your anxiety levels are going through the roof.

Use this template to talk yourself down from the ceiling.

1) **"Josh, there's no need to be nervous about giving this talk. You've done this a hundred times before."**
   Remember to get distance by addressing yourself by your first name and providing supportive advice just like you would to a friend.

2) **"Just remember what points you can and convey your love of the subject. People will respond to your passion and enthusiasm."**
   Remember to soothe yourself and tell yourself a truth about the situation.

3) "Josh, you're an accomplished, professional, and seasoned speaker. You're going to do great – this is what you do." Remember to use the power of affirmations to expand your perceptions of yourself. Give yourself a final positive stroke to make it all stick.

Regardless of the circumstance, you can adapt this template to self-encourage as needed and transform your self-talk into a tool that will take you to new heights.

# Break On Through To the Other Side

*"Your mind is your instrument. Learn to be its master and not its slave."*

— **Remez Sasson,** *author*

In continuing to take back our power to create and questioning the source of these harsh inward criticisms that we have started to dismantle, we need to get at some deeper parts of the Inner Critic. How will we do that? We're going to give the brain a little workout by forcing activity in the nondominant hemisphere.

We'll do this for several reasons. First, using our nondominant hand forces us to use a part of the brain that is related to feeling, intuition, inner wisdom, and creativity.[46] I like to think this means it's the part of the brain that is more closely connected to younger parts of the psyche. Second, while the brain often only uses one hemisphere when doing familiar tasks with the dominant hand, forcing use of the nondominant hand activates both hemispheres simultaneously. The unfamiliar physical motion improves communication between the two sides of the brain, enhancing mental processing. Finally, using our other hand encourages the formation of new neural connections and pathways. The more we use our nondominant hand, the more we can not only reach harder-to-reach emotions, but also simultaneously amplify the brain's capacity for creativity.

## Creative Dose: Inner Critic Undoing

*Purpose: To use the other side of your brain to get at the roots of your Inner Critic*

### Part 1: Give Your Inner Critic The Third Degree

For this exercise, use both your dominant hand and your nondominant hand.

Sit down with a piece of paper, and write the following questions to your Inner Critic with your dominant hand. Be sure to leave enough space for the answers:

- Who are you?

- Where do you come from?

- What do you want?

- What do you believe you're protecting me from?

- So, what's your point?

- What does it matter if I am _____ or not?

Take a moment to sit with the questions, then write the responses with your nondominant hand. What comes up for you?

### Part 2: Erasure

With your nondominant hand, draw a picture of the meanest, nastiest, most vicious version of your Inner Critic. Drawing your Inner Critic takes it out of your head and puts in front your eyes, helping you to distance from it.[47]

Now, while telling your Inner Critic that you don't need it to be so zealous and that you are creating new terms for your relationship with it, take the picture and rip it into shreds. Dispose of the shreds. Or if you have the means to burn the shreds, then do so.

How did it feel to make your Inner Critic visible? Did it make it feel less threatening?

How did it feel to physically destroy your representation of it?

## Change Your Mind By Hand

*"Often the hands will solve a mystery that the intellect has struggled with in vain."*

— **Carl Jung,** *psychologist*

As we increase awareness of our thoughts to gain better control of them, we'll invariably notice more negative ones and greater amounts of self-criticism. In addition to relying upon mindfulness to notice them and self-compassion to think more supportive thoughts, we can also make use of the mind-body connection and use gesture to spark a change.

A wide body of research shows the use of the hands "enhances cerebral capacity, elevates mood, and elicits creative thought."[48] Indeed, physical movement holds the potential to be a major part of stimulating the imagination and the brain for problem-solving and creative work. However, most exciting to me is one research finding that "body movements are involved not only in processing old ideas, but also in creating new ones."[49]

It turns out that gestures and thinking are far more connected than we realize. Susan Goldin-Meadow, a professor of Psychology at the University of Chicago and author of *Hearing Gesture: How Our*

*Hands Help Us Think*,[50] studies the effect of gestures on learning with children. What her research has revealed is absolutely fascinating.

First, gestures have a strong effect on our mindframe. Goldin-Meadow's studies found that gestures reflect what is on our minds and often give a better indication of what we are thinking than what we say verbally.[51] Second, the gestures that we see others do can change our minds: she found gestures that suggest information are almost as leading as verbally stating the same. Third, the gestures that *we* make can change *our* minds as well. And it gets even better: not only can we use gestures to change what we're thinking, but we can also use gestures to activate deep-seated knowledge.

Finally, in addition to showing what's on our minds or guiding it toward change, gestures enhance learning. Goldin-Meadow's findings reveal that when children use gestures to accentuate concepts – either those taught to them or those they naturally create themselves – they learn better. Children who use gestures to learn math problems far outperform those who do not, and babies who learn gestures at fourteen months old have dramatically expanded vocabularies by fifty-four months old.[52] Gesture, then, is an overlooked powerhouse of a tool.

As adults, our gestures are well-established and many of them already have strong mental associations. One very strong one that is the gesture of swiping to the left to signal subtraction or taking away. It's easy to think that "swiping left" came into being with the development of swiping apps, but this gesture far precedes them. It's been a part of human communication for a very long time, with almost universal common meaning. The motion of moving your hand in front your body to the left has long had the meaning of "Take it away/get rid of it," "Go away," "I don't want it," and even, "It's not good enough." The deeply established connection between this gesture and our brains is the perfect vehicle to lessen our self-criticism.

In our process of banishing the Inner Critic, we're going to co-opt this already ingrained body-mind connection and put it to work to transform the power of our self-criticisms. That's right: we're going to use gesture to change our minds from being highly self-critical to becoming more approving of ourselves.

## Creative Dose: Swipe Left

*Purpose: To quickly delete negative thoughts*

We can counter self-critical thoughts by "deleting" them. No, I'm not talking about trying to "not think" them – we've already discovered in Chapter 2 that thought-stopping doesn't completely work. It's only when we halt the process of turning thoughts and feelings into self-criticism, and also stop replaying the self-criticism that is already there, that we will start becoming less self-critical and more self-supportive.

To cease censoring our creative ideas, we will use our hands and mind together to censor self-critical thoughts and create new thought patterns. This exercise is so quick and easy that you can start using it right now.

### Option 1: Delete

When you start going into a self-critical litany of how everything you create sucks, or any other toxic self-criticism, think or say "Delete" or "Cancel" and use the gesture of swiping left with two or three fingers in the air, the same way you would do on your smartphone to delete an email.

Doing so will leverage a strong association that already exists in your brain and start applying it to thoughts to help you delete them and move on.

### Option 2: Delete and Replace

You can take this practice step further by creating or using a second gesture to anchor the positive thought that replaces the negative one. If your negative thought is "My work sucks," first think or say "Delete" and swipe left.

Then think a new thought, such as "My work is constantly evolving and improving," and combine with a nod yes, or even combine nodding yes and touching your hand to your heart.

## CEASE SELF-CENSORING

*"You must be unintimidated by your own thoughts because if you write with someone looking over your shoulder, you'll never write."*

— **Nikki Giovanni,** *poet*

Some of our most precious time is during the moments of ideation, brainstorming, musing, and contemplation. These are times when we are playing with ideas and seeing how they connect and inform each other. During these times in particular, we need the Inner Critic to be unobtrusive and quiet. As we are all too aware, this is when it tends to weigh in the most and we become the most self-critical. Instead of easily accessing ideas, we feel they are maddeningly just out of reach.

As an over-zealous protector, your Inner Critic does its job a little too well. When we think self-critical thoughts like, "This idea is dumb, so I'm not going to attempt it. I'll wait until a better idea comes along," or "I'm wrong," or "it will be boring and suck," we are making either a conscious choice to withhold ideas or an unconscious one that inhibits the generation of ideas.[53] When we do that, we are committing what writer Matthew May refers to in a recent online article as "ideacide," a process of self-censoring he considers "the highest crime against creativity."[54]

It's the Inner Critic in the form of High Self-Criticism that causes us to commit ideacide and to "reject, deny, stifle, squelch, strike, silence and otherwise put ideas of our own to death, sometimes even before they're born."[55] We do this for fear that we'll be judged, criticized, or ridiculed and that our ideas will be evaluated negatively. The resulting self-doubt and over-control interfere with our ability to be creative. If any ideas do make it past the Inner Critic's stalwart efforts to block them, they are stunted and weak from their ordeal.

Ironically, being overly self-critical and committing ideacide heightens the likelihood that the very outcomes we fear will come to fruition.

But ideacide is detrimental to more than ideas. When we commit ideacide, while destroying the sprouting seedlings of ideas before they reach the light of day, we also mentally beat ourselves up and destroy our self-confidence. Furthermore, ideacide also affects the people we work with. Being highly self-critical blinds us to the prospect that even if our ideas are not fully formed or brilliant, others could benefit from them. Our ideas could be a catalyst that sparks variations to build upon, or even other great ideas.

For writers especially, poet Nikki Giovanni's quote about being "unintimidated by your own thoughts" is spot-on, but because not all of us are writers, I will be so bold as to alter her quote to make it more applicable to everyone: "You must be unintimidated by your own thoughts, because if you create with someone looking over your shoulder, you'll never create."

Think back to the last time you were in the creative zone with your work and remember the thoughts you were thinking and the feelings you were having then; what do you find?

Were you concerned about how interesting your ideas were or afraid they were intrinsically wrong? No!

Were you panicked or anxious about bringing your idea into the world or afraid you wouldn't do it justice? No!

Did you feel like you could learn what you needed to bring your idea to fruition? Yes!

Did you feel like you could do it? Yes!

You were able to feel positive and confident because no mental critic was looking over your shoulder. Your Inner Critic was, at least for several shining moments, deliciously and beautifully silent.

When you are so highly self-critical that you commit ideacide, you've let your Inner Critic stand over our shoulder and assume the role of a manager or director you can never impress. Your Inner Critic is far too high on the organizational chart of You Incorporated.

Let's demote the Inner Critic from director/manager of your creative life to a position lower on the org chart, and reassign it to a support role that is more commensurate with the level of responsibility and importance that we want it to have.

How do you reorg your Inner Critic? Let's look at some ways to do this so you can move to a place of criticism-free creating.

## Question and Challenge

*"Self-criticism, when it isn't useful in the way any self-correcting approach can be, is self-hypnosis."*

**— Adam Phillips,** *"Against Self-Criticism" essay*

The Inner Critic has been operating in the background and under the radar in the form of High Self-Criticism for years now. Hoping to protect us from others' criticism, it's been surreptitiously blindsiding us by throwing wrenches in the works of our equilibrium when we least expect it. Our High Self-Criticism paints a patina over everything we do, and causes us to not see ourselves or our creative capacities clearly. We forget our creative core and begin to doubt, second-guess, or overlook our skills and talents. The worst part is that we don't even know that we are doing it.

Some indications are obvious, like causing us to criticize everything we do or shooting down every idea we come up with from the get-go. But others are more subtle. Don't believe me? Check to see whether any of the following sound familiar:

- You suddenly lose interest when you were previously highly engaged.

- You're working on something, and all of a sudden you start questioning yourself.

- Out of nowhere, you feel your energy decreasing and maybe even start to feel inordinately sleepy.

- You're making great progress but then suddenly become stuck and unable to problem-solve your way past your block.

- You "know," "are sure that," or "are certain that" something won't work, won't be accepted, or will be criticized.

Any of these scenarios are a pretty sure sign that the Inner Critic, in the form of High Self-Criticism, was kicking in.[56] We all have fallen prey to these crafty ploys at some point.

High Self-Criticism also convinces the Inner Critic that it is fully aware of our capacities – it knows the extent of our limits, is intimate with our weaknesses, and is conversant with our strengths. But this is categorically untrue. Despite the fact that it often feels otherwise, the Inner Critic voices stories about the things we fear, not the truth about who we are. Our self-internalized criticisms came from people who could not see the extent of our magnificence, could not see the depth of our brilliance, and did not have the capacity to understand that we are only limited by our perceptions of what is possible for us. Are you going to let someone else's limited vision of you determine the parameters of your being?

The Inner Critic has become far too comfortable in its position as saboteur. By this point it probably doesn't believe that we will a) recognize its handiwork, and b) shine a light on it and make it answer for its actions. Instead of allowing the "authoritative" Inner Critic to rely on the beliefs, values, and motivations of the people from whom our younger selves took our cues and criticisms, the Inner Critic needs a firm talking-to and update on exactly what our true beliefs, values, and motivations are now. We need to stand up and challenge our Inner Critic's authority to show it the vast expanse of the potential that we hold and are meant to realize.

We can follow the lead of writer and jazz singer Katy Bourne, who wrote an open letter to her Inner Critic with very clear instructions on how she wished to be treated moving forward. She writes, "...I just don't hang with people who talk to me like you do. You're going to have to figure out a different way to be with me, Mademoiselle Critic. I'm tired of your shrill banter. I don't want you to poke me in the ribs anymore. If you try to kill my buzz again, I'll swat your hand."[133]

Sometimes, the best thing we can do with our Inner Critic is to use a little "tough love" like Katy. Let's look some ways we can start taking back our power by standing up to the Inner Critic.

## Creative Dose: Get Up, Stand Up

*Purpose: To take back control by standing up to your Inner Critic*

Even though we're all about compassion, sometimes we just have to stand up for ourselves. If your Inner Critic just won't quiet down when you are in the middle of trying to create something – or even worse, it tries to covertly sabotage your efforts – then it is time to get tough and defend your right to creative flow.

Here are three options for showing the Inner Critic who's boss and setting the tone for how the relationship will work best for *you*.

### Option 1: Acknowledge and Thank

When you recognize a self-critical thought, you can acknowledge your Inner Critic for its efforts. However, while being appreciative of its efforts, you must also stay firm in showing it its place and being clear how you would like to work together moving forward.

Your inner dialogue could go something like this:

"I appreciate all of the work you do to try to keep me safe, and I thank you. However, you are not needed right now."

### Option 2: Establish the Tone

Your Inner Critic has grown accustomed to you taking its litany of self-criticisms without a peep. But actually talking back and setting the tone will totally catch it off guard and give it pause.

Let's say for the sake of argument that the essence of your self-corrections that have turned into high criticisms has merit and could be useful for you.

To get a more inspiring and positive version to use for motivation, ask your Inner Critic to rephrase.

You could think or say something like this: "I hear what you're saying, but I don't appreciate your tone of voice. Can you say it again, but in a way that makes me want to do it?"

### Option 3: Get Hard-boiled

If asking your Inner Critic nicely to change its tone doesn't work, you can always face the Inner Critic with your aggressive, tough-as-nails side. Turn the tables on the Inner Critic and catch it off guard with defiance, using this exercise adapted from "5 Immediate and Easy Ways to Silence Your Inner Critic," by Lynn Newman.[57]

When you've had enough of your Inner Critic's incessant self-critical bullying, challenge the messages by coming back with these rebuttals:

- **"So what?** I don't care that you think that – that doesn't make it true."

- **"Who cares?** Your judgments don't matter to me."

- **"Big freakin' deal!** So, you think I'm (insert insult here)? WHATEVER."

- **"Why not?** So, you're telling me that I shouldn't try something new because you say I can't do it or don't deserve it. Thanks for your input. Despite what you say, I'm doing it anyway and will learn what I need to from the process."

Certainly, being compassionate is ideal, but sometimes enough is enough. You can show the Inner Critic that you are the boss of you.

## Tune In to Tune Out

*"Choice of attention - to pay attention to this and ignore that - is to the inner life what choice of action is to the outer."*

— **W. H. Auden,** *poet*

In the past, the Inner Critic may have seemed like a huge, intimidating presence in your mind, with your stringent self-criticisms appearing as if they are the sole truths about you. However, now that we've started becoming more aware of the mistaken beliefs that underlie our strongest self-criticisms and are regaining the power that we've given up by believing them, we start to see through the Inner Critic's thin veneer and perceive its lack of substance and dimension. In his essay "Against Self-Criticism," psychologist Adam Phillips eloquently and accurately describes the Inner Critic: "...the self-critical part of ourselves... has some striking deficiencies: it is remarkably narrow-minded; it has an unusually impoverished vocabulary; and it is, like all propagandists, relentlessly repetitive."[58]

When we are being overly self-critical and falling prey to the Inner Critic's worst messages, it often feels like the Inner Critic takes over our entire awareness. Like being at a party stuck listening to the most self-absorbed, tiresome guest in the room, giving too much attention to the Inner Critic in the form of High Self-Criticism is a misappropriation of your valuable mental resources and time.

To get a handle on our thoughts and emotions and to take back the power of our time and attention, we need a way to put high self-criticism into perspective. Again, managing our attention and making use of a built-in tendency of our brains comes to the rescue.

Speaking of parties, you know how when you're at a party and you're so absorbed in a conversation with someone that you really only hear what that person is saying and none of the other conversations around you – but if you wanted, you could tune into the other conversations around you? Humans have the impressive ability to be able to focus on one voice amid countless others, regardless of the environment. This phenomenon is referred to as "selective hearing," also known as "the cocktail party effect."[59]

One of the aspects of the cocktail party effect that we'll make use of is this: while our brains are outstanding at honing in on the one conversation that we're engaged in, we absorb little to nothing of the ones that we decide to ignore.[60] Perfect! We've already heard enough of what the Inner Critic has to say and know the list of self-criticisms by heart. Once you've learned what the Inner Critic is ultimately trying to protect you from, there's precious little to be gleaned from continuing to listen to its self-critical diatribe.

Using the power of attention and focus and choosing where to place them, combined with a commitment to mindfulness, we'll practice the internal equivalent of the cocktail party effect. The same mechanism is at work here, except instead of tuning in to someone's voice externally, we will choose which of our thoughts we listen to. By shifting to other more relevant "conversations" in our heads, we'll begin to break our habit of generating so much self-criticism. The circuit and the broadcast will grow weaker – and the Inner Critic will lose its audience.

 ## Creative Dose: Turn Down Da Noise, Turn Down Da Funk

*Purpose: To choose other thoughts over the self-critical voice of the Inner Critic*

Here are three ways to shift your focus to other messages that have been getting drowned out by the strident droning of the Inner Critic.

### Option 1: Tune Out

The Inner Critic can be a lot like a parrot on your shoulder, sitting there chirping away, droning on about all of the reasons why your work is allegedly no good. Here's how you can use the cocktail party effect to your advantage.

Imagine that, just as if you were at a party wrapped up in a conversation with someone fascinating, the annoying voice of your Inner Critic starts to fade into the background. It's still there, and if you decide you want to tune back in to it, you can whenever you want.

But instead of listening to your dull Inner Critic, who tells the same stories all of the time, you're attending to the far more interesting perspective of your Creative Self.

## Option 2: Tune In

Imagine that your brain is like a radio. You're currently on WHSC–the high self-criticism channel, nothing but self-criticism all day and all night, and advertisement-free to boot. But good lord, what a boring station! All it plays is oldies in the form of criticisms you've internalized from what people have said to you in your deep past. Isn't there something *else* you could listen to?

Imagine turning the dial, pressing buttons, or swiping left to find and pick up a new station, for instance, one that broadcasts accurate messages about who you are as a person and about your abilities.

There is even a station that broadcasts messages of comfort and kindness as well.

You have a choice of where to put your listener support. Which station will you tune in to?

## Option 3: Inner Critic Shrinky Dinks

When I was a growing up, there was a wacky toy called Shrinky Dinks. It was special plastic that you could either draw on yourself or use preprinted designs, put in the oven, and with heat shrink them down into smaller plastic pieces that you could turn into pendants and other things. (Yes, that's a form of creativity: someone thought of that idea, pitched it to an exec at a company, they marketed it, and people bought it. Wild, isn't it?!)

Close your eyes. Imagine your Inner Critic in as much grandiose detail as possible, passionately recounting all of the ways in which you are falling short, slacking, and being a disappointment.

Then imagine your Inner Critic slowly but surely shrinking. You could even imagine putting it in an oven or a really hot room like a sauna, or melting like the water-soaked Wicked Witch of the West in the Wizard of Oz.

It is shrinking, shrinking, shrinking, and its voice is getting smaller and more difficult to hear — until it is so small that it can fit in the palm of your hand.

What is your Inner Critic like now? Is is as scary as before?

Can you even hear what it's saying to you without bending down to listen really closely?

Can't hear that self-critical voice anymore? Great! Now you can go and get into your creative groove.

# Reassign Duty

*"Change is the end result of all true learning."*

— **Leo Buscaglia,** *author*

Much of what people think of as the Inner Critic is precisely what we are dealing with in this book: the voice of self-criticizing, self-doubt, and self-berating. However, there is another part of our psyche I think of more as "the Inner Editor," or even more accurately as, "the Inner Evaluator." This part of ourselves is the expert at what we do, who genuinely knows the pearls of our work that grow from our preliminary "SFD" (Sh*tty First Draft) product.

Personally, I trust my Inner Evaluator. She has a seasoned eye and is all about discernment. She's the part of my brain that takes in everything that I read and makes note of the prose that I find compelling and that I do not, and uses that information to keep me on track with my writing. She's the one who loves earrings as much as I do, and guides me toward making the earrings that she and I both would love to see more of in the world. She is a foodie, a lover of indie films, adores good neo soul music, and has a weakness for soft fabric.

She is the one who helps me uphold my standards of quality. And I appreciate her for it.

This Inner Evaluator is in stark contrast to the mean Inner Critic, who browbeats me for not doing everything "perfectly," who drives me to exhaustion, and who wakes me up in the middle of the night in anxiety about something that I could wait to fix until the next day – all in the name of supposedly keeping me safe from potential future threat. *That* one is my Inner Critic. She's the one who needs another job.

We can put the position of the Inner Critic as the hypervigilant protector of your mental well-being to good use. It wants to be useful and do its job and fulfill its duty. What most people don't know is that the Inner Critic is actually trainable. What we need to do is to give it other jobs that it is better suited for.

 ## Creative Dose: The Inner Critic As An Intern

*Purpose: To assign your Inner Critic another job to give yourself mental space*

Just because the Inner Critic is desperate to distract you with thoughts of potential future doom doesn't mean you have to shift your focus from what you're working on and listen to it.

As the Inner Critic tries to be useful by protecting you, you can enlist its help by telling it that protecting you actually doesn't mean blocking ideas by distracting you with your fears. You can tell it that being useful means being cooperative and giving you the space you need to initially let as many of your ideas out as possible so you have more to choose from and can pick out the best later.

## Part 1: Ask for space

Usually, when you need someone to give you some space, the easiest and most effective way to get it is to ask for it. In the sage words of the old adage: "If you don't ask, you don't get."

Because the Inner Critic is clearly very eager to help, tell it that the best way to do so is for it to be quiet to help ideas flow more freely. Thank your Inner Critic in advance for its assistance, and return to what you were working on.

## Part 2: Plus Ten

Put the practice of mindfulness into place. Gently yet respectfully tell your self-critical thoughts to come back later. When you are in the midst of working on something and your Inner Critic pops up and starts to steer you off track, task it with giving you unfettered space to create.

Tell it, "I'll be with you in a moment – just give me ten more minutes."

Much in the way you would deal with a spunky intern for whom you haven't had time to organize any work, or an annoying coworker looming over the edge of your cubicle when you are trying to focus, every time your Inner Critic returns, tell it the same. The practice of pushing it away should make it quiet down enough for you to continue creating.

## Part 3: The Inner Evaluator Internship

If your Inner Critic is particularly enthusiastic when it comes to upholding its duties by making you super self-critical, then trick it and then retrain it. Because the Inner Critic is masterful at critiquing and editing, strike a deal: tell it you are going to give it a promotion to assist your Inner Evaluator so that it can help you with quality control.

Tell it you don't have anything for it to do right now, but it should come back to help you and your Inner Evaluator at a later stage of the process when you are ready for feedback, vetting ideas, critiquing and editing.[71] Tell it that it will get promoted if it gets good at being quiet when you are ideating, and then weighing in when you need help seeing which ideas are the strongest.

When it is the appropriate time, ask your Inner Critic as Inner Evaluator wannabe, "What do you think this work needs instead? What can be done to make it better?"[72]

This exercise will start to train your Inner Critic to apply the skills that it is particularly good at only when needed and not before, which will help it move to the position of the Inner Evaluator instead. It will take to its new responsibilities like it was made for them, and all will be a lot quieter on the self-critical front as well.

# WALKING AWAY FROM THE HAMMER

Thankfully, we've brought the tendency of High Self-Criticism to light. Now we are better equipped to cease self-attacking, stop rumination in its tracks, get distance from self-critical thoughts, and put a kibosh on self-censoring. We are beginning to break out of our Inner-Critic induced haze and to loosen the dam we have on our ideas. We've successfully put down the hammer, and we are finally walking away from it with our heads held high.

However, there are more guises of the Inner Critic we have yet to discover.

Because High Self-Criticism is so focused on our alleged weaknesses, one of its byproducts is feeling like there's something intrinsically wrong with us, which leads to Deficiency Anxiety. Let's progress to those times when our Inner Critic tells us we're not enough and find out what we can do to assert that, in fact, yes we are.

*I am not creative enough — one idea wonder.*

# CHAPTER 5 | "I'M NOT GOOD ENOUGH" - *DEFICIENCY ANXIETIES*

**This chapter examines:**

*Cognitive Reappraisal*

*Inventory of Self*

*Self-Trust*

*Befriending Yourself*

*Competence Model of Learning*

*Information Distillation*

*Deliberate Practice*

*Active Listening*

*Collaboration and Plussing*

*Remixing Ideas*

*"When are we enough for ourselves?"*

—**April White,** *Waging War*

One aspect that I love about doing this work is all of the incredibly talented people I get to meet and become friends with. Through my overseas travels I met my friend Darren, who is a gifted visual designer. For the past two years, Darren has been taking a rigorous professional design degree program. Even before his studies, I was blown away by the visual problem-solving skills that he applied to his design projects and his ability to expertly execute really lovely work. One of his projects on color was so visually stunning and masterfully done that a mutual friend, who is a professional photographer, beseeched Darren to turn the project's photographs into a poster series. Despite all of the encouragement that he received, Darren continued to doubt his own abilities and did not fully own his creative talents.

At the beginning of summer his final exams were coming up, and Darren was becoming progressively more stressed at the prospect of having to keep the previous two years' worth of knowledge in his head and then apply it to the practical exam project. He was working all day and studying every free moment during the night, leaving him very close to burnout. Darren's Inner Critic was stimulating his fear of "not enough." We scheduled an emergency coaching session to help him shift into a more positive mindset.

When I got on the Skype call with Darren, I encouraged him to recognize that in doing design, he is only being who he has been all along. Therefore, with this exam and all design work, he needs to act from a place of self-trust instead of self-doubt. In terms of making sure the information sticks in his brain, I suggested that he organize the information in a way that he understands it best: visually. Finally, I encouraged him to rest, because it's when we stop putting information in our heads that our brains are actually able to process, make sense of, and access the information later. At the end of the coaching session, seeing Darren's anxious shoulders drop and his furrowed brows relax into a look of relief told me that my words had hit home.

# ENOUGH IS ENOUGH

Fears of not being good enough, not knowing enough, and not coming up with original enough ideas keep us from reveling in our innate creative abilities. See if any of these statements resonate with you.

Are you afflicted with **Deficiency Anxiety**, the belief that you or your ideas aren't good enough?

- ❏ "I'm not creative, smart, clever, and/or hip enough."

- ❏ "Whatever I do won't be good enough."

- ❏ "My creativity is, and never will be good enough."

Do you suffer from **Proficiency Anxiety**, afraid of not knowing enough and not being good at what you do?

- ❏ "There are too many holes in my knowledge to make it good enough."

- ❏ "I'm afraid I won't be able to learn what I need to."

- ❏ "I can't come up with ideas fast enough."

- ❏ "I can't keep up with new tech/trends/evolving technology. I'm not learning fast enough."

- ❏ "I'm just not good enough at what I do. I don't have enough expertise."

Has **Originality Anxiety** gotten the best of you, seducing you into believing that everything you do must be new, unique, and groundbreaking every time?

- ❑ "I'm just rehashing old ideas – everything I do is from someone else. Nothing is original enough. All of my ideas have been done before and done better."

- ❑ "I can't come up with new innovative ideas constantly."

- ❑ "I fear that I have no original thoughts. I'm just a copycat who takes creative shortcuts."

## USE YOUR BRAINPOWER FOR GOOD

The common element all Deficiency Anxieties share is self-doubt: doubting the value of your ideas, doubting your ability to acquire new information and skills, doubting your ability to come up with anything original, and even doubting your own inherent value. That's a lot of doubt!

Regular negative self-talk reinforces this self-doubt. As you know, worrying about how we are lacking creates habitual negative thoughts. These thoughts are the product of our Inner Critic reflex: our brains firing electrical signals through well-worn channels of neurons that have fired and wired together through years of repetition.

We have committed to using our brainpower for good now, though. Let's continue to harness the power of thoughts to make significant changes around our beliefs with this initial tool that you can use immediately to improve thought management.

# Think Like a Scientist

*"When you change the way you look at things, the things that you look at change."*

— **Max Planck,** *Nobel Prize-winning Theoretical Physicist*

Constantly feeling inadequate and battling self-doubt puts us on the defensive emotionally – except that it's with ourselves. In order to turn down the emotional intensity so that you can think more clearly and objectively, we need to diffuse our feelings and create mental breathing space. We can do this using a mental training technique known as cognitive reappraisal. The practice of cognitive reappraisal regulates emotions by reframing thoughts so that they are based in reality. This reframing then alters the intensity of the emotional response to the thought.[1] The way it is done is much like mindfulness: one non-judgmentally observes thoughts and then redirects them by recognizing habitual thinking patterns and changing them to a different pattern.[2]

Using the techniques of cognitive reappraisal will not only help us to begin to lessen the amount and frequency of negative thoughts, but we'll also be able to better remember emotional situations, and our ability to interact with others in relationships of all kinds will improve as well.[3] This can be a great boon to your capacity for creative collaboration, which I will I talk about later.

 ## Creative Dose: Emotion and Thought Inquiry

*Purpose: To transform thoughts of inadequacy by examining them*

Earlier in the book I mentioned that the Inner Critic uses hyperbolic language to distract you from the work of creating to make you pay attention to it. Keep this in mind: most of what we tell ourselves when we are ruminating – thinking the same negative thoughts over and over again – is patently untrue. To shift our internal narrations to something less debilitating and more constructive, we need to question our thoughts and put them up for rigorous examination.

## Step 1: Question and Answer

Turn your self-critical thought about yourself into a question.

Instead of "I'm X." Ask yourself, "Am I X?" then look at the answer.

For example, let's say one of your constant thoughts is "I don't have any good ideas."

You would change this statement to the question "Do I not have any good ideas?"

Then, you supply answers to the new questions that are more accurate.

For example, the answer to "Do I not have any good ideas?" is most likely "Yes, I do have some good ideas."

Here's a framework for you to use:

Constant thought: _____.

Statement: I am _____.

Question: Am I _____?

Play with this practice and see how turning these thoughts that you have taken as truth into a question transforms both the meaning and the validity of the original criticisms.

## Step 2: Refute

Set a time each day to write a brain dump of your self-critical thoughts and their triggers.

Make three columns.

In the first column, write down the situation that triggered your self-doubt.

In the second column, write down the self-critical thought triggered by the event.

In the third column, write down a refutation of the critical thought, and make sure it has the following characteristics:

1) it needs to be neutral or positive, and

2) it needs to be both based in reality and accurate.

The goal is not to formulate some overly optimistic affirmation, just the positive truth. [4]

By writing down the truthful refutations, you will start to see the fallacy of your thoughts, and will start to create new connections in your brain.

Here's an example:

| TRIGGER | SELF-CRITICAL THOUGHT | REFUTATION |
|---|---|---|
| Being on deadline and having limited ideas | "My ideas aren't good enough." | "The client actually loved the idea I had for the last project." |
| Coming out of a brainstorming meeting | "I'm not as talented as everyone on my team." | "One of my co-workers told me today that she appreciates the ideas I come up with." |

# SHIFT TO AMPLE

*"When you realize there is nothing lacking, the whole world belongs to you."*

— **Lao Tzu,** *philosopher, writer and father of Taoism*

When we focus on something, everything falls away until only that one thing exists for us, and we see that item clearly to the exclusion of everything else. This can be true when we reach a state of creative flow, but unfortunately is equally true for the times when we are in the throes of negative self-talk and rumination. Fixation on where we feel we are inadequate is due to a mentality of lack, and is the basis of Deficiency Anxiety. Being so intent upon that which we believe we don't have enough of, whether it be talent, ideas, or creativity, blinds us to that which we have in abundance. Concentrating on our shortcomings bars any thoughts of what we actually are good at from entering our consciousness. To begin to see where our cup runneth over, we need to manage our attention and shift focus.

There's a well-known parable of us all having two wolves within us who constantly fight each other for the upper hand. One wolf is the positive: kindness, benevolence, acceptance, truth, compassion, and generosity. The other wolf is the negative: self-doubt, inferiority, envy, sorrow, despair, self-pity, resentment, greed, superiority, and ego. Which one will ultimately win the fight? The one we feed.

Let's feed the wolf of positivity to start reversing the feelings of lack and inadequacy that are the roots of Deficiency Anxiety.

# You Are Enough

*"You alone are enough. You have nothing to prove to anybody."*

— **Dr. Maya Angelou,** *author and poet*

What would happen if you stopped doubting yourself and tuned in to the fact that you've got this? That everything you've seen, experienced, learned, thought and accomplished has come together to create a unique, singular, and extremely capable you?

When I had my great insight into doing creative work that I shared in the preface, one of the best things that came from it is that my self-doubt was replaced with deep conviction and knowing. This sense of self-trust pervaded all of my actions, and enabled me to channel all the energy that formerly had been devoted to self-doubt and negative self-talk to getting my ideas out into the world. Did it last forever? No. But for the several months that I was in that space, I felt on fire with creative inspiration, and I was so engaged with researching, compiling, and developing new talks on creativity that self-doubt was unable to enter the picture.

Let's shift focus away from self-doubt by homing in on how great and capable you truly are.

## Creative Dose: Take Inventory

*Purpose: To shift focus to what you have in abundance and discover hidden pockets of your creativity*

Rather than spending time and energy worrying about how you're not smart or talented enough, interesting enough, or expert enough, make time to internally validate yourself and all that you have done instead.[5] Break out your journal and settle in – we're going to do some great remembering with this exercise.

### Part 1: Your Successes

First, become aware of and inventory your own successes. You are going to make three lists:

1) Talents and Abilities

2) Skills

3) Accomplishments/Achievements

Your talents can range from something like being able to easily recognize patterns to having a good memory for music. Your skills can range from being able to sharpen a knife to being able to build a log cabin. Your achievements can be big, like being the first in your family to get a university degree, to small, like how you save spiders from drowning before you take a shower.

Don't censor, downplay, or dismiss anything; put as much on these lists as you can remember and in as much detail as you can.

The goal is to capture as much as possible of what makes you *you*, so that you can get back in touch with what sets you apart from everyone else on the planet.

**Part 2: Your Intrinsic Qualities**

Now that you are more in touch with your accomplishments, bear in mind that being enough isn't about what you do outwardly, it's about who you are as a person internally. For this exercise, we'll shift the focus from outward abilities and achievements to the human qualities that are your essence.

Think of and list your intrinsic qualities. Here are a few words to help you get started:

Able • Ambitious • Analytical • Astute • Attentive • Aware • Balanced • Brilliant • Cautious • Certain • Charitable • Confident • Considerate • Consistent • Courageous • Conscientious • Courteous • Decisive • Disciplined • Driven • Efficient • Erudite • Faithful • Flexible • Focused • Graceful • Grateful • Industrious • Innovative • Modest • Nurturing • Outgoing • Perceptive • Persevering • Poised • Practical • Professional • Punctual • Resourceful • Respectful • Responsible

There are several great lists online that you can use for further ideas.

Write down on your list all of the qualities that you associate with yourself . You can even enlist the help of close friends for any words that they feel describe your essence, and add those words to your list if they resonate with you.

## Part 3: Your Esteemed Self

Act as if the person that you described in part 2 is a completely new person outside of yourself that you've never met before. Imagine talking to this person and how the interaction would go.

- In what regard would you hold this person, and how would you treat this person?

- Would you be impressed?

- Would you have a lot of respect for this person?

- How would you talk to this person, and what would you say to someone with your lists of accomplishments and qualities ?

How different is how you treat this "new" person from how you treat yourself now?

Return to this practice whenever you find yourself focusing on where you believe you're lacking and discounting who you are.

## Part 4: Where's Your Creativity?

It bears repeating: when you are focused on how you aren't creative, you won't be able to see where you have been creative in the past, and where you are inherently creative overall. So let's look at your tableau of past accomplishments and play the creativity version of the Where's Waldo? game.

Review the lists you created in parts 1 and 2. Look at the items and ask yourself these questions:

- In which instances did you exercise creativity?

- How exactly were you creative at those times?

- What qualities inform and enhance your creativity?

Remember that being creative is NOT limited to art, music, or writing – think of when you brought something new into the world or you felt the thrill of the creative spark running through you.

Mark or tag the accomplishments in which you employed creativity.

Then, mark and note which talents, abilities, and qualities within you lend themselves to your creative capacity.

If you are hard-pressed to think of when you were creative, then do this:

Think of a time when you reached a state where you lost time, had a peak experience, and/or felt empowered from what you accomplished.

What did you find from this process of structured recollection?

Are you surprised at just how much creativity you've exercised in your life?

# Readjust to Trust

*"Can you remember who you were before the world told you who you should be?"*

— **Danielle LaPorte,** *author, speaker, entrepreneur*

Have you encountered a four-year-old lately? At this age, many children are very much themselves. They are clear about their likes, dislikes, and wants. They are wonderfully opinionated and sassy. They are in a fabulous place in their lives: full of self-assurance and blissfully unaware of the impending self-doubt that will drive them to start trying to become someone they think they should be.

It's beyond our control – almost everything in the world tells us from an early age that we need to place our trust in authorities outside ourselves: parents, elders, teachers, doctors, the government. We learn early on to turn a deaf ear to the grounded voice of our souls and our knowing gut and start to listen solely to society's messages coming through the mouthpiece of the people in our lives.

When I was 24 years old, I had just graduated from the University of Washington with a bachelor's degree in international studies with a minor in French. Throughout my college career, several professors had taken me aside and applauded my skill in writing – one even got me a job as a writing tutor in a campus learning center. Right around my graduation, I hesitantly shared with my father that I thought I would like to become a writer as a profession. His immediate response was, "Do you know how hard it is to get published?"

Now, let me be clear about one thing: my father was no slouch. In 1957 at the age of 20, he completed his flight training and got his pilot's license – no small feat for a young African-American man growing up essentially without parents in inner city Detroit before the Civil Rights Movement. He was the first person in his family to graduate from college with his degree in aeronautical engineering. As a hobby, he built and flew experimental aircraft. My father was brilliant, driven, and accomplished. Yet, despite all of the barriers that he broke in his own life, my father still believed and proliferated the lies that run rampant throughout society: that artists starve, that creativity is what you do in your free time and not as a job, and that very few writers ever get published.

Even though deep inside myself I knew that my ability to write was genuine and deserved to be respected, cultivated, and expressed, I was unsure of my abilities, nervous about my future, and wracked with self-doubt. I took my father's advice to heart, and spent three dismal years after college that felt like an eternity doing soul- and creativity-stifling office temp work, until I taught myself HTML and boldly entered the tech world.

When the economy crashed in 2008, I was let go from my well-paying project management job at a local software company. Despite just having bought a house two months previous, I knew that the layoff was largely fortuitous. Instead of continuing to do work that I despised but thought I "should" do, it was my chance to finally pursue my dream of becoming a writer and a speaker. I dug down to unearth the deeply buried self-trust that had lain dormant within me for more than 15 years. Five months later, I had a conversation at a tech conference party that led to my first book publishing deal practically falling into my lap. Fast forward to the present, and you are reading the product of my second serendipitous book contract.

Self-doubt equals an absence of self-trust. When we don't trust ourselves, we second-guess our own thoughts, opinions, likes, wants, and desires. When we lack self-trust, the life we're living is not authentic to our own soul, but is based on the goals, values, and dreams of people outside of ourselves.

Getting back to the level of trust in ourselves that we had when we were younger is a critical component not only of allowing our creativity to flow, but of making magic happen in our lives. We've put our trust in the rules of the world – often prescribed by uninformed and fearful people – and many of us have lost our way. Let's relax back into our own skins and learn to trust in ourselves, our abilities, and our truth again, and in doing so, return to center and come home to our creativity.

## Creative Dose: The Parallel Trust Universe

*Purpose: To return to trusting yourself and your capabilities*

Being focused on what we're afraid we don't know and what we fear we can't do – in other words, not trusting ourselves – blocks us from accessing what we actually do know and can do.

The next time you are anxious about not having a good enough idea, or that your work won't be good enough, or that you don't have enough expertise, stop.

Take a deep breath, and recognize where you have been focusing: on lack. Realize that by being anxious about the potential of lack, you are preventing yourself from accessing what already does exist there and is available for you in terms of ideas, skills, expertise, and performance.

Take another deep breath, and imagine this alternative reality:

What would I feel like if I trusted that I had the answer or capability?

- What mode of thinking would I be in right now?

- How would I physically feel in this mode of thinking; how would it feel different from how I am feeling now?

- In place of being anxious, what are the actual thoughts that I'd be thinking now?

- Take another deep breath, and make a conscious decision to adjust to a place of trusting yourself and to operate from that mindframe.

# Be A Friend Indeed

*"Self-trust is the essence of heroism."*

— **Ralph Waldo Emerson,** *poet*

Elizabeth Gilbert, the author of the bestselling books *Eat, Pray, Love* and *Big Magic*, shared in a recent speech that even she has moments when she beats herself up for perceived shortcomings and has to consciously work to stop her brain from doing so. Her suggestion to break out of the cycle is to "be kind to yourself." She continues, "you must give yourself unconditional self-friendship."[6] In other words, practice self-compassion and self-kindness.

Unfortunately, when our feelings of anxiety about alleged deficiencies are at the forefront of our consciousness, we become the opposite of a friend – we become our own worst bullies. Consequently, we have lost trust from the deeper, more vulnerable parts of ourselves.

Learning to be more consistently supportive of yourself is the key. By showing yourself that you will make a conscious and conscientious effort to be a friend, champion, and boon companion to yourself again, you can win this trust back. As a bonus, you'll bolster self-confidence through breaking the tendency to seek external approval and will be better able to interact with others while you move from being a bully to yourself to being a hero.

## Creative Dose: Quantum Companionship

*Purpose: To be abundantly kind to yourself, past, present, and future.*

When I started really working on my own Inner Critic and tuned into to my self-talk, I was (and sometimes still am) shocked at how mean I can be to myself. I realized that my internal hypercritical reprimanding was being said to the equivalent of a child: 3 years old, 7 years old, 12 years old, etc. When I see someone in public talk to an actual child that way (and we have all seen this), I'm frequently moved to angry tears. Practically sick to my stomach, I have to hold myself back from rushing in to shield the child from the verbal chastisement with a hug and soothing him/her with kinder words.

I think indignantly, "how can someone speak to a child like that?!" The answer is: because that's what people learned from experience, and that's how they now internally speak to themselves – just as I was doing to myself.

The adult that the world sees now is merely a box that contains the child that we were before.

To remind myself to be more compassionate and gentle to my internal kid, I've hung my favorite photo of myself as a baby on the wall of my office so I can see it while I'm working. I've changed the lock screen photo on my cell phone to a picture of myself at age four: with a sweet, spunky smile on my face, braids in my hair, full of wonder at the world, and naturally overflowing with my own unique version of creativity. Now, every time I pick up the phone I'm further reminded to have the same fierce protectiveness for that little girl as I would for any other.

To help ourselves truly understand that we are enough and to continue to build self-trust, we need to start thinking of ourselves as a friend[7] and act accordingly.

**Part 1: The Way-Back Machine**

Close your eyes, and imagine that you go back in time to visit yourself as a child. Imagine yourself as a mentor who sees this child's rich potential.

What makes this child unique?

- What would you encourage this child to do?

- What advice and warnings would you give her/him?

- What would you tell the child if s/he beats up herself/himself over a "mistake" or "failed" at something?

- What message(s) do you know that the child desperately wants and needs to hear around her/his creative abilities, but doesn't hear enough of?

Tell this child everything you feel s/he needs to know to realize her/his greatness.

## Part 2: Present Advocate

Close your eyes again, but this time, imagine yourself as your own best friend.

You're watching as your friend is being berated and bullied by a manager or a boss (it may help to imagine that the bully looks like the image of the Inner Critic that you drew and ripped up back in Chapter 4). If you knew you had absolutely nothing to lose, what would you say to the bully?

Become a sworn defender – of yourself. Come to the defense of your friend and tell the bully exactly why the bullying is wrong, and why and how your friend is amazing, does great work, has fabulous ideas, and is an asset to the team and company.

How do you talk to your friend afterward?

What would you say to her/him to help process this incident?

## Part 3: Future-Trip

Close your eyes a final time, but this time, imagine yourself at the end of your life, looking back at what you've created in this one and the legacy you are leaving.

- What do you feel are the experiences and accomplishments that have been the most important to you?

- What are you most proud of?

- What impact have you left on other people and the world?

- What kind of person can you say you have been and how was this reflected in your life?

- What do you want people to remember about you?

- What do you regret that you did not accomplish, create, develop, or experience?

This is a great exercise for getting back in touch with what is really important to you and even with your soul's desires.

The good news is that you can use this information to start directing your life from this point on.

*Bonus Action:* **Write Yourself a Letter**

Another way we can be a friend is to write ourselves a compassionate letter.[8] It may be helpful to bring to mind your Future Compassionate Self that you generated in Chapter 2, and imagine this version of yourself writing the letter, while you merely take dictation. Either way, the language and tone of the letter should be loving, comforting, and full of empathy and warmth for yourself and the distress generated by your self-doubt.

The letter might be structured like this:

"Dear Jim, I heard that you've been afraid that your work isn't good enough and have been beating yourself up over it, which makes me sad. I want you to know that I trust in your abilities."

You can write this letter in your journal so that you can revisit it regularly.

Or, you could even go so far as to email the letter to yourself by using a great service called FutureMe.org, where you can compose an email to yourself to be mailed to you at whatever date you choose in the future.

*Super Bonus Action:* Make writing emails to yourself a self-kindness habit and regularly write and schedule emails for yourself!

No matter which method you choose, writing self-compassionate letters or emails to yourself helps to undo your self-doubt and your Inner Critic.

## LEARN, EXPAND, AND MIX IT UP

*"As we grow in awareness, our fear of loss, not having enough or being insufficient matures into love of giving, sharing and collaboration."*

— **Joseph Rain,** *author and entrepreneur*

Think back to a time when you were excited to learn something new. Your focus was on the experience of gaining knowledge and skill – and probably also on what you would be able to do with that knowledge in the future. Similarly, think back to a time when you were completely wrapped up in executing an idea that you had, and you were so excited about it that you completely got into flow, lost track of time, forgot to eat, and were completely enamoured with what you were creating.

In either scenario, did doubt-ridden thoughts of whether it had been done before or better enter your consciousness? No, because the only thing that mattered to you at that moment was the experience of creating and seeing your concept come to fruition.

In continuing our efforts to shift our focus to where it needs to be, the objective is to relinquish self-doubt so that we (re)learn to trust ourselves: our intelligence, skills, experience, knowledge, and originality, and cultivate methods through which we can joyfully expand all. When we do that, we can then put our efforts into using our knowledge, expertise, and creativity to help others.

Here are two methods – quick learning and deliberate practice – that you can employ to learn information and build skill more quickly, while stimulating your creativity and potentially achieving flow as a bonus.

## Believe That You Can Be Informed and Able

*"They are able who think they are able."*
— **Virgil,** *classical Greek poet*

Futurist and inventor Buckminster Fuller developed the Knowledge Doubling Curve to describe the rate at which human knowledge has been increasing. According to the curve, until 1900, human knowledge doubled approximately every 100 years. By 1945, the rate changed to 25 years. At the present, the rate of knowledge doubling is estimated to be every 12 months.[9] With the rate of change and innovation these days being so dramatic, your sense of not being able to keep up is arguably based in fact. But even without the rate of knowledge doubling, you simply can't learn everything – so get that out of your head right now as an unnecessary point of frustration. Your ability to grow and expand your knowledge whenever you need it is completely independent of how much there is to know.

You can shift into feeling confident about your capacity to learn by keeping these three things in mind:

1) **Trust in your intelligence and ability to learn.** Studies have shown that believing in your own intellectual capacity actually improves it.[10] Starting out with the conviction that you have the ability to understand a new subject or skill is almost half the battle.

2) **Be patient with yourself during the learning process.** Remember at the beginning of the book when I talked about

neuroplasticity? When we are learning, we are pushing our brain to create new neuron connections. We are quite literally forcing our brains to think differently than before.[11]

3) **Get clear about your motivation.** Why do you want to learn the new knowledge or skill, and what do you want to achieve through learning it? The more you are motivated by positive outcomes, such as how the information will be useful for you and you believe it will have a positive impact on your community, the easier and more enjoyable the entire process will be. But if you come from a place of fear and anxiety, not only do those feelings adversely color the learning experience, but they will actually stunt the process on a neurological level, as negative stress suppresses the brain's ability to create new neural connections. Keep your positive outcomes in mind during the learning process.

An additional benefit will come from your commitment to learning something new: the very process itself sparks creativity! Curiosity is a precursor of creativity; it is through curiosity that we stimulate and push our brains to take in information that gives our mind fodder for new associations.

## Know the Four Stages of Competence

Before you set yourself to the task of learning anything, keep in mind the four stages of learning using the competence model of the stages of learning[12] to help quiet your Inner Critic by mitigating frustration and helping you stay the course.

Starting off, you're in **unconscious incompetence**, where you don't know what you don't know. You don't know how to perform a new skill or even when you are doing it incorrectly.

The next stage of **conscious incompetence** is where you can see what you are doing incorrectly, you are very aware of gaps in knowledge and skill, and whatever you are learning feels awkward. You'll also make a lot of mistakes. Beware: this is often the place where people get frustrated and abandon acquiring the new skill.

Now you'll move to **conscious competence**, where you understand the information or skill and have achieved a certain level of proficiency. However, executing the skill still requires concentration and conscious effort. Continuous practice is the key to building even higher proficiency at this stage.

Finally, you reach **unconscious competence**, where with practice and effort, your skill is now second nature and can be performed or accessed easily, even to the degree of executing it while doing another task. Performing the skill or drawing on the knowledge is now natural, comfortable, and habitual.

Here is a method that you can employ to learn information more quickly.

## Creative Dose: Quick Learnin'

*Purpose: To learn new information fast*

When trying to learn something for work or a project on a tight deadline, none of us have time to wade through huge amounts of content or the luxury to read our sources a second time. We need a way to thoroughly assimilate information in a short timeframe.

If you feel anxious about your ability to take in and apply new information and then turn around and apply it immediately, this process for accelerated learning will help.

These five steps for learning a subject in a number of days[13] are adapted from a recent article on the blog of Nir Eyal, best known as the author of *Hooked: How to Build Habit-Forming Products*.

## Step 1: Research

Do your research, but put a limit on it. Find all of your sources of information in one sitting. Strive to keep the number of sources (both online and offline) to around 20, and then *stop*. You want to get an overview of information.

When researching, think beyond articles: expand your search to images to leverage the pictorial superiority effect – the brain's ability to understand pictures faster than text – to get the gist right away. Be sure to include multiple types of media (written articles, audio, video, infographics, pictures) to create multiple memory points in your brain and also to have a better chance of catering to your personal learning and retention style.

## Step 2: Sketch

Draw a diagram or mindmap so that you can start to see the overview of information that you have and chart the relationships between concepts. Take as many sheets of paper as you need to create your sketches until you feel that they encompass the information you've processed.

## Step 3: Connect

Mentally link the new information to knowledge that you already have. In other words, try to think of how the new information is similar to something you already know well. For example, if you are learning Portuguese, and are already familiar with French and Spanish, you can think that the some of the sounds of Portuguese are similar to French but with the rhythm of Spanish. Your established points of mental reference will help you contextualize the new content better.

### Step 4: Ask

If you can, talk to several experts on the subject. Let them tell you what they feel is relevant. After the experts tell you what they feel is relevant, ask them if there's anything else you really need to know about the topic.

### Step 5: Explain

Finally, write out all of the information you've gathered about the new subject as though you were explaining it to a child. Resist the urge to use your new vocabulary of topic-specific terminology, which typically obscures rather than clarifies. This process will help you zero in on the parts of information that are still unclear to you and need to be rounded out, or further simplified. To stay on track, keep the words of Albert Einstein in mind: "If you can't explain it to a six-year-old, you don't understand it yourself."

When you've taken these steps, you'll be well on your way to getting a good handle on the new subject.

# Build Skills With Intention

From the Creative Dose exercises earlier in the chapter, you should be well on your way to feeling more confident about the skills that you have. However, if you truly would like to expand your skill set, I wholeheartedly encourage you to go for it.

Let's break down a few myths surrounding building skill before starting, though. Talent is irrelevant; it means nothing. An alleged lack of "natural ability" is no excuse. Your supposed "limitations" are meaningless. Forget the "it takes 10,000 hours to achieve mastery" truism: unless you are specifically looking to become the next Tiger Woods or a chess grandmaster, the 10,000-hour rule is inapplicable for most people looking to improve their skills. In short, building skill doesn't have to do with ability or talent, nor does it require years of practice. You can build enough skill to become really good at something in far less time; in roughly 20 hours, if structured correctly. [15] Developing proficiency at a skill really boils down to practice, a very particular version called deliberate practice.

When our performance is automatic, we are unable to improve it. To shift our skills to the next level, we need to place ourselves back into the stage where we regain conscious control over the skill we're honing. With deliberate practice you practice to the point of failure, and then learn from that failure to adjust and try the skill again until you've mastered it.

The amount of practice is not as important as how you practice: in fact, it's the deliberateness that drives progress. Your practice must be intentional, aimed at improving performance, designed for your current skill level, combined with immediate feedback, and repetitious. It's best if you are intrinsically motivated: driven by interest, enjoyment, and satisfaction in the skill itself. [16]

## Creative Dose: Practice Deliberately

*Purpose: To increase skill through deliberate practice*

Here are some key pointers for setting up your deliberate practice.

1) Know your starting skill level, and build each step in the skill acquisition sequence accordingly.

2) Perform each task repeatedly, but remember that each subskill should be masterable in one to three practice sessions. If it takes longer than that, then the skill is too complex and needs to be broken down into smaller segments.

3) Focus on failing so that you can learn from it; make sure you receive immediate feedback that is directly applicable – without it, you won't know how to make adjustments to improve.

4)  Commit to at least 20 hours of focused, deliberate practice. Your practice must be carefully scheduled but also limited to avoid burnout and long-term fatigue.

To maintain momentum, make sure you revisit the fundamentals if you feel your skill slipping, stay aware of working on the next step once you've mastered the previous one, and always be thinking of what you might be missing and how you can continue to learn and grow in your skill.[17]

A fantastic side effect to deliberate practice is that it actually is a setup for achieving flow! By hitting the sweet spot of not being so far beyond your skill level that you are overwhelmed (and thus demotivated), and not so easy that you go into autopilot because you've already mastered it, you have the proper conditions for being in the flow channel,[18] continuously balanced within the magical space between skill and challenge.

# Amp Up Your Ability to Listen

*"When people listen, creative waters flow."*

— **Brenda Ueland,** *On The Fine Art of Listening*

One of the most underrated ways of feeling confident about ourselves and abilities actually has nothing to do with us, but instead is about being present for others by listening to them. Effective listening is the foundation of positive human relationships, and being an adept listener is one of the keys to being both a valued team member and leader. But not only that, being a good listener goes hand in hand with being creative. Why? Because listening to other people's ideas sparks ideas for you! And by reflecting back to the listener their own idea and creating connection, you also lay the foundation for creative collaboration. It is a win-win situation: in giving the person your full attention, you create connection with the other person, social value for yourself, and they can spark ideas for you!

Improved listening skills have also been shown to have a positive effect on self-esteem, personal confidence, and increased well-being in general. In her lovely essay, "On The Fine Art of Listening," writer Brenda Ueland speaks of the power of this practice: "We should all know this: that listening, not talking, is the gifted and great role, and the imaginative role. And the true listener is much more beloved, magnetic than the talker, and he is more effective and learns more and does more good." [19] It is the listener who has the power, creating a safe space and foundation upon which the talker can begin to share themselves.

If you are experiencing Profiency Anxiety, then developing your listening skills will be another highly effective method for establishing your value to both yourself and others.

 ## Creative Dose: Take In, Reflect Back

*Purpose: To increase your value by developing strong listening skills*

Here are tips for becoming a power listener:

1) Relax yourself and relax your agenda and be present to your talker.

2) Make sure they feel they have the space to speak.

3) Stay focused on what is being said verbally, but also be attentive to what is being communicated in other ways.

4) Flex your empathy muscle and make an effort to understand where they are coming from.

5) Remember to be patient and let the speaker say his or her piece.

6)   When giving feedback, rephrase what you've heard the talker say in your own words.

What you will find is that by focusing on the talker, you stop focusing on yourself and your anxieties. This alone will often help creativity flow. Additionally, by listening, you will be able to learn who has strengths that complement your own, helping you to further increase your effectiveness, value, and creativity.

# Raise A Barn

*"None of us is as smart as all of us."*

— **Kenneth H. Blanchard,** *author and management expert*

Feelings of deficiency can foster competitiveness and jealousy, which tend to shut down your creativity. When we are overcome with feeling like we don't know enough and that we'll never be able to keep up with our peers, here's a thought to consider: maybe we aren't supposed to know it all. Maybe the reason we feel that we have gaps in our knowledge is because there is someone else whose knowledge complements ours with whom we can join forces. Maybe, just maybe, we're not supposed to try to do it all by ourselves: instead of feeling like we need to compete with others, we are really destined to work together and collaborate to create something amazing.

Wouldn't you rather have collaboration and connection, which are key ingredients in creative synergy and teamwork with others? We need to let go of our DIY (Do it Yourself ) mindset and start to embrace a DIWO (Do it With Others) perspective instead.

Bruce Nussbaum, the author of the book *Creative Intelligence*, says, "...creativity is social...and comes out of small teams of twos and threes and fours and fives and sixes. Instead (of brainstorming) you need 'magic circles,' small teams of people who trust each other, are familiar with each other, and play together."[20] Set yourself to the task of tapping into the "superlinear scaling" of creativity[21] by assembling a group of people who will create better together.

## Creative Dose: Join Forces and Plus It

*Purpose: To leverage collective creativity*

What a relief: you don't have to do all of the creative heavy lifting yourself! Create a circle of creativity compatriots and then use the technique Plussing, which is often attributed to Walt Disney and is actively used by Pixar Studios. With Plussing, you give feedback in a way that is not only helpful but that also provides a new additional suggestion that helps the first idea, ensuring that creativity is nurtured and not stymied.[22]

Ready to start creating magic?

### Step 1: Create Your Circle

Remember that having a lot of people is not the goal, but trust is.

Gather people who not only inspire your creative thinking, but who you also trust.

The group members need to feel comfortable enough with each other to feel safe risking looking stupid and making mistakes.

The focus as a group should not necessarily be on generating a lot of ideas together. Rather, the group's focus should be on building upon each person's experience and individual expertise to create and play with new ideas.

Got your group together? Great! Now you're ready to amplify ideas.

**Step 2: Plus It**

When you are together, build upon and iterate ideas through the use of the supportive language of Plussing.

To start using Plussing with your magic creative circle, follow these simple guidelines:

1) **Accept every offer.**
   Start with whatever you've got and don't shut anyone's idea out. You want to employ a "do onto others" mentality.

2) **Yes, and!**
   When giving feedback, add a constructive suggestion using language like "yes, and…", "what if…", or "how might we do (x)?". Using phrases like "yes, but…" or "that will never work" will only shut down the flow of ideas and will break trust.

3) **Make your partners look good.**
   By accepting their suggestions and adding to them, you validate their ideas. And when the next person "plusses" what you've said, that person makes you look good, and so on.

By employing this structure for increased creative synergy, you'll be amazed at what your group members contribute and what you'll be able to produce collectively. You'll find that not only will collaborations get better, but the circle of your group (or team) will indeed start to play together and create magic.

# Steal Like An Artist to Remix

> *"Nothing is original. Steal from anywhere that resonates with inspiration or fuels your imagination… Authenticity is invaluable; originality is non-existent."*
>
> — **Jim Jarmusch**, *film director, screenwriter, actor, producer, editor, and composer*

From the data on creativity that I have collected from my keynotes and workshops, one of the most universal fears that people have is the fear of not being original enough, of having ideas that have been done before and better, and the fear that they are just rehashing someone else's ideas. I was amazed at how many people suffer from this fear, so I've given it a name: Originality Anxiety.

Not only is this belief founded in a quixotic ideal, but more importantly, like the other Deficiency Anxieties, it hinders what originality and creativity you do have. Listen: searching for an idea that no one has ever had is like looking for a unicorn. I'm not saying that you'll never have an original idea. But committing ideacide by blocking your ideas just because you feel they aren't original enough or because your initial concept plays off of another's work doesn't serve anyone, especially not you and your creative spark.

There's nothing new under the sun. But there is only one you. So anything that has been done before that comes through the filter of you will be a changed version of what existed before: different and uniquely yours.

 ## Creative Dose: Be a Mixmaster

*Purpose: To create originality from remixing*

For those who appreciate dance music of any sort, you know that there is nothing like a great DJ. A great DJ can take an assembly of songs, beats, and sounds, and through layering and interweaving, turn them into a completely new experience from the original.

Don't beat yourself up about doing something that is derivative. Remember and realize that everything is a remix.[23] When you let go of the idea that being creative means doing something completely new, you can let yourself play with what's already available, much like a DJ.

The process of creativity relies on elements of copying, transformation, and combining. Use these elements to change the starting idea into something that is authentically yours.

Instead of trying to come up with a completely original idea, I encourage you to shamelessly use other people's ideas as a springboard for your own. Use others' work as inspiration and as a jumping-off point upon which to build your ideas and get your remix on.

## BEYOND ENOUGH

With our new knowledge, we're making the effort to shift our attention away from what we fear we lack in order to rediscover what we are rich in: our accomplishments and our wealth of experience, our natural talents and skills, and our intrinsic qualities, in a combination that no single other human in the world has. And with further tools to let our ideas out into the world and develop our knowledge and skills, we're making great headway.

Let's move on to learn how to break away from comparisons.

*I am not as smart / creative as others.*

**6**

# CHAPTER 6 | "I'M NOT AS CREATIVE AS EVERYONE ELSE" - *COMPARISON SYNDROME*

*This chapter examines:*

Envy v. Jealousy

Media Detox

FOMO and JOMO

Tools for Eliminating Distractions

Becoming Self-Referential

Determining Distinctiveness

Learning from Envy

Activating Admiration

Celebrating Success

Taking Action

*"Comparison is the thief of joy."*

—Theodore Roosevelt

I grew up in an environment of perpetual creativity and inventiveness. My father Dennis built and flew experimental aircraft as a hobby. During my entire childhood, there was an airplane fusilage in the garage instead of a car. My mother Deloria was a self-taught master artisan who could quickly acquire any skills that it took to work with fabric and weaving. She could sew any garment she desired, and was able to weave intricate wall hangings just by looking at a black and white photos in magazines. My older sister Diane blossomed into a consummate fine artist who drew portraits with uncanny likeness, painted murals, and studied art and architecture. In addition, she loved good food and had a genius for cooking and baking, which converged in her creating remarkable art pieces out of cake that were incredibly delicious to boot. Yes. This was the household in which I grew up.

While there countless positives to being surrounded by people who were compelled to create, there was also a downside to it. I incessantly compared myself to my parents and older sister and always found myself lacking.

It wasn't a fair comparison, but tell that to a sensitive kid who wanted to fit in to her family by being creative as well. From my early years throughout my teens, I convinced myself that I would never understand how to build an airplane or at least be as proficient with tools as my father, the aeronautical engineer. Even though my sister was six years older than I was, I lamented that I would never be as good a visual artist as she was. And I marveled at my mother's seemingly magical ability to make and tailor clothes and was certain that I would never attain her level of mastery.

This habit of comparing myself to others grew over the years, continuing to subtly and effectively undermine my sense of self. I had almost reached an uneasy truce with my comparison habit when social media happened.

As an early adopter of Twitter, I loved staying connected to people I met at tech conferences. However, as I began to realize my aspirations of being an author and a speaker, Twitter became a dreaded hall of mirrors where I only saw distorted reflections of my lack of achievement in other people's success. Every person announcing a publishing deal caused me to drown under waves of envy over the imagined size of her or his book advance as I struggled to pay my mortgage. Every announcement I read of someone speaking at a conference led to thoughts of, "I wish I were speaking at that conference – I must not be good enough to be invited." Twitter was fertile ground for my Inner Critic to run rampant.

One day in 2011, my comparisons to people who I didn't even know rose to a fever pitch. I saw a series of tweets that sparked a wave of self-loathing so profound that I spent the day sobbing and despondent, as I chastised myself for being a failure. I had fallen into the deep pit of Comparison Syndrome, and to return to anything close to being productive took a day or two of painstakingly clawing my way out.

## COMPARISON SYNDROME TAKES DEFICIENCY ANXIETY TO ELEVEN

Do any of these scenarios ring true?

❑ You frequently feel like a failure when viewing the success of others.

❑ You feel dispirited and paralyzed in moving forward with your own work because it will never measure up to what others have done.

☐ You discount your ideas because you fear that they aren't as good as those of your colleagues or industry peers.

Are you making yourself miserable by thinking thoughts like these?

☐ "I'm surrounded by people who are so good at what they do, how can I possibly measure up?"

☐ "Compared to my partner, my musical ability is childish – and music is no longer fun."

☐ "Why haven't I accomplished more by now? My peers are so much more successful than I am."

# UNENVIABLE ENVY

Many people use the terms envy and jealousy interchangeably, but they are two distinct emotions. Jealousy is the fear of losing someone to a perceived rival: a threat to an important relationship and the parts of the self that are served by that relationship. Jealousy is always about the relationship between three people. Envy is wanting what another has because of a perceived shortcoming on your part. Envy is always based on a social comparison to another.[1]

Envy is a reaction to the feeling of lacking something. Envy always reflects something we feel about ourselves, about how we are somehow deficient in qualities, possessions, or success.[2] It's based on a scarcity mentality: the idea that there is only so much to go around, and another person got something that should rightfully be yours.[3]

A syndrome is a condition characterized by a set of associated symptoms. I call it Comparison Syndrome because a perceived deficiency of some sort – in talent, accomplishments, success, skills, etc. – is what initially sparks it. While at the beginning you may merely feel inadequate, the onset of the syndrome will bring additional symptoms. Lack of self-trust and feelings of low self-worth will fuel increased thoughts of not-enoughness and blindness to your unique brilliance. If left unchecked, Deficiency Anxieties can escalate to full-blown Comparison Syndrome: a form of the Inner Critic in which we experience despair from envy and define ourselves as failures in light of another's success.

The irony is that when we focus so much on what we lack, we can't see what we have in abundance that the other person doesn't have. And in doing so, we block what is our birthright: our creative expression. Envy shackles our creativity, keeps us trapped in place, and prevents forward movement. The Inner Critic in the form of Comparison Syndrome caused by envy blocks us from utilizing our gifts, seeing our path clearly, and reveling in our creative power.

There are two parts to keeping a grip on reality and not falling into the abyss of Comparison Syndrome. First, we'll quell the compulsion to compare before it happens: we will free the mental bandwidth to turn our focus inward so we can start to see ourselves clearly. Then from there, we'll be ready to reverse Comparison Syndrome by transforming envy into motivation.

## BREAK THE COMPULSION TO COMPARE

*"Why compare yourself with others? No one in the entire world can do a better job of being you than you."*

— **Krystal Volney,** *poet and author*

At some point in time, many of us succumb to moments of feeling that we are lacking and comparing ourselves unfavorably to others. As social animals, much of our self-definition comes from comparison with others. This is how our personalities develop. We learn this behavior as children, and we grow up being compared to siblings, peers, and kids in the media. Because of this, the belief that somehow, someway, we aren't good enough becomes deeply ingrained. The problem is that whenever we deem ourselves to be "less than," our self-esteem suffers. This creates a negative feedback loop where negative thoughts produce strong emotions that result in self-defeating behaviors that beget more negative thoughts.

Couple this cycle with the messages we get from society that only "gifted" people are creative, and it's no wonder that many of us will fall down the rabbit hole of Comparison Syndrome like I did on that fated day while reading tweets. Comparing ourselves to others is worse than a zero-sum game, it's a negative-sum game. No one wins, our self-esteem deteriorates, and our creative spark dies out.

With effort, we can break the compulsion to compare and stop the decline into Comparison Syndrome by turning the focus of comparison inward to ourselves and appreciating who we've become. But first, we need to remove some of the instances that trigger our comparisons in the first place.

## Arrest: Stop the Triggers

*"Right discipline consists, not in external compulsion, but in the habits of mind which lead spontaneously to desirable rather than undesirable activities."*

— **Bertrand Russell,** *philosopher*

After my Twitter post meltdown, I knew had to make a change. While bolstering my sense of self was clearly a priority, I also knew that my ingrained comparison habit was too strong to resist and that I needed to instill discipline. I decided then and there to establish boundaries with social media.

First, to maintain my sanity, I took this on as my mantra:

*"I will not compare myself to strangers on the Internet
or acquaintances on Facebook."*

If you find yourself sliding down the slippery slope of social media comparison, you can do the same: repeat this mantra to yourself to help put on the brakes.

Second, in order to reduce my triggers, I stopped reading the tweets of the people I followed. However, I continued to be active on Twitter through sharing information, responding to mentions, crowdsourcing, and direct messaging people. It worked! The only time I'd start to slip into darkness were the rare instances when I would break my rules and look at my Twitstream.

But we can do even more than calm ourselves with helpful mantras. Just like my example of modifying my use of Twitter, and more recently, of separating myself from Facebook, you can get some distance from the media that activates your comparison reflex and start creating the space for other habits that are more supportive to your being to take its place.

## Creative Dose: Trigger-free and Happy

*Purpose: To stop comparison triggers in their tracks*

Mindfulness is a wonderful tool, but sometimes you have to get hardcore and do as much as you can to eliminate distractions so that you can first hear your own thoughts in order to know which ones you need to focus on.

Here are four steps to becoming trigger-free and happier.

### Step 1: Make a List

Pay attention when you get the most triggered and hooked.

Is it on Twitter, Facebook, Instagram, or Snapchat?

Is it YouTube, TV shows, or magazines?

Make list of your top triggers:

My primary trigger is: _____

My second trigger is: _____

My third trigger is: _____

Now that you have your list, you need to get an idea just how often you're getting triggered.

## Step 2: Monitor

It's easy to think that we should track our activity on the computer, but these days, it's no longer our computer use that is the culprit: most people access social media and news from their phones. Fortunately, there are apps that will track the usage for both.

Seeing just how much you consume media from either or both will show you how much of an accomplice the use of devices is to your comparison syndrome, and how much you need to modify your behavior accordingly.

For tracking both computer use and tablet use, this app works great:

- **RescueTime.com** tracks app usage and sends a productivity report at the end of the week via email.

For your phone, there are many for either platform.[4] Athough I recommend fully researching what is available and will work for you best, here are a few recommendations:

- For both platforms: **Offtime, Breakfree, Checky**

- For Android only: **Flipd, AppDetox, QualityTime, Stay On Task**

- For iOs only: **Moment**

Install your app of choice, and see what you find. How much time are you spending on sites or apps that compel you to compare?

## Step 3: Just Say No

Now that you know what your triggers are and how much you're exposing yourself to them, it's time to say No.

Put yourself on a partial social media and/or media detox for a specified period of time; consider even going for a full media detox.[2] I recommend starting with one month.

To help you to fully commit, I recommend writing this down and posting it where you can see it.

I, _____, commit to

avoiding my comparison triggers of _____,

_____, and _____ for the

period of _____, starting on_____

and ending on _____.

To help you out, I've created a social media detox commitment sheet for you.[6]

## Step 4: Block

When I decided to reduce my use of Twitter and Facebook to break my comparison habit, initially I tried to rely solely on self-discipline, which was only moderately successful. Then I realized that I could use the power of technology to help. Don't think you have to rely upon sheer willpower to block, or at least limit, your exposure to known triggers. If your primary access to the items that cause you to compare

---

[2] You can download your Media Detox Commitment sheet here: creativedo.se/media-detox-commitment

yourself to others is via computers and other digitalia, use these devices to help maintain your mental equilibrium.

Here are some apps and browser extensions that you can use during your media detox to help keep yourself sane and stay away from sites that could throw you into a comparison tailspin.

These apps are installed onto your computer:

- **RescueTime.com** works on both computer and mobile devices, and does a lot more than just prevent you from going to sites that will ruin your concentration, it will also track your apps usage and give you a productivity report at the end of the week.

- **HeyFocus.com** and **SelfControlApp.com** (Mac-only)

To go right to the source and prevent you from visiting sites through your browser, there are browser extensions.

Not only can you put in the list of the URLs that are your points of weakness, but you can also usually set the times of the day you need the self-control the most.

- Google Chrome: **StayFocusd, Strict Workflow**, and **Website Blocker**

- Firefox: **Idderall** and **Leechblock**

- Safari: **WasteNoTime** and **MindfulBrowsing**

- Edge (or Explorer): Unfortunately, there are currently no website blocking extensions for these browsers.

I currently use a browser extension to block me from using Facebook between 9:00am – 6:00pm. It's been a boon for my sanity: I compare tons less. A bonus is that it's been terrific for my productivity as well.

Which tool will you use for your media detox time? Explore them all and then settle upon the one(s) that will work the best for you. Install it and put it to work.

Despite the tool, you will still need to exercise discipline. Resist the urge to browse Instagram or Facebook while waiting for your morning train. You can do it!

### Step 5: Relax

Instead of panicking from FOMO (Fear of Missing Out), take comfort from this thought: what you don't know won't affect you. Start embracing JOMO (Joy of Missing Out), and the process of rebuilding and maintaining your sanity.

What will you do instead of consuming the media that compels you to compare? Here are some ideas:

Read a book • Go for a walk • Have dinner with a friend • Go watch a movie • Learn a how to play the harmonica • Take an improv class

Really, you could do anything. And depending on how much of your time and attention you've devoted to media, you could be recapturing a lot of lost moments, minutes, hours, and days.

### Step 6: Reconnect

Use your recovered time and attention to focus on your life and reconnect with your true value-driven goals, higher aspirations, and activities that you've always wanted to do.

## Assess: Become Self-Referential

*"Don't compare yourself to others. Compare yourself to the person you were yesterday."*

**— Anonymous**

External achievements are a limited way to measure success. Accomplishments that everyone can see, like getting a degree, starting a company, or having a baby represent enormous amounts of internal shifts, learning, and growth. Comparison is a filter that prevents you from seeing yourself clearly. When you apply your measuring stick against everyone else's external achievements, you get a wildly inaccurate reading of your progress. A well-known adage wisely instructs, "Do not compare your insides to someone else's outsides."

However, the mind is predisposed to compare.[7] So let's work with it. Instead of externalizing the comparison by unfairly judging yourself against someone about whose life you have limited (or even inaccurate) information, redirect the comparison to someone whose life you are an absolute expert on: yourself!

In other words, become self-referential. Determine your success by looking at who you've become over time.[8] Once you've done that, you can focus your energies on continually becoming the best version of yourself.

 ## Creative Dose: Apples to Apples

*Purpose: To compare yourself to yourself to recognize your growth*

Instead of focusing only on external accomplishments, which could potentially lead back to comparing yourself to others, think about your internal growth. This exercise is adapted from the article "Stop Comparing: An Alternative to Competing with People" by Sonya Derian.[9]

How have you evolved and developed as a person? Choose a period of time, for example: one month, one year, five years, or ten years. You're going to make note of how far you've come in various areas.

Hunker down with your journal or some paper and reflect upon these questions and then respond – your answers will create an outline of your growth.

1) Skills

- What new skills have you acquired?

- What are you doing today that you couldn't have done five years ago or even one year ago?

2) Commitment

- How have you shown up more consistently for your own success?

- What negative behavior have you stopped?

- What positive behavior have you added?

3) Expansion

- What have you done recently that you never thought you could do?

- What new decisions or actions have resulted in you moving in a new direction in your life?

- Where and when have you exercised courage?

4) Emotional Growth

- How have you grown emotionally?

5) Self-care

- How have you taken better care of yourself physically, emotionally, and mentally?

- How have you fed your soul?

6) Overall

- How have you become, and how do you continue to become, the best version of yourself?

Look at how much you have grown, what you have achieved, and what progress you have made toward your goals. Can you see how far you've come?

Regularly revisit and amend your list to instill a habit of focusing on yourself and gain perspective on your development. Do this consistently (once a month is great!) and you'll see tremendous change over time in your self-appreciation.

## Creative Dose: Keep Your "But" Out of It

*Purpose: To use improv to keep from dismissing your accomplishments*

If you find yourself saying "yes, but..." when thinking about how you've grown (indicating that you are still comparing), you need to apply the improv technique of using "Yes, and."

"Yes, but" is the Inner Critic's way of trying to pull your attention back to your fears. This is just your brain's attempt to get back to a well-worn neural pathway.

"Yes, and," however, mutes the Inner Critic by forcing your brain to come up with new ideas and associations. It uses improv to start changing your negative self-talk to positive.

So, when you are thinking about how much you've grown over the past several years, replace your "yeah, but" with "yes, and" to shift yourself out of a deficiency mindset that will leave you susceptible to comparing yourself to others.

For example, if you're thinking, "I should list the triathlon I did 10 years ago," and your Inner Critic responds with, "Yeah, but you didn't make a great time and you walked during part of the run," then change it to this:

"...yes, and I'm so proud that I finished my first triathlon ever!"

Use the approach of "yes, and" to counter the Inner Critic's attempts to discount your achievements.

# Attune: Embrace Your "Onlyness"

*"There is a vitality, a life force, an energy, a quickening that is translated through you into action, and because there is only one of you in all of time, this expression is unique. And if you block it, it will never exist through any other medium and it will be lost. The world will not have it. It is not your business to determine how good it is nor how valuable nor how it compares with other expressions."*

— **Martha Graham**, *The Life and Work of Martha Graham*

What you produce with your creativity can't be produced or replicated by anyone else. Comparisons focus on the wrong person and block the expression of your unique brilliance. The Martha Graham quote above practically makes me want to stand up and testify. Ya-uuussss! What you bring forth into the world can only come through you. Amen!

To break away from comparing, I encourage you to acknowledge what author, speaker, and innovation strategist Nilofer Merchant has coined your "Onlyness": "the space in which only you can stand."[10] Tuning into your Onlyness means truly understanding and appreciating that you are a singular combination, a totality of talents, experiences, and wisdom that no one else in the world has.

Embracing your Onlyness is a powerful practice: the more you become aware of and appreciate just how incomparable you truly are, the less you will compare yourself to others.

## Creative Dose: Determining Distinctiveness

*Purpose: To discover and own your uniqueness*

Recently, I learned the saying, "When you're in the frame, you can't see the picture." I loved how apropos and timely this discovery was.

In the previous chapter, the Creative Dose: Take Inventory got you in touch with your achievements, intrinsic qualities, and successes. But this assessment was all from your perspective. That is your "frame."

To get a better idea of the things about you that everyone else can see but you can't (your "picture"), you are going to enlist help from others. Their feedback will to help you to determine your Onlyness.

I've adapted this exercise from the process that Nilofer Merchant used to successfully transition from being the founder and CEO of a leading strategy firm to becoming a sought-after international speaker, author, and innovation consultant.[11]

### Step 1: List

Make a list of 5-10 people with whom you have strong professional connections (think mentors, former managers, and colleagues), who know you well, and – most importantly – *who will be completely honest with you.*

### Step 2: Ask

Ask them these questions:

- In your opinion, what am I distinctly good at?

- What do you think the world would be missing without my contribution to it?

- What can you see in me that I cannot see, but that you wish I could see and act upon?

### Step 3: Glean

Compile their answers and find the common threads. Use the information to open your eyes to your distinctive qualities that you've overlooked or dismissed, and as impetus for you to start putting your Onlyness to good use.

## MOVE FROM STAGNATION TO ACTION

*"Be so busy improving yourself that you have no time to criticize others."*

— **Chetan Bhagat,** *author*

Comparison may have been useful as a tool for personality development when we were younger, but the habit hurts us as we grow older. Think back to the last time you compared yourself to someone. Did it leave you feeling elated and motivated? Or was it the fast track to a pit of despair that you had to work to escape? I'm certain that it was the latter. Research supports this: one study showed that amongst students, comparisons destroyed motivation and severely compromised the students' ability to achieve goals.[12]

Here's the good news: instead of allowing comparisons to monopolize our consciousness and co-opt our feelings, we can get back into the driver's seat to regain control of our attention. We can change the course of our conscious thoughts and make comparisons serve our needs. By letting go of our preoccupation with the trajectory of other people's lives, we can transform our envy from a stagnant, blocking force into a powerful motivator for growth.

Let's look at ways to employ the energy of comparing to propel us forward rather than keeping us mired in comparison quicksand.

# Ascertain: Learn from Envy

*"Negative emotions like loneliness, envy, and guilt have an important role to play in a happy life; they're big, flashing signs that something needs to change."*

— **Gretchen Rubin,** *The Happiness Project*

Despite the stigma that envy is a "bad" emotion, it is part of the human experience.[13] It's okay to feel envious at times. But more importantly, envy (like all strong emotions) has the potential to be a great teacher. Just as physical pain alerts you to a problem in your body that needs to be tended to, the mental distress of envy alerts you to a problem in your psyche calling for your attention.

Emotions are messengers. They give us information about how we are responding to our thoughts and experiences. This is easier to accept with positive emotions such as happiness, joy, or euphoria. The challenge comes when we experience strong so-called negative emotions such as anger, sadness, or fear. From an early age, we are taught to suppress or ignore negative feelings and to deal with them later – if at all.

The very essence of emotion is movement: the word emotion originated from words that mean "to set in motion; to move feelings." The real problem with strong emotions is when we don't fully acknowledge, feel, and express them — they don't move. These emotions end up staying past their welcome, building up in our psyches. Then one day a seemingly minor event triggers an overblown reaction, as the emotion finally dynamites its way out.

Sadly, through the practice of denying and suppressing strong emotions, we miss their message and their original purpose gets lost. In contrast, when we acknowledge and feel a strong emotion, two positive things happen. First, the felt and expressed emotion typically quickly diminishes in intensity. Second, we learn something about ourselves from its presence.

Take heed and learn from your envy. By acknowledging this important message from your inner self and acting on it, envy will serve its purpose, helping to form a positive vision for your future.

## Creative Dose: What Lies Beneath Your Envy

*Purpose: To treat envy as a messenger and learn what it's trying to teach you*

Use the comparison trigger of envy to your advantage to find out what lies beneath it.

One of my favorite sayings is, "You want something because it wants you." Envy can be a messenger to not only tell us of our innermost desires, but also provide clues to our highest potential.

Instead of allowing your envy to make you miserable, treat it as a clue leading you on the path to becoming more of who you are.

Think of a person or someone's circumstance that you have envy towards.

Reflect upon these questions, and then write down your answers in your journal or on paper:

- What is your envy trying to tell you? Is there is something missing in your life that it's time for you to start working toward?

- What does your envy have to teach you about the deep aspirations of your soul?

- For example, if you are thinking comparison thoughts such as, "I'll never be an award-winning dev/designer/CEO like my colleague," then look at that thought as a message. Maybe deep down inside, you actually want to be recognized for your work. Capture what you've discovered.

My envy tells me that I really want to:_____

If that's what you truly deeply desire, there's no reason in the world why you shouldn't have it, or at the very least, put forth effort towards it. See your envy, then, as a call to action.

If this is a deep desire, then how can you make it manifest? Maybe you need to enter yourself into a contest, start writing articles for popular websites or speaking to raise your visible profile, or have people start to recommend you for awards. Write some ideas on how you can start moving in the direction of achieving your desire.

Ideas on steps I can take to achieve my desire:

1. _____

2. _____

3. _____

Don't just stop at three, keep going until you exhaust all of your ideas.

In essence, envy may be lighting a path for you towards the life that you actually want to live. Follow the breadcrumb trail to discover the deeper truth that your envy is trying to communicate.

## Admire: Transform Envy

*"When emulation leads us to strive for self-elevation by merit alone, and not by belittling another, then it is one of the grandest possible incentives to action."*

— **Samuel Johnson**, *author and poet*

We tend to overestimate the positivity in the lives of others, but that's because most people will only share the positive.[14] In other words, what we get from people – what we see and what they share – is an incomplete picture. What we see are people's highlight reels.[15] We don't see anything behind the scenes: the bloopers, the struggles, and the failures. We don't know the full truth. Keep this in mind: when you compare yourself to others, you're comparing yourself against incomplete or even inaccurate information: an idealized version of the other person. Comparisons are selective, exaggerated, and unreal.

The striking thing in my keynotes, talks, and workshops is the universality of the feeling of self-doubt and the internal voice of chastisement. I've said it before, and I'll say it again: to have an Inner Critic is to be human. Feelings of inadequacy and disappointment are shared by everyone. When we feel ashamed and less than, we don't focus on what we have in common with others.[16]

While it may seem like there are certain people who have everything together on the exterior level, know that inside they are wrestling with their own inner critical voices as well: their own special version of mistaken beliefs and distorted thinking about themselves. The Inner Critic is universal. We all – every single one of us – have one. Some of our Inner Critics may be more vitriolic than others, but they all have left their hurtful imprint upon our psyches. And it's this element of commonality that also helps us to be more compassionate to ourselves: we actually all belong. We are all suffering from similar mental wounds. We are all trying to work it out, trying collectively trying to figure out this thing called Life. The next time you feel particularly put upon by self-critical thinking and mired down by harshly judging or criticizing yourself and comparing yourself to others, remember that other people are feeling similarly. You're not the only one. Give yourself a pass, and extend yourself some kindness for being human.

The alternative to Comparison Syndrome is to look at the success of others with approval, pleasure, and wonder. From this new standpoint, we can use their success as an impetus for admiration, emulation, and celebration.

## Creative Dose: A Comparison Syndrome Intervention

*Purpose: To prevent you from going into a comparison spiral*

If you find yourself going down the comparison rabbit-hole, stop and ask yourself these questions:

*Q: Do I have all of the information about these people and how they got to this point?*

A: No, I don't.

*Q: Is comparing my insides to their outsides really fair?*

A: No, it's not.

*Q: Is it a waste of my brainpower and time to continue comparing myself to them?*

A: Yes, as a matter of fact, it is.

Repeat as needed.

## Creative Dose: To Admiration and Beyond

*Purpose: To move from envy, to emulation, to celebration*

Despite knowing that what we see on the surface of a person's life isn't the full story, with an ingrained comparison habit, we still allow the outward success of others to adversely affect us.

Here are four methods that you can employ either individually or in combination to transform the success of others into a source of inspiration and motivation.

## Option 1: Acknowledge

Give the person the same consideration that you'd like for yourself. Recognize and acknowledge all of the incredibly hard work that invariably has gone on behind the scenes of their highlight reel: their aggravations, setbacks, failures, and yes, even dealing with their own Inner Critic.

Instead of sitting in envy, which hurts you on multiple levels (but doesn't affect the person at all unless you interact with them regularly and your envy sours the dynamic of the interaction), use a mindful approach to shift your thinking. Activate your empathy and extend compassion towards what the person went through to get where they are.

## Option 2: Differentiate

Separate yourself from the other person by focusing on the differences between you and her or him, rather than the similarities. Examine the situation itself and find differences as well. [17]

You'll most likely find that you've been comparing apples to oranges.

You can use this framework to help you think through this.

The person I envy is _____, and I am

_____.

The person I envy had _____, and I had

_____.

The person I envy does _____work, and I

do _____work.

Be conscious of focusing on de facto differences, rather than leaning towards listing what advantages you believe that this person has over you.

## Option 3: Emulate

To transform envy into a motivating force that will help you attain your goals, learn from another's trajectory.

Look at the people that you envy. Instead of a "role model," which makes what a person has accomplished feel unobtainable, make someone your "Opportunity Model": someone who is showing you that the opportunity is available for you to achieve,[18] as well as a potential method to do so.

Learn from your Opportunity Model's achievements.

* What steps has this person taken to achieve their success?

* How can you emulate what she or he has done to achieve success for yourself?

Focus on her or his process and steps to success.

* Are there parts of the process that you can replicate? What are they?

Think about the qualities that your Opportunity Model has.

* How can you learn from the qualities that s/he exhibits?

Here is a framework to help you out:

My Opportunity Model is: _____.

She/He is successful at: _____.

She/He achieved success by: _____.

My Opportunity Model has these qualities that contributed to this person's success: _____.

My Opportunity Model has these qualities that I admire:

_____

Take the responses from all of these questions, and start devising how you can take their strategies and combine them into an even better approach that is uniquely tailored to you, your talents, skills, and ambitions.[19]

You can use this framework:

It is my intention to be successful at:

_____

Here are ideas on how I can start:

_____

Here are the qualities I have that will contribute to my success:

_____

Here are the qualities that I will develop to accelerate my success:

_____

**Option 4: Celebrate**

Another's success does not diminish what we are doing and who we are. Remind yourself that the success of others does not reflect on you and does not take away from you. Instead of comparison, find inspiration. Transform your envy into congratulations and celebrate another's success.

Here are some ways you can celebrate someone's success:

- Send them a congratulations card

- Send them a congratulations gift

- Post about their achievement on social media

- Recommend them for a podcast or interview

- Recommend their work to other people

*Bonus Action:* Go one step farther and applaud people's efforts instead of their achievements, for an accomplishment is merely the product of many smaller tasks. Doing this for others gives you a template for how to cheer yourself on and celebrate your own successes, and will make you open to receiving it from others.

## Acknowledge: Recognize Effort and Reward Success

*"A person who feels appreciated will always do more than what is expected."*

**– Author Unknown**

Speaking of cheering on others for their success, consider this: You may be critical and envious of another's success because you don't acknowledge your own.

It's easy to get stuck in the loop of Comparison Syndrome when we feel that we haven't done enough. But maybe one of the reasons you feel that way is because you haven't fully celebrated the big things that you have accomplished. Trust me, I speak from experience.

When my book the The *CSS Detective Guide* came out in early 2010, you'd think that the fact that I was finally a published author – particularly given my inherited belief that becoming a writer was hard and becoming a published author was even harder – would have caused me to shout it from the rooftops and celebrate at every moment possible. But that was not the case. When the box of books arrived from the publisher, I snapped a couple of photos and posted one to Twitter, and that was it. I took my book with me to a local tech meetup to show my friends, and when people asked if I would have a reading, I said that I would eventually set one up. But I never did. In fact, the excitement about the book, to which I had slavishly devoted eight months of my life to writing, was completely overshadowed by my focus on my next big goal of making my first international speaking engagement happen the next month. Seriously – I didn't even have a party with my friends. As I wrote in a post for the Pastry Box Project, "my celebration of having accomplished one of my life's Big Goals of being a published author consisted of a few clicks of a digital camera, a couple of tweets, and a buried blog post."[20]

Part of the reason that I moved on so quickly was due to my own Comparison Syndrome. I was so busy feeling that I was "behind" my peers in terms of being successful and that I needed to "catch up" to the people whom I admired. Because I didn't fully recognize and celebrate my own major accomplishment, it seemed almost as if it hadn't happened. To this day, having written that book still hasn't fully registered in my mind as the achievement that it was.

When we don't acknowledge or celebrate success, good performance, or even progress, our motivation flags, and achieving long-term goals become more difficult. Whereas when we acknowledge our efforts, not only do we feel great, but we are then inspired to tackle even more. This is because acknowledgment and celebration activate the reward system in the brain and release the feel-good neurotransmitter dopamine.[21] Activating the reward system is a huge part of motivation: the more we receive pleasure from rewarding our efforts, the more inclined we are to continue the activities that engender the pleasure of the reward. In short, we develop an addiction to exerting effort toward and achieving goals.[22]

In an online article, coach Emma-Louise Elsey recommends celebrating achievement and success[23] when:

1) **You've taken steps towards a big goal.** Have you started learning Portuguese for your three-month sabbatical in Brazil? Have you changed your treadmill workout to steep inclines in preparation for a trip to Tanzania to hike Mount Kilimanjaro? Have you gathered up all of your portfolio pieces and written

your application to get your work into the Smithsonian? Maybe you haven't reached the ultimate goal yet, but the work that you've put in so far needs to be recognized and celebrated. And then you can celebrate again when you've hit your goal!

2) **You've had a personally significant success.** Regardless of size, if you've reached some sort of personal milestone, then you absolutely must celebrate it. Maybe you've been wanting to learn how to knit and you've knitted your first scarf. Maybe you've been wanting to learn how to drive stick shift since you were a teen, and you've finally mastered it through driving lessons. Maybe you've been wanting to rearrange your living room for years, and you've finally done it. Whether or not an outsider would think it's a big deal, it's a big deal for YOU. Celebrate the heck out of it.

3) **You've learned from mistakes, difficulties, and failures.** Celebrate failure? Yes! But really, what you're celebrating is the learning. What have you learned from realizing that you've been approaching something all wrong? How has it helped you grow and gain clarity about yourself and your direction? Celebrate the fact that you are learning, growing, and expanding, and that your mistakes only make you stronger and more powerful, not less.

To break the habit of looking at the achievements of others and feeling that our own pale in comparison, we need to direct a laser-like focus toward acknowledging and basking in our own successes. But it's not just the big things that we need to acknowledge and give ourselves credit for. It's just as important (if not more so) for us to congratulate ourselves for showing up every day and putting in the work that moves us ever closer to our goals and aspirations. Building the habit of and addiction to forward progress will keep us motivated and on-track with achieving our goals.

When we're busy working towards our goals and celebrating our efforts, we won't have the time, mental bandwidth, or inclination to compare ourselves with others.

## Creative Dose: A Celebration of Effort and Achievement

*Purpose: To shift focus to your own efforts and successes*

You may be critical and envious of another's success because you don't acknowledge your own. My recommendation? Celebrate your successes, both large and small, and do so with abandon. You'll get in touch with just how much work you put forth and will also be less inclined to be as focused on what others are doing. You'll also be more present to revel in the success of others.

### Step 1: The Self-Talk of Reward

Now that we know the power of self-talk and particularly talking to ourselves in the third person, we need to use it as much as we can. To keep ourselves motivated by everyday progress, we need to make sure that our self-talk is that of encouragement, not berating.

Just like we would encourage a kid to keep them motivated to take on big projects, we need to encourage the younger part of ourselves that is sensitive to self-criticism and recognize our own efforts.

Here is an example of what you can say to yourself to acknowledge your efforts, even when everything's not finished or perfect[24]:

"Wow, Amy, you're working really hard on this project! You're doing great!"

And when you're done:

"Great job, Amy! You kick butt!"

You'll spur yourself on to continuing doing the work because it's important to you, it interests you, and because you like it.

## Step 2: Take A Success Inventory

You may be so in the habit of barely taking heed of your successes that they rush past you, and you forget them almost as quickly as you achieved them.

First, review your lists that you generated from the Creative Doses: Take Inventory and Apples to Apples in the previous chapter to refresh your memory on what some of the wonderful things you've accomplished.

Then, let's get even more in more in touch with both your small and large successes to help you celebrate both. This exercise is adapted from the article "Celebrate Success!" by the team at LeadFearlessly.com.[25]

Go back into your calendar and look at the past 12 months. For each week, try to remember:

1) What new ideas did you dream up?

2) What did you initiate or start?

3) What did you get done or complete?

4) What did you launch?

5) What strengths, talents, and skills did you put to use?

6) What abilities and knowledge did you develop or acquire?

7) What relationships did you initiate, grow, or strengthen?

8) What challenges and obstacles did you overcome?

9) What are you most proud of?

10) What surprised you?

Don't worry if you can't remember everything perfectly, the goal is really to bring as many as you can to mind. The answers to these questions should be a rich trove of situations that deserve recognition and celebrating!

Now that you know what to reward yourself for, it's time to actually do something about it.

## Step 3: Reward and Celebrate

How will you celebrate? The choices are endless. Here are some tips for you:

- **Buy Yourself A Present.** Treat yourself to something that you love. While an experience is great, such as getting a massage or taking yourself to a concert, also make an effort to you treat yourself with an object. Looking at and/or using it will be a constant reminder of both your hard work and an embodiment of how you are respecting yourself.

- **Hold a Retroactive Celebration.** You don't have to limit yourself to celebrating things that have happened recently. Just because your success was 10 years ago doesn't mean you can't finally give it its due and celebrate it now. It's your life – you can do whatever you want. And besides, people love parties and celebrations. Your friends and colleagues will be happy for the excuse to come together and support you! Put together a get-together potluck or a barbeque, host a dinner party or a gathering at a fancy restaurant, or go bigger and hold a bona fide party. Whatever you do, make sure you bring in people who are important to you to share in celebrating your accomplishment.

- **Achiever's Choice.** How would you most like to honor yourself? Choose whatever resonates the most with you and then commit to it. Choose a day and time, and schedule it on your calendar so that it has as much importance as everything else that you block time out for.

### *Bonus Action:* **Get A Success Buddy**

You don't have to celebrate by yourself. Team up with someone who is working on acknowledging their successes as well, and agree to be "Success Buddies." Share your successes with each other, no matter how large or how small. Agree to remind each other of dismissed or forgotten successes as well.

With all of this celebrating of how great you are, who has time to bother thinking about what others have done?

# Act: Start Your Own Adventures

*"Do you want to know who you are? Don't ask. Act! Action will delineate and define you."*

— Thomas Jefferson

Clearly, comparisons keep you stuck and they don't help you accomplish anything. But I will go one step further. Your envy may be a safety crutch: a vehicle and excuse for staying stuck in the deceptively safe place of "woulda/coulda." Yeah, I said it. Instead of going and "doing the damn thing," you're spending your valuable brainpower watching others kick ass, then you berate yourself for not having done enough. It's time to snap out of it: there's a solution for comparison-fueled paralysis. The antidote for envy is action.

### Creative Dose: Take Action

*Purpose: To create the distraction of action*

What have you been longing to do that you've been putting off until the right time? What have you always wanted to do? When you pursue your interests, you don't have the time to be envious. Shut down Comparison Syndrome by creating the distraction of action. It's time to cultivate your own successes.

To start pursuing activities that probably would otherwise stay on your bucket list with no checkmarks by them, join (or create!) a club focused on action. Luckily, you don't have to look far, there is a new organization called Akxen that does exactly that.

### Step 1: Create the Group

Gather several people to meet every week to create support, give accountability, and create community.

### Step 2: Make a Bucket List

Get a notebook. Write a list of 150 things that you've always wanted to do or activities that sound intriguing.

For example, here's my list: take voice lessons, take an acting class, go learn to scuba dive, learn how to speak Mandarin, travel to Bali, bench press my body weight.

You will stick with an action item until it is achieved; then you can move on to the next one.

### Step 3: Share and Support

During the meetings, each person has an equal amount of time to report on her/his progress on her/his actions and goals.

Successes are celebrated by a high-five around the table that ends at the achiever.

## Step 4: Meet Regularly

The way that Akxen clubs work best is for people to feel supported and to be with a group of like-minded individuals who are interested in having experiences rather than simply thinking about them. Weekly meetings help all of the group members stay on task and also be held accountable for their intended goals.

Here are some tips to make the experience of taking action even better:

- Instead of focusing on the outcome of the goal itself, look for the resulting feeling of the outcome. For example, the point of going deep sea fishing may not be to catch anything, but the feeling of contentment you have being out on the water and the experience of feeling closer to nature.

- Focusing on the feeling rather than the goal itself also helps keep you from having your goal be a moving target. For example, it could feel like you've never achieved learning Mandarin if your criterion is speaking it fluently.

- Similarly, remember that it's not about the goal, it's about all that you experience and learn in the process of pursuing it.

- Your group members will be a constant source of inspiration and information. You also will get a healthier perspective on what people go through to achieve their goals, and go beyond the Facebook and Instagram view of people's lives.

- As a bonus, you get to connect with others who are going after their dreams, which will put you in an environment of success.

Surprisingly, Akxen clubs are a new concept, and you may not have a local group. If that's the case, start one, and let me know how it goes!

To get more information on how Akxen clubs work and how to start one yourself, check out their website: creativedo.se/akxen-club, and their Facebook group: creativedo.se/action-club-facebook-group. You can also see their Meetup.com group: creativedo.se/action-club-meetup, and create your own.

# LEVELING UP

Because my own compulsion to compare was so deeply ingrained, I know how deterimental the habit can be: it puts a kibosh on your ideas and stops you dead in your creative tracks.

Through using the tools in the chapter to eliminate triggers that can spin you into a downward comparison spiral, and then get you to a place of really appreciating the confluence that is you, you'll develop a deep understanding that you can't be compared to anyone. From this improved perspective, you'll be able to turn envy into something grander and greater that not only celebrates the accomplishments of others, but lays the foundation for your own future success.

Let us continue to move onward to quell our doubts about not being creative at all, feeling too busy and overwhelmed to even think about being creative, and our fear of not having any original ideas. That's right: our final destination on our journey is Creativity Denial.

*I'm not creative at all.*

# CHAPTER 7 | "I'M NOT CREATIVE" - *CREATIVITY DENIAL*

**This chapter examines:**

*Owning Your Creativity*

*Activating Your Imagination*

*Granting Permission*

*Stress v. Eustress*

*Regaining Time*

*Power Pose*

*Finding Inspiration*

*Generating Ideas*

*"The essence of being human is being creative."*

— **Joel Garreau,** *author*

One of the things I love about speaking at conferences is getting to know the other presenters during the speakers' dinner. I always have a great time and learn new things. There was one dinner in particular at a conference last year which was no exception, but as a bonus, I also got to see the Inner Critic in action.

Someone at the table asked about my work, and I shared that one of the methods that I use to teach is Applied Improvisation. The natural follow-up question was "is there an improv exercise that we can do at this table?"

Soon we were playing a game which I call "What is this?"[3]. Everyone puts a random object in the middle of the table, then the person who starts chooses an object. Next you describe the object in detail to your neighbor and then give it to him/her. Here's the catch: *you cannot say what the object actually is.* You must create something completely out of your imagination. For example, say I chose a tube of lip balm. I take the lip balm, turn to my neighbor, and say "This is the jeweled sacred holder of the ancient pen nib of the most amazing writer in history on the planet Betelgeuse. It has traveled through a wormhole, and has been passed down from generation to generation in my family. I want you to have it." And then that person would do the same for her/his neighbor, fabricating something entirely different.

Almost everyone was having a wonderful time devising completely different and outrageous descriptions, but I could sense my friend Joelle sitting beside me becoming increasingly anxious as it neared her turn.

---

[3] Honestly, I don't know what the game is called – improv games tend to have a lot of different names for the same thing.

When the object got to her, she lamented, "I'm totally going to mess this up. I don't know what to say. I'm really bad at this kind of thing! Seriously, I'm really just not good at this stuff."

My Inner Critic radar went off! It took me several times of giving Joelle support by telling her "just say whatever comes to mind. It's okay. You've got this. You'll be *fine*," before she relaxed enough to tentatively try her hand at fabricating a mini story for the object.

Naturally, she ended up creating something delightful, unexpected, and entertaining. Her anxiety about "not being creative in that way" had created an enormous block that she had to break down before she could come up with anything. Even though we were playing a game, she was so anxious about not being creative that she inhibited her powers of imagination.

The most fascinating part of watching Joelle deep in the throes of Creativity Denial was seeing how much of a self-perpetuating cycle it is. The more anxious Joelle got, the more she denied her ability to be creative, and the more she blocked any potential ideas that she may have had by either stopping their flow or by dismissing her ideas before she even attempted to share them.

It was a textbook case of the Inner Critic in the form of Creativity Denial, in which, despite evidence to the contrary, you are convinced that you aren't creative at all. It's a state of self-imposed creativity paralysis that eventually becomes a self-fulfilling prophecy.

## WHAT STATE ARE YOU IN?

Are you cutting yourself off from your creativity like Joelle did? Are you blocking creativity that could be flowing? Let's find out by seeing if any of the forms of Creativity Denial ring true for you.

**General Creativity Denial** is when you're in full-on denial about having any creativity at all.

Have you ever caught yourself saying these things, denying your creativity completely?

- ❏ "Oh, I'm not creative at all."

- ❏ "I'm analytical, not creative."

- ❏ "I don't have original ideas or the creative eye."

- ❏ "I don't feel as creative as I would expect in order to create."

- ❏ "My family and friends tell me I'm creative, but what do they know?"

**Overwhelm Obstruction** is when you are so caught up with and focused on the stuff you feel you "have" to do that you don't have the bandwidth to divert to creative thinking.

Are you feeling too overwhelmed to create anything and have these thoughts running through your head?

- ❏ "Creativity?! Who has time for <u>that</u>?!"

- ❏ "With these tight deadlines, I'll never come up with something."

- ❏ "Why bother being creative? I don't have enough time to create what I envision."

- ❏ "I can't find the clarity and focus I need to be creative."

You may actually think of yourself as creative, but you don't trust it. You have **Creativity Misgivings** that cause you to see your creativity as fleeting, unreliable, and capricious. You deeply fear creative drought: that your creativity will run out and that you will lose the ability to come up with any more ideas.

Do you distrust your creativity and inspiration, fearing that it won't come back when needed? Which of these thoughts have you had?

❑   "I won't find my creative outlet."

❑   "My creativity will run out eventually."

❑   "My creativity will never hit."

❑   "I'll never fully explore the limits of my creativity."

❑   "I'm completely uninspired now, and I'll be completely uninspired when I need it."

Did you see yourself in any of these descriptions? Don't worry, help is on the way. To reverse these cycles and access your ideas, I've got several tools to break through the barriers in your brain to the other side where your creative power lies.

# CONFIRM YOUR CREATIVITY

*"The desire to create is one of the deepest yearnings of the human soul."*

**— Dieter F. Uchtdorf,** *aviator, executive, and religious leader*

Although we established in the first chapter that everyone is creative, if you suffer from Creativity Denial, you're probably a skeptic on this point. Believing that being creative has to look and feel a certain way is narrow, limited thinking that is detrimental to your creative identity. Through self-censoring we create a state in which we feel intrinsically uncreative, and the process becomes so quick and so automatic that we view it as truth. This behavior starts a self-perpetuating habit cycle where the more you believe that you aren't creative, the less able you are able to come up with original ideas. By holding on to this belief, your negative confirmation bias makes it true, and you block the generation of creative ideas. For the few ideas that do make it through, your self-judgment and self-criticism causes you to dismiss and discount them.

Part of the problem with seeing yourself as creative may be that you are trying to match the image of creativity in your head with what creativity is in your experience. When the two don't match, then the obvious conclusion is that you're not creative, right? Wrong. If you're plagued with the feeling like you aren't creative at all, it's time to expand your definition of what being creative looks like and find your unique version of it.

## Acknowledge Your Abilities

Maybe you're stuck on the belief that being creative equals being an artist. But let's look at other ways people are creative. People exercise creativity physically as talented athletes who are able to do things with their bodies that often seem unreal. People practice creativity in business, forming companies from ideas to create products that we use every day and growing the economy by creating jobs. People can be creative in the areas of finance, social solutions, strategy, technology, math, science, food, the environment – the list is endless. Creativity is about bringing something new into the world that didn't exist before, and it comes in many sizes, flavors, and variations.

Wouldn't our lives lack dimension if the only place that creativity happened was through the arts?

Instead of focusing on *if* you're creative, I invite you to look at **how** you're creative. Look at the ways in which you've come up with something new and really enjoyed doing it, because this is precisely where *you* are creative. Maybe you are amazing at bringing people together through creating social events. Maybe you are gifted at reusing building materials. Maybe you are a fantastic parent. These are all areas where creativity can, and does, flourish.

## Creative Dose: "Yes, I Am"

*Purpose: To recognize where you are creative and affirm it*

Take several minutes to write down three to five situations where you have created something new and where you have been in a flow state while creating some or all of it.

Think back to how you felt in those situations.

- What did you create?

- What do the situations have in common?

- When you find the thread(s), you have found where and how you are creative.

# Use Your Imagination for Good

You may be like my friend Joelle at the conference dinner: so convinced that you have not one iota of creativity that you go into a mode of self-censoring creative paralysis, completely blocking any flow of ideas when you feel put on the spot to "perform" creatively.

However, all of us have imagination and use it at practically every moment of the day, whether we are conscious of it or not. In fact, Creativity Denial is actually your imagination and creativity running wild – but in an unhelpful, negative way! Think about it: what you are doing is envisioning all of the bad things that will happen if you don't come up with an idea, right? You're falling into anxious rumination. Your focus on the prospect of not coming up with an idea is what obstructs the flow of ideas.

Let's truncate this process by getting you back in touch with the wonders that your brain can actually produce when not forced over to the dark side.

## Creative Dose: What's in the Box?

*Purpose: To discover the endless nature of your creativity*

Take a moment to close your eyes and imagine that there is a present sitting on your desk.

Use all of your senses to experience it: notice its size and how it is wrapped; pick it up and feel how heavy it is; smell the wrapping paper, the package, and maybe even the contents.

Without opening it, imagine what is inside the box. Then, slowly open the box to see what is inside.

You're surprised to find the present is not what you initially expected at all!

What did you think it was, and what did you find instead?

Look into the box again.

Guess what? There is yet another gift that you did not notice before. What is it?

Repeat one more time. What were your presents?

Congratulations, you've just exercised imagination, the precursor to creativity!

I recommend using this exercise whenever you feel stuck for ideas, as a way to prove to yourself that your imagination is alive and well: still intact, fully functional, and ready to be put to use.

# Bestow Upon Yourself

*"Quit waiting to get picked; quit waiting for someone to give you permission; quit waiting for someone to say you are officially qualified and pick yourself."*

**— Seth Godin,** *author, entrepreneur, marketer, and speaker*

For as long as I can remember, I wanted to be creative like everyone else in my family. In the previous chapter, I shared that my father was so passionate about flying that he not only became an aeronautical engineer but also built full-size experimental airplanes in the garage as a lifetime passion project. My mother delighted in spending Saturdays combing fabric stores for interesting fabrics and chic patterns to make into exquisitely tailored outfits for the whole family. My sister showed an early talent for visual art and gourmet cooking.

I struggled with my own artwork. I didn't want to be making any old thing – I wanted what I did to be considered "good" by others. My thinking was: "What's the point of doing something creative if it isn't considered good?" I was highly protective of my artwork, only sharing it with selective people. I was skeptical of my ideas and distrusted my ability to realize them. For fear of producing something that wasn't any good, I'd go for months without making anything, and then would produce several sketches in a creative spurt.

No matter how much positive feedback and reinforcement I got from my drawing, sculptures, or creative writing, I would think, "They're just saying that to be nice," or "Thanks, but what do you know?" I waited and waited to be dubbed an "Artist" (or more accurately, "A Person Who Does Good Creative Work," since I create in multiple media) by some all-powerful, all-knowing authoritative source. But that anointing never came.

The seedlings of creative confidence that I possessed died away until I wasn't sure that I had much creativity at all. I reverted into being a "closet creative," suppressing my creative proclivities and only expressing it in fits and spurts with long lapses in between. I was so unsure of my abilities that I still believed that someone outside of myself decided my creative identity. Waiting to be deemed as creative by some panel of extraordinary judges, I dismissed the feedback that actually did affirm exactly what I wanted to hear.

Until recently, this was my own form of Creativity Denial. It wasn't until I finished writing my first book and was in the midst of designing the book website that I *finally* got it: I'm the one who decides! I realized that I could be like the character Eva Luna in Isabelle Allende's book of the same name, who decided that she was beautiful for the simple reason that she wanted to be[2] – I could decide that I was creative, because that's who and what I wanted to be. Yes, at the tender age of 42, I finally claimed my identity as a creative.

If only I knew the previous 40-odd years what I know now! In his book *The War of Art*, Steven Pressfield says, "If you find yourself asking yourself (and your friends), 'Am I really a writer? Am I really an artist?' chances are you are."[3] For years I went from person to person seeking validation of my creative and artistic skills.

*But the person who I truly needed validation from was myself.*

Once I truly recognized my creativity as existent and valid, I was finally able to step into my creative power.

There is no "them", no magical panel of judges, no moment when you will know you have "arrived." We need to let go of the story that we tell ourselves that our creativity is determined by an authority outside ourselves. We need to recognize and validate our creativity from the inside out, not from the outside in, and claim what is our birthright.

## Creative Dose: "I dub thee..."

*Purpose: To validate your creative self*

If you are still waiting to be picked before you can allow yourself to be creative, this is what you need to do: pick yourself, and give yourself permission.

### Option 1: Give Yourself Permission

If you have been waiting for permission to be creative, then you can do one of two things:

1) Take permission from me:
   "You now have my permission to be creative."

OR

2) Grant yourself permission.
   "I now give myself permission to be creative."

You have now been bestowed with the permission to be creative!

I recommend that you celebrate this new state of being with a ceremony. Print up a fancy proclamation[4] and post it in your workspace, take yourself out for your favorite kind of cupcake, or plant a flower to remind you that from this point on, your creativity will blossom.

### Option 2: Dub Yourself a Maker

If you find that thinking of yourself as creative is too difficult, then try using a term that is gaining popularity, and think of yourself as a "Maker."

Try writing it out:

I am a Maker of _____.

---

[4] You can download your Creativity Permission Slip here: creativedo.se/creativity-permission-slip

Write this out as many times as you can providing a different answer each time. What can you now see that you Make?

Seeing yourself as a person who makes things may relax any fears you have around creativity performance anxiety or having to fit certain criteria.

## OVERCOME OVERWHELM

*"Creative minds have always been known to survive any kind of bad training."*

– **Anna Freud,** *psychoanalyst*

In this age of information overload, overcommitment, comparison-driven ambition, and constant distraction, overwhelm is no longer the realm of Type-A overachievers, but instead is the current spirit of the times. So it's not surprising that you feel inundated by too many projects to do at work, tight deadlines, and a heavy workload. Of course it seems like 24 hours simply isn't enough. And naturally you feel angst at the prospect of having to come up with so-called fresh or "cutting edge" ideas at the drop of a hat.

I refer to this form of Creativity Denial as Overwhelm Obstruction. With Overwhelm Obstruction, we feel too overburdened by work and life to be creative. The problem with Overwhelm Obstruction is that because overwhelm is today's zeitgeist, people often don't recognize how much of a creative block it is, and more importantly, that we actually have the capacity to shift our habits in favor of respecting and feeding our creativity.

## Transform Imposition into Opportunity

Feelings of overwhelm stem from stress, but did you know that there are actually two kinds of stress? There is negative stress, the kind that is the result of external pressures and internal anxieties with which we are all too familiar. However, there is also positive stress, which is called "eustress." What's the difference? Interestingly, from a brain and body chemistry standpoint, very little. They both produce adrenaline and both activate the attention centers and reward mechanisms in the brain.

The difference then, is perception. With negative stress, the pressure, fear, or sense of danger is perceived as coming from an external source, triggering a fight-or-flight response. In contrast, eustress emerges from challenges that we have deliberately taken on, and makes us feel motivated, confident, and optimistic.[5]

Because the difference is a matter of perspective, that means that we have a lot more control over feeling stressed than is generally believed. Changing your stress from negative to positive can be done by making a conscious choice. By making a shift to choosing, you will become a stress alchemist, transmuting negative stress into eustress.

## Creative Dose: Word Choice

*Purpose: To shift out of an imposition mentality to an opportunity disposition*

We often talk about how "busy" or "slammed" we are, or how much work we "have" to do. However, these seemingly small figures of speech are indicative of an important perceptual orientation: that of put-upon victimhood. In *The Now Habit*, author Neil Fiore talks about "the images of powerlessness and passivity...created by negative self-talk."[6] I call this mode of thinking "Imposition Mentality." We can switch out of the mode of imposed-upon powerlessness and resistance by exercising the power of choice, making up our minds, and fully committing to doing a task.

The year before last, I joined a local mastermind group which meets regularly for the members to help each other work towards their big life goals. During the first meeting, one of the group members shared how he was training for a marathon to raise money for tuberculosis research. It turns out that he was a shining example of surviving tuberculosis himself. Just two years earlier, he was so weak and near death that he couldn't move out of his hospital bed and required brain surgery. He asked the group for ways he could motivate himself to train more regularly. I said, "So two years ago, you weren't sure if you were going to live, right? I offer this: that you don't 'have to' run to train for this marathon, but instead you '**get to**' run to train for this marathon." My words struck a chord with him, and he recommitted to running with gusto.[7]

The upshot? The easiest way to consciously and deliberately take on a task (rather than feel put upon by it) is to change your language. This exercise is adapted from the book *The Now Habit* by Neil Fiore.[8]

**Part 1: Replace**

For what it's worth, should/ought/must are common cognitive distortions, which the Inner Critic uses to twist reality to fit its means. Don't fall for it! Make a stronger choice of words.

Swap out new words for old ones to break out of Imposition Mentality. In place of "I have to", use "I choose to" or " I get to" or "I want to."

In place of "I must (x)", reframe it by saying "When can I (x)?".

More power phrases to employ: "I will" and "I decide."

These self-statements turn those who are paralyzed by the Overwhelm Obstruction into more active producers.

**Part 2: Reframe**

Take a look at where you feel like you "have to do" something. Reframe this sentiment by making a list of all of the ways that are you *privileged* to be able to do it.

For example:

Are you on deadline because you "have to" put together a presentation for your manager? Think back to how happy you were when you first got the job and how fortunate you felt to do the work.

Do you "have to" write an article for an online publication? Think about how your words will potentially help people and how the article may also boost your exposure.

Here's a framework for your reframes:

I'm privileged to _____because

_____.

I'm grateful to be able to _____because

_____.

I choose to _____ because _____.

For more suggestions on reframing, go back to the Creative Dose: Focus on the Work in Chapter 3.

With practice, you'll find that becoming grateful for the opportunity to do something changes the energy around it dramatically.

# Reclaim Time, Create Mental Space

In our age of distraction and overwhelm, it's all too easy to forget that *time is a mental construct*, and what our brains are actually keeping track of is where we put our attention. If you have simply too much going on to be creative, then you need to shift attention, especially as the management of attention is one of our main means of reclaiming our creative power. This means readjusting priorities.

What does this look like? Trying not to "do all of the things," asking for help, and (gasp) relinquishing control. Don't worry, this process can be a lot more satisfying and enjoyable than you think.

### Creative Dose: To Don't List

*Purpose: To free up time and mental energy to do more of what you love*

You can free up time by writing a To-Don't List — a list of things that you have decided you will no longer do, and therefore no longer devote attention to.

To create your first To-Don't List, you need to write down 3-4 items that you commit to stop doing within the next 30 days. Pro-tip: four is a great number to shoot for, so you have one time to focus on one for each week in the month.

Which tasks are candidates?

- If a task is so onerous and/or repugnant that you can't reframe it no matter how hard you try, that's a great place to start.

- If there is something that you feel that you have to do, but really don't enjoy, that is a candidate as well.

- If it is a task that is neutral, but takes up time you'd rather spend on something else, that's a good one too.

All of these tasks will go on your list and you will figure out how to **Delegate**, **Alt**(er), or **Delete** them.

1) **Delegate**
   Maybe the task can be *delegated*. You can find someone else to do it. For example, maybe there is someone else on your team

who is really good at proofreading. Or, you break down the numbers and find that hiring a housekeeper is more affordable than you think. Outsourcing can save a lot of headaches and time!

2) **Alt(er)**

Maybe the item can be *alt(ered)*. Do you really *have* to balance your bank account by hand like you've done for years, or can you sign up for a service like Mint.com and reconcile items online or on your phone as you make purchases?

3) **Delete**

Finally, the item could just be something the you *delete*. You just stop doing it and thinking about it completely. For example, if you're not a drinker and you'd really rather head directly home after work, then bow out of going to Happy Hour with your co-workers.

Now that you've determined which tasks go on the To-Don't list, how will you either Delegate, Alt(er), or Delete them?

Here comes the fun part: ask a friend to kick around ideas on how you can eliminate each item from your life by either delegating/outsourcing the tasks or stopping them.

Date your list, and over the next month, start putting your solutions in place.

At the end of the month, review your list and ask yourself these questions:

- Where have you decided that being in control was no longer important and delegated?

- How and where have you asked for help?

- How many tasks have you let go of completely?

- Figure out what you need to continue to stop doing, and create another list for the upcoming month.

Take your newly reclaimed time and devote it toward a creative project — particularly one that you keep pushing off because you "don't have enough time." Keep this practice up for six months to a year and see how it changes both your time and the quality of your creative life.

## Hack Your Body-Mind

*"Our bodies change our minds, our minds change our behavior, and our behavior changes our outcomes."*

**– Amy Cuddy,** *"Your Body Language Shapes Who You Are" TED talk*

In the absence of the Inner Critic, self-judgment, self-criticism and self-doubt are replaced by self-confidence, which is one of the strongest contributors to higher levels of creative expression at work and elsewhere. Self-confidence can be seen as trusting oneself and not having the need to prove oneself to others. When we already feel like we are okay, on top of things, and succeeding, we are less susceptible to the inner critical voice. One study conducted at the University of California showed that Ivy League students set up to fail a test, but pre-prepped with affirmations about feeling proud and confident, had a better sense of their self-worth afterwards.[9] People who are self-confident have less fear around generating their ideas, which allows them to generate a greater number of creative ideas.[10]

But self-confidence and the Inner Critic are not just a product of what's going on in your head. It's easy to forget that we are comprised of both the mind and the body, which are inextricably linked. Our minds are not solely contained within the confines of our craniums. Indeed, body movement can affect how we take in information, process it, and learn, and takes an active role in our thinking processes. And as we learned earlier with the power of gestures, the motion of our bodies helps to facilitate mental problem-solving.[11]

Thus, we can leverage this strong mind-body connection to have our bodies control our brains, and correspondingly, our thoughts. Using the knowledge, wisdom, and processing power of our body-mind as a whole, we can replace our habit of lacking creative self-confidence and consequently distrusting our ability to generate ideas.

In a TED talk by Harvard Business School faculty and social psychologist Amy Cuddy entitled "Your Body Language Shapes Who You Are,"[12] Cuddy shares her research on how the body and mind are connected, and how the nonverbal signals of body language accurately communicate how a person is feeling, even if they aren't conscious of it. While people lacking confidence slump, hunch over, or cross their legs and arms; confident people stand up straight with their chests out or place their hands on their hips. When feeling a sense of triumph, or "fiero" – the rush that you feel when you have succeeded over adversity, taken from the Italian word for "pride" [13] – people universally thrust both arms in air over their heads in the shape of a "V."[14]

In order to trick our minds into feeling confident, Cuddy suggests reverse-engineering confident people's body language. The key is in physically "opening up" and taking up as much space as you can. In doing this "power pose" and mimicking the stance of physical power, we can actually make ourselves feel powerful as a result.

Employ the power pose when you need an extra boost of confidence. It's a great exercise to do before meetings, presentations, and even dates (who doesn't need to feel empowered for that?!). By using this tool, you'll give yourself the opportunity to use your behavior to change the outcome for the better.

## Creative Dose: Cop a Power Pose

*Purpose: To empower yourself by physically generating a sense of capability*

If your Inner Critic is being particularly vociferous, causing you to be highly self-critical while you are in the midst of doing creative work, then you can fend off the lies with a power pose. This exercise is adapted from Amy Cuddy's TED talk.[15]

1) Stand up. Assume a pose that embodies your Inner Critic telling you that you can't do it, it will never work, that you suck, your work is crap, that you're no good, and that your ideas are lame and you can't come up with any more. Really take on the stance of being critical and judgmental.

2) When you've channeled your Inner Critic to the max, shake it off and move yourself to where your Attacked Self was on the receiving end. To reject the negative message of your Inner Critic, have your Creative Self step in and STRIKE A POWER POSE! Stand with your arms on your hips, arms in the air in triumph, or imagine flying with a cape behind you.

3) It is you as your super Creative Self throwing off all of the inaccurate messages of the Inner Critic. Channel your favorite superhero or badass: think Wonder Woman, Superman, Xena the Warrior Princess, Deadpool, Luke Cage, or Daenerys of Targaryen (and if you want to envision a protective dragon behind you to complete the vision, go right ahead). The Inner Critic will not be able to withstand the force of its negativity coming back to it, and it will beat a hasty retreat.

4) Now that you've successfully repelled the Inner Critic, imagine yourself as the superhero of your Creative Self looking off into the distance seeing your destiny of major creative butt-kicking.

5) Make an effort to hold the power pose for as long as you can
– Cuddy suggests that you need to remain in a power pose
position for 2 minutes to really feel the change. This amount of
time allows your body to communicate back to the brain that it
is safe and can therefore feel empowered, raising testosterone
levels and lowering levels of the stress hormone, cortisol.[16]

Two minutes may be more than you have, however. If two minutes
seems like an eternity, then shoot for 30 seconds.

Are you feeling a little more "fiero" now than you did before you did
your power pose? Now go forth and kick some creative butt!

# DISPEL CREATIVITY MISGIVINGS

*"Creativity isn't about talent, it's a way of operating."*

— John Cleese, *actor*

With the mystique that still surrounds creativity and creative
inspiration, it's easy to see where a kind of distrust develops. The fear
that creativity and inspiration will run out and become a thing of the
past, leaving us in the creative lurch, is perpetuated by the stereotype
of the tortured artist whose muse has abandoned them.

However, having more creativity is about actually exercising
creativity. The more you use your capacity to be creative, the stronger
it gets and the easier it is to keep using it. The fact is this: creativity is
a skill that is more like a muscle, and needs active regular training.
Getting into the habit of being creative, then, is more like the training
that athletes do. Yes, it's the irony of all ironies: creativity takes
intention, practice, and discipline.

Instead of living in constant fear that your muse will decide to take a
permanent vacation on Bora Bora and that your creativity will dry up

like the Sahara, you need to know for a fact that you can make it rain both inspiration and ideas. We'll do this by beginning to practice some of the art of disciplined creativity to cultivate strong creativity habits.

# Intend Inspiration

*"Being creative is not so much the desire to do something as the listening to that which wants to be done...."*

— **Anni Albers,** *textile artist and printmaker*

Like a favorite flamboyant aunt with a big personality, inspiration can feel like an unpredictable force of nature that sashays into your mental home unannounced, demanding all of your immediate attention and a glass of dry sherry. However, I believe that inspiration can be more like a loyal companion who, with regular attention and intention, can be encouraged to show up when wanted and needed. I'll share a story to demonstrate.

One thing that I am particularly proud of is my great parking karma. I find a parking space about 95% of the time. But I will let you in on a little secret: I'm convinced that the reason I find the spaces is because I genuinely believe that they will be there. When I get near my destination, I announce out loud, "I am finding a *great* parking space!" Because I already believe the space to exist, my job is merely to find it, and most often, I do.

It's using some of the forms of cognitive bias – specifically, a combination of selective attention and confirmation bias – for a positive and helpful outcome.

Leveraging our natural tendency towards cognitive bias, we can find creative inspiration using the same mindset and approach that I use to find a parking space to generate similar results.

# Creative Dose: Inspiration-Hunting

*Purpose: To discover that inspiration is all around you at all times*

When feeling stuck for ideas, activate your cognitive biases and know that inspiration is out there waiting for you to find it.

### Option 1: Intend Inspiration

Leave where you are and go walking for 10-20 minutes with the conviction that a source of inspiration is waiting for you, and you just have to find it.

Keep in mind that even mundane locations that you go to all of the time can hold inspiration, like the grocery store or your favorite coffeehouse.

While walking, open your fields of perception (visual, auditory, smell, touch, taste, and even emotions), and see what sparks your interest.

What did you find? Capture what was sparked in your journal:

Inspiration Spark 1: _____.

Inspiration Spark 2: _____.

Inspiration Spark 3: _____.

I'm fairly certain that confirmation bias was on your side and that by expecting to find something, you did. Use this trick whenever you feel you lack creative inspiration.

### Option 2: Tune in to Your Subconscious Radio

Another technique is this:

Tell your brain that you are open to whatever ideas it has.

Then, go take a walk and see what songs pop into your head.

Take the lyrics, meaning, or feel of the song as a message from your subconscious about what to focus on creatively.

What songs came up? What lyrics stood out for you? How can you use them to inform your creative process?

Capture what came up in your journal.

# Become an Idea Machine

If you are afraid that you'll run out of ideas, then the obvious solution is to come up with a lot of them regularly. Serial entrepreneur James Altucher calls this regular practice to keep the idea muscle of your brain from atrophying "idea therapy." Don't let your brain get flabby – exercise your "idea muscle."

 ### Creative Dose: 10 Ideas a Day

*Purpose: To train the idea muscle of your brain*

This exercise has been adapted from the recommendations in James Altucher's article "The Ultimate Guide to Becoming an Idea Machine"[17] and the exercise "The World's Worst Ideas" by Jessie Shternshus, author of *CTRL+Shift: 50 Games for 50 \*\*\*\* Days Like Today.*[18]

Keep a small notebook and write down 10 ideas a day. Don't know where to start? Here are some prompts to help you focus and generate your ideas more easily:

- Make "bug lists": things that bug you.[19] Every annoyance, every point of friction, everything that rubs you the wrong way hides an opportunity to apply creativity!

- Have your 10 ideas go along the lines of a theme, such as 10 blog posts you would write, 10 movies that would be fun to spoof, or 10 things I'd like to build by hand, or 10 businesses that would be fun to create.

- You could generate your ideas based on areas of interest, such as transportation, appliances, or devices.

- Generate your ideas by trying to make them as silly, unrealistic, crazy or absurd as possible.

- Channel the spirit of your favorite thinker and innovator and generate ideas like George Washington Carver, Buckminster Fuller, Nikola Tesla, or Marie Curie would.

- Do a mash-up: take two seemingly completely unrelated areas and generate ideas from their point of confluence. What do eco-tourism and vitamins have to do with each other? Go!

- If you need to, go for the absolute worst ideas that you can think of.

The point is to generate your 10 ideas every day and to capture them. Struggling to get past idea 6 or 7? Then push yourself to come up with 20 ideas to push past self-censoring.

Remember that your ideas do not have to be amazing, unique, or wildly creative. As a matter of fact, deliberately *don't* strive to make them perfect or good.

Will they be good ideas? Maybe. Will they be bad ideas? Possibly. Will you build a habit of using your brain and start proving to yourself that you can indeed come up with ideas? Most definitely.

About this process, Altucher says this: "Practice doesn't make perfect. But practice does make permanent."[20] And building a new habit to break the cycle of Creativity Denial and specifically Creativity Misgivings is precisely what we are shooting for.

# A CHANGE OF STATE

By recognizing and claiming our creativity, establishing our value, getting the upper hand on overwhelm, and beginning to strengthen and flex our idea muscles, we move to a much more empowered place: a state of flow-ful creativity.

Congratulations! You are well on your way to returning to your Creative Self.

*I've got this!*

# CHAPTER 8 | STEP INTO YOUR CREATIVE POWER

### This chapter examines:

*Self-fullness*

*Supporting Others*

*Being Your Brilliance*

*Finding Your Strengths*

*Sharing Your Expertise*

*Being a Connector*

*Sharing Your Brilliance With the World*

*Teaming Up For Success*

*Giving and Getting Validation*

# THE ROAD HOME

*"Home is where you go to find solace from the ever changing chaos, to find love within the confines of a heartless world, and to be reminded that no matter how far you wander, there will always be something waiting when you return."*

— **Kendal Rob,** *author*

You've been on a long journey to return to your Creative Self.

The well-meaning but untrue messages of the Inner Critic forced you to wander far and wide, putting more and more distance between you and your source of power.

You've wanted to get back to where you came from because down deep, you always have known how powerful creativity is. And maybe, just maybe, when you experienced moments of it shining through, you were a little frightened of just how much you could do with this source of power. But there's been a part of you that has always known that you were capable of more – that life in general, and your life in particular, is about far more than just "dialing it in." You have experienced the frustration and low-level stress of not exploring your capabilities. And you have felt the underutilized potential inside of you gradually start to fester and contaminate your soul.

You've made the decision to change, to return to your Creative Self so that you can tap back into your creative power. Now every shift in thought from negative to positive that you make to rebuild your brain, every new practice you do that opens your eyes to how wonderfully unique you are, every time you stand up for yourself to the mean inner voice and make it slightly less vicious, has brought you closer and closer to home.

As a matter of fact, you're close enough now that you can tune into the station of your Creative Self, and as you continue on, the signal is getting increasingly more clear and static-free. No longer out of range of the voice of your Creative Self, you're now respectfully listening and trusting it enough that you act upon its directives. Your Creative Self's message is clear: "Come on home. I'm waiting for you. And I can't wait to see you again when you get here."

Now that your Inner Critic is quieter, you can hear the voice of your Creative Self, and your creativity is starting to flow, let's look at what we can do to step into your creative power. Here are some final concepts and practices you can incorporate to help you keep on with the process and continue to expand back into your creative skin, start to thrive, and start a ripple effect of the same with others.

# BE MORE OF YOURSELF

*"Our job in this lifetime is not to shape ourselves into some ideal we imagine we ought to be, but to find out who are already and to become it."*
— **Steven Pressfield**, *The War of Art*

One regret of those at the end of their lives is of not living up to whom they believed themselves capable of becoming – of not fully actualizing themselves.[1] So many people spend their lives fighting themselves, limiting themselves by being self-judgmental. They spend their time and energy trying to change and improve themselves, because they want to be someone, anyone, other than who they are. It's no wonder that they are unhappy and unfulfilled.

You, however, have committed to a different destiny. Through the process of banishing your Inner Critic, you've recognized where and how you've been beating yourself up, and you've been able to send kindness and compassion to the battered and bruised parts of your psyche in order to start feeling like it's okay to be you again.

You've become more aware of your self-critical thoughts and are now managing them better through refocusing your attention and also thinking kinder, more supportive ones. Both your tendency to compare yourself to other people and your wish that you were better are starting to fade in the face of seeing your value, getting in touch with your deep desires, and taking action. Your reserve of emotional resilience and self-trust is deepening. And you're starting to appreciate yourself, your skills, and your talents so much more – to the point that your creativity is starting to flow.

You are becoming more of who you are, and by starting to expand and push the limits of your creativity, you will continue to bring the fullness of all that you are to the fore.

In positive psychology, the focus is on achieving maximum human potential by actualizing ourselves – becoming fully who we are. I think of this as thriving. When we silence the Inner Critic, we can begin to dive into the wellspring of power that is creativity and lose ourselves in the process of bringing new ideas into the world. When we emerge from the other side of the creative process, we come out as an enhanced version of ourselves – as more of ourselves, with much more to give to the world. In other words, we start to thrive.

## Become Self-full to Become Self-less

*"Be kinder to yourself. And then let your kindness flood the world."*
— **Pema Chodron,** *Buddhist nun and author*

When you're on an airplane, you know what to do when the oxygen masks fall from the ceiling, right? Of course you do: put the mask on yourself first, and then assist anyone else who needs it. I like to call this approach the "Oxygen Mask Theory." I also refer to this as "self-fullness."

In contrast to being self-centered, where you are completely engrossed in your own affairs at the expense of others, or selfish, where you only care for the welfare of yourself, and therefore withhold from others, "self-fullness" is caring for the welfare of oneself *in order* to also care for the welfare of others. Banishing your Inner Critic is actually an act of self-fullness, not selfishness.

The beauty of self-fullness is this: when you feed your soul and fill up your creative well, something amazing happens: self-fullness transforms into selflessness. Take, for example, Tesla Motors founder and innovation wunderkind Elon Musk. By reveling in his passion for tech, business, and physics, Musk has created forms of transportation that rely on clean energy to help combat global warming. Now *that's* self-fullness transformed to selflessness on a grand scale.

Self-fullness is not just a neat idea – it can be seen in brain activity. When we become more aware of our internal environment, such as through paying attention to the breath, we build up a part of the brain that also helps us to become better at sensing feeling. Incidentally, this is also the part of the brain that is important for empathy. Sensing the emotions of others stimulates this feeling part of the brain.[2] When we get more in touch with ourselves, we are able to be more in touch with others. It is in developing and practicing compassion for ourselves and our own struggles that we develop the resources within ourselves to be able to give more to others.

To become more of who we are, we first need to feed our own creative souls. After we've done that, then we will be able to feed others.

 ## Creative Dose: Refilling the Cup

*Purpose: To fill our creative cups so that we have more to give*

Working with a writing coach recently showed me how critically important filling up our creative cup is. To be at our creative best, we need regular sessions of creative expression and regular infusions of self care.

You may think: Wait! If I use creativity, won't that use up my reserves? Nope, not really. Creativity is like a self-charging battery: the act of tapping into it and expressing it enables you to tap into and express it even more. Maya Angelou has put it this way: "You can't use up creativity. The more you use, the more you have."[3] As for self-care, think back to the Oxygen Mask Theory. How in the world can you be useful if you don't properly care for yourself?

For me, giving myself time to make earrings in the mornings before writing was like taking creativity vitamins. The process relaxed my brain and taught me to trust that ideas would come to me, particularly when I didn't push for them. And stretching in the morning was like a long hug that I was hungry for, showing me that I was cared for and mattered.

To make sure you are stoking your creative fires so that you can use your creativity as a force for good, you must take time for creative play and valuing yourself through self care.[3] Then, and only then, will your energetic, mental and emotional coffers be full enough to share your gifts with everyone.

This exercise is adapted from the process outlined in the book *Around the Writer's Block* by Rosanne Bane.[4]

### Step 1: Brainstorm

Here are a few suggestions to get you started for creative play time:

Join a lindy-hop dance class • Start coloring in coloring books • Take a drawing class • Start tinkering with electronics • Develop your singing voice like you've always wanted • Take up guitar • Build those raised beds to start your organic vegetable garden

• Strap on your rollerblades again • Dust off that novella you've put away and design a cover for it while you're at it • Sketch out those designs you've had in your head for years (even if you can't sketch)

Just starting to express your creativity will rekindle that dimmed spark back to a brightness that will light you up.

And here are some suggestions for self-care:

Take a bubble bath • Go for a walk in the woods • Go to the beach • Take yourself to a movie • Have brunch with friends • Make yourself a fancy dinner • Get a massage • Get your nails done • Spend extra time in the gym steamroom • Have a spa day

How will you feed *your* creative soul? What creative play and self-care will you schedule and incorporate regularly into your schedule?

Don't think I'm going to let you off easy by letting you just think about it. Now it's time to put your ideas where your creativity is.

## Step 2: Make a List

Now that you've got some ideas about what you could do to for fun creative time and self-care, take a piece of paper and write a list of at least five activities that are creative and fun for *you*. As a matter of fact, you can start with five, but what you really need to do is to keep a running repository of ideas. Uplevel from the piece of paper to a small notebook that you carry with you so that whenever you think about, see, or hear of something that sounds enjoyable, you add it to your running list.

Do the same with what feels like good self care to you as well. Start with five items. But don't limit yourself to only five – as new ideas come to you, add them to your notebook.

**Step 3: Mark Your Calendar**

In order to take this endeavor seriously, making a list is not enough. When the pressure's on and stress comes up, these items are typically the first to go. But this is precisely when you need them the most! You need to commit to making these activities a regular part of your day (Trust me, it's true! You can thank me – and Rosanne – later).

For each item, note what it is and when you will do it.

Do you plan to sign up for that improv class you've been looking at for years? Great. Note what it is and what days and times you will attend.

Creative play: _____

When? _____

Planning to get a massage once a month? Fantastic! Schedule the appointment, and then mark it on your calendar.

Self-care: _____

When?_____

Do this for each creative playtime and self-care item to show yourself that you've got your own back. The payoff for making this commitment is two-fold: first, having fun and taking great care of yourself feels great. Second, in helping yourself by refilling your cup, you end up being able to start helping others.

# Use Your Creativity for Good

*"Creative work is not the selfish act or bid for attention on the part of the actor. It's a gift to the world and every being on it. Don't cheat us of your contribution. Give us what you've got."*

— **Steven Pressfield,** *The War of Art*

In addition to becoming more of who we are, through creativity we also have the power to transform the world around us. This is not just feel-good blather, but profound truth. Think about every single object in your life. Each one of those was first an idea, for which someone then put forth the effort to make it tangible, and then further made the effort to share it with the world.

Seriously, think about it – I mean *everything*: from the chair you may be sitting on, your electronic devices, and the clothes you're wearing, to the sport you play or are a fan of, the books you read – the list is practically endless. All of those items are products of someone's imagination and effort. If that isn't powerful, I don't know what is.

Moving past the fears that hold us back to exercise and express our unique creativity creates a strong base of "creative confidence." David and Tom Kelley of the international design consulting firm Ideo, who originated the term, define creative confidence as our innate ability to come up with new ideas and solutions that no one has had before and the courage to try them out. The more our small but regular creative successes build self-confidence and self-trust, the more we come into our creative own. Developing creative confidence starts a cascade effect of good. David Kelley says, "...when people regain this creative confidence...they start working on the things that are really important in their lives. They go in new directions. They come up with more interesting, more prolific ideas, so they can choose from better options. And they make better decisions."[5]

Let's use our growing creative confidence to start effecting positive change on a grand scale by applying ourselves to envision a better future that we can start bringing into being now.

### Creative Dose: Where Experience, Skill, and Need Meet

*Purpose: To determine how you can use your creative skills for the greater good*

What are you going to do with your newfound burgeoning creative power? Now that you're nurturing your Creative Self, who else can you help?

This is a great time to start envisioning where you can put your creative skills to use that will feed your soul and help others as well.

Take several minutes moments to close your eyes and meditate on these questions:

- What's something you've always wanted to work on?

- What's a problem that you want to solve?

Get any ideas? Write down whatever came to you.

If nothing comes to mind, then try this visualization:

Imagine yourself in your mind's eye. Then start expanding your view outward as though you were a camera that's pulling away.

What issues really concern you? Can you see anything that moves you to get involved in your neighborhood? How about in your town or city, state, or region? Is there a particular group that you would like to help? Whose pain do you feel that you would like to help because you've been there too?

Keep in mind that you're not trying to solve everything. You are, however, looking to see where there is a logical fit. Where does what you are naturally good at and how you creatively problem-solve fit with an issue that you could apply it to and feed your creative soul while helping others?

When you open your eyes, write down whatever insights and ideas came to you:

People often experience the most profound, self-actualizing, and life-enhancing experiences when they use their skills and talent to help others. Sometimes focusing outside of yourself, also causes you to see yourself, your talents, and their power more clearly.

# SHINE YOUR LIGHT

*"Let your light shine. Be a source of strength and courage. Share your wisdom. Radiate love."*

— **Wilferd Peterson,** *author*

Another wish of people nearing death is that they had touched more lives and had inspired more people.[6] By getting to a place of expressing your creativity, you may not only touch people with your work, but you can inspire them to have the courage to share their creative gifts with the world too. In this way, you not only contribute to making the world a better place with your own contribution, but by inspiring others to follow suit, embrace their creativity, and share their gifts with the world, which benefits humanity even more.

## Be Your Brilliance

*"You have brilliance in you, your contribution is valuable, and the art you create is precious. Only you can do, and you must."*

— **Seth Godin,** *author, entrepreneur, marketer, and speaker*

In his book *Release your Brilliance*, author Simon Bailey describes being your brilliance as "letting out the genius within you."[7] You may think to yourself, "Brilliance? Genius?! These are not words that apply to me! The stuff I'm good at is easy – anyone could do it!"

The interesting thing about being your brilliance is that it seems counter-intuitive, because it's not "hard." It's more like breathing: you really have to pay attention to notice it. For example, do you think about your eye color? No, because you can't see it. However, it is still a distinguishing characteristic about you to others. Similarly, because it is so second nature, your brilliance is probably invisible to you. However, others absolutely marvel at your ability to seemingly effortlessly execute said skill, looking at you with awe.

Like your eye color, your vocal pattern, and your genetic code, you are 100 percent completely unique. No one has the combination of experience, interests, talents, and skills that you do. They are singularly yours and they endure – your talents and aptitudes are not going anywhere. But if you don't know what that special something of yours is, it will be that much harder for you to accentuate it and share it with others.

How do you "be your brilliance"? Instead of focusing on making yourself better at skills you're weak at and don't enjoy, focus on your natural talents. By focusing on the areas in which you have natural potential, you will more quickly develop them, thereby setting you up for success and reconnecting you with your value. Being your brilliance will not only give you increased clarity and inspiration in your work; it will also provide a boost in your self-esteem.

## Creative Dose: Tune In To Your Strengths

*Purpose: To discover your strengths in order to leverage them*

Tom Rath, the author of *StrengthsFinder 2.0*, defines a strength as the combination of talent, knowledge, and skills.

**Talent** consists of natural patterns of thought, feeling, or behavior that can be productively applied. These are the abilities that come so easily to us that we don't acknowledge them as talents, abilities that we believe everyone has and that are intrinsically enjoyable – exercising your talents just feels good.

**Knowledge** is the culmination of information obtained by both learning and experience.

**Skills** are the sequential steps to help you to perfom a given activity gained through practice.

To build your strengths, you need to identify your primary talents. When you've identified these, then you can further strengthen them by increasing your knowledge in that arena, and then by building skills to help you express them.

## Option 1: Take the StrengthsTest

To quickly zero in on your top strengths, I recommend taking the StrengthsTest online, which will help you zero in on your strengths and help you begin to shift your focus to where you are naturally amazing.

There are numerous free StrengthsTests as well as the official one that you have to pay to take. Whichever you choose, make the commitment. The only thing you have to lose is continuing to do work that doesn't fit you.

## Option 2: Think Back and Remember

Think back to times in your life where doing something was enjoyable and nearly effortless . Focus on these two items:

1) **Excitement**
   You felt alive, motivated, and compelled by what you were doing. You were deeply interested in it or even fascinated by it. You couldn't wait to learn more about it and apply that knowledge immediately.

2) **Standing out**
   Your execution was unique, and people's responded to what you produced by being highly impressed or even with awe.

Make a list of the situations where you have experienced this and list what you did and how you felt. The common dominators will be your talents.

Be diligent about making sure that you no longer spend your valuable life energy on trying to get better at things that you don't enjoy or care about, and instead focus on building your strengths.

## Share Your Brilliance

*"Hide not your talents, they for use were made. What's a sundial in the shade?"*

— **Benjamin Franklin**

There are two kinds of brilliance that I encourage you to share:

1) Knowledge that you have.

2) Ideas that you are working on – those that are yet to be fully formed and that you are playing with in your head.

Despite feeling that you still have so much to learn, at this very moment, you have an enormous amount of knowledge and experience that can be enormously beneficial to your colleagues and other people. Don't be stingy with this information – share it! Sharing your knowledge helps you remember and solidify what you already know while enabling you to expand upon this knowledge and simultaneously increasing your professional value by establishing you as an authority.

Sharing ideas – especially ones that aren't fully formed – can seem a bit daunting. However, it is through this process that you will begin to connect with and leverage other people's creativity, using theirs to spark your ideas and to help your ideas to take better shape and develop into what they are supposed to be. This also means respecting your inklings: making sure that you acknowledge and respect any little sparks, nudges, or information that piques your interest by capturing them and keeping them in a place and format where you can regularly review them. Keep them in mind in conversations, and share something you find intriguing, yet perplexing. You may not hit gold every time, but at some point you are bound to connect with someone's else's related wonderings and find a synergy in your shared interests.

## Creative Dose: Share Your Expertise

*Purpose: To increase your value to yourself by sharing your talents*

In that wonderful head of yours, there is a treasure chest of information. Don't wait until you know everything about everything or have an advanced degree – or until someone asks you for it. Step up, give yourself permission, and share your cranial wealth.

### Part 1: Distinguish

Here are five ways to start establishing your expertise, not only making it clear that you're an authority, but also enabling people to raise their own level of expertise in the process of discovering your knowledge.

1) **Write or blog**

   Write articles, white papers, blog posts (as a guest or for your own blog) about your passionate expertise, interests, and what you are currently learning.

2) **Teach/Train/Present**

   If you like the interaction of teaching or being in front of people, then take your knowledge and put it in the form of a Lunch and Learn or a more formal presentation. You could also conduct a workshop or trainings. Be sure to leverage the collective wisdom of the audience and facilitate conversations so that others may share their expertise as well.

3) **Mentor**

Make yourself available to mentor someone junior to you. Give them guidance and share your hard-earned lessons.

4) **Be a Resource**

When possible, weigh in on issues for which you have knowledge and experience. Share articles, books, videos, or other resources that you find useful to those who may be interested.

5) **Lead**

Take the lead on a project. Your guidance can help others avoid problems in the long run – and will probably prove to be invaluable.

## Part 2: Cross-Pollinate

To initiate the magic of social sharing and help ideas spread like seeds, start by leveraging the power of your social ties and be a Connector. As suggested by Malcolm Gladwell in his book, *The Tipping Point*, Connectors are people with ties to disparate groups of people who regularly bring them together or pass information between people in these different groups. "Connectors," says Gladwell, "are people who link us up with the world."[8]

For those who are naturally social, here's the task: create a gathering where you bring together groups of friends, acquaintances, colleagues, clients, and others to mix and mingle.

If the thought of bringing a lot of people together at once is intimidating (if not terrifying), then take a cue from the call to action "Introverts Unite! Occasionally, in small groups, for very limited periods of time." Even if large groups are daunting, you can still be a Connector, bringing together a smaller, more comfortably sized group. Another tip is to make sure that you have a safe space, like the kitchen, where you can interact with people one on one at your own pace.

Whether your gathering is large or small, first focus on connecting people with potential commonalities, then take the time to share some of the ideas you've been working on. You'll find through this process that you will not only get your ideas out in the wild, letting them take on a life of their own, but that you will also become an idea magnet yourself. In the book *The Ten Faces of Innovation*, author Tom Kelley says, "There's magic in cross-pollination – and in the people who make it happen."[9]

Start being a Connector to become a locus of ideas and an initiator of magic.

# BE STRONGER TOGETHER

*"Coming together is a beginning. Keeping together is progress. Working together is success."*

— **Henry Ford,** *industrialist*

Banishing your Inner Critic and working your way back home to your Creative Self need not be a journey that you embark upon all by yourself. In fact, getting help is a huge part of being able to make lasting change. Instead of holing up during the process, make an effort to connect with others so that you can become stronger together.

A dear friend of mine gave me this nugget of insight about the process of writing this book, which I feel applies well to creativity in general. With a look of utter conviction, she said "It was never meant to be your sole responsibility." I felt an immediate sense of relief upon hearing that, and from that point on made an effort to reach out to people for support and accept help when offered. Similarly, while your creativity is yours, it can also be a means to build connections with others on multiple levels.

We're all in this together. We are all wrestling with learning to be better to ourselves and also to other people and the world. Invite people to join you on your journey back to your Creative Self, and endeavor to participate in theirs. Remember that most often we are not only stronger together than alone, but we can also do even more good.

# Have (At Least) Two Heads

*"Two heads are better than one."*
— **Proverb**

Through the years, I've learned something very important about myself: if I really want to make change in an area, I work best either when I commit to having someone that I am doing it with or when I have someone to check in with regularly and share my progress. If I want to start working out again, having a workout buddy with whom I have a standing date for meeting at the gym works wonders. If I want to change my behavior, having a coach and weekly check-ins is highly motivating and makes me feel supported.

The concept of rugged individualists – people who can pull themselves up by their bootstraps, are tough and can go through challenges alone – is a hurtful myth that separates us from each other. We all need people, and strong connections are even more helpful when we start on the path of personal growth and development.

In her TED talk "Listening to Shame," Brené Brown says that vulnerability is the path to finding our way back to each other. She goes on to say that empathy is key, and when someone is going through something, the two most powerful words you can say are "Me too."[10] During this process, you are bound to have moments when being able to be vulnerable and having someone say "me too" will not only make you feel worlds better, but will also fuel your growth. If making a promise to yourself by committing to other people works for you too, then let's leverage the heck out of it.

 ### Creative Dose: The Buddy System

*Purpose: To get and give support*

There was a Schoolhouse Rock teaching cartoon on television in the seventies that stated that "3 is a magic number."[11] However, two ain't so bad either. To lay the foundation for your success with this process, find a person to team up with and help to hold you accountable for your progress and commitment to growth and change. Get a coach, check in with a mentor, and/or talk to a wise and insightful friend about your process and journey. Share your insights and realizations, and get their thoughts and feedback. Or get an accountability buddy while you are both working through the book, and check in regularly. Both you and the other person will be better for it.

Alternatively, you can leverage the collective genius of a group. Start a Banish Your Inner Critic reading group that meets regularly to discuss the book together, do the Creative Doses, and then share what comes out of the process for each of you.

# Give Validation, Get Validation

*"We have a responsibility to treat ourselves kindly. Then we will treat the world in the same way."*

— **Natalie Goldberg,** *Writing Down the Bones*

Many of us have a deep need for validation, and the advent of social media has only made this more evident. We now live in an age of "like" addiction, in which the hook that gets us to return to using an app is to see how many and which people have liked our posts, Tweets, and photos. The term addiction is not used lightly. For "like" addicts, a lower than expected number of likes can lead to negative feelings toward the self, loss of self-esteem, and heightened self-criticism.[12] Whereas getting "love" on a social media platform can provide not only a sense of accomplishment, but a rush of dopamine in the brain that ensures the continuance of the validation-seeking behavior – and lays the foundation for the addiction. In fact, brain scans of people who can't stop using Facebook show patterns similar to those of drug addicts.[13]

The search for validation on social media is just a reflection of how starved we are for the strokes we need in real life. Everyone wants to be seen for who they are, valued, and respected. To truly get these needs met, searching for "likes" on social media is an empty pursuit. All of the "likes" in the world can't replace what it is we most deeply crave: true in-person human connection and appreciation.

To nurture your Creative Self, commit to a return to real social connection and to being around people who support who you are. Make an effort to find and develop your Creative Tribe. Start gathering your creative companions, compatriots, and co-conspirators. And because you've been filling yourself up by building your self-fullness and valuing your own creativity, make good use of your freed-up mental and emotional energy. Apply it to helping other people feel better about themselves by letting them know about how much you appreciate and value their creativity as well.

 ## Creative Dose: Give What You Didn't Get

*Purpose: To validate people, their work, and their creativity*

When we get the true kind of validation we crave so deeply, the security that it fosters within us helps to spur us on to greater creative heights. We need ways to bolster our sense of self from the interactions that we have with the people who mean the most to us – those within our real-life circle and whom we actually know. Furthermore, knowing that real people like and support us, and also *how* they do, is a powerful combination.

The messages that others tell us and that we tell ourselves dramatically influence how we see our place in the world. Most of us didn't get the encouragement we needed in order to feel empowered around being creative. In order to allow people to hear this needed positive validation around their creativity, try this group exercise, which I learned from participating in a workshop given by the motivational speaker and entrepreneur Lisa Nichols. It is my absolute favorite, and is one of the most powerful exercises I've ever experienced. I've done it with groups as small as seven and as large as 50, and every single time the effect this exercise has on people is profound.

Make sure there is space for people to move about the room. Split into two groups. The first group will be the Receivers. Each Receiver needs to find a spot in the room where he or she stands with eyes closed.

The second group will be the Givers. The people in this group need to think of positive and encouraging messages about creativity and being creative that they have always wanted to hear themselves, but never heard enough of.

Maybe it was, "You're brilliant," or "You have great ideas," or "I know you will be successful using your creativity," or "I believe in you."

Keeping those messages in mind, the Givers go around to all of the Receivers, whispering one of those messages in their ears. It's important that as a Giver, you don't tell them something that you think they want to hear, but rather stick to the *messages that you've always wanted to hear yourself.*

If you are a Receiver, it is important to mentally accept the message that the Givers say to you. To really take it in, it may help to mentally say a simple "Thank You" in response.

When all of the Givers have spoken to all of the Receivers, the groups will switch places and repeat the process.

How did it feel to give those messages? How did it feel to receive them?

# WELCOME HOME

*"True power comes from standing in your own truth and walking on your own path."*

— **Elizabeth Gilbert,** *author*

Like seeds, the potential for greatness lies dormant in all of us until we find the proper environment in which to plant ourselves and flourish. Banishing your Inner Critic is the first step in creating that ideal environment for yourself. With the tools that you've learned in this book, you've courageously started the process of shaking loose the mental and emotional blocks that have dammed up your creative flow. You're getting back in touch with the part of you that sees possibilities, connections, and meanings where you didn't before.

You're becoming the embodiment of the creativity that you'd like to see in the world. You have finally accepted that you are creative. Now there is nothing else to do but to create.

I hope this book has helped you get back in touch with the creative badass that you are. And I hope you continue to nurture your creative talents and skills so that you can apply them to be a force for good and to create positive change in the world.

Welcome home to your Creative Self.

# AFTERWORD

Some people say you teach what you most need to learn. If that's the case, then I am guilty as charged.

I wish I had known a lot of the straight talk, encouragement, tips, and techniques in this book when I was younger and making decisions about my future – particularly career decisions that revolved around my identity as a creative person. At that time, I didn't realize how strongly my Inner Critic affected my life. Despite how desperately I wanted to be creative, I couldn't see how much I sabotaged my own creative efforts by holding myself back, judging myself and my creativity, not truly giving myself permission to play creatively, not taking care of myself, and pushing myself to the point of burnout.

Having had this book earlier in my life probably would have done me so much good. With my current 20/20 hindsight, I could have completely sidestepped so much self-questioning and mental anguish, had I had sound guidance from an unbiased source. To make up for what I missed then, this book is a love letter from my future self talking to my current and past selves, giving each of them encouragement and cheering each on to her creative best.

Unsurprisingly, because of working with this subject, I'm now super-aware of my own Inner Critic. Through my writing progress this year, I have tuned into the subtle ways I still dismiss, discount, deny, and block my own unique expressions of creativity. Indeed, while writing this book I went through moments of being highly self-critical, feeling as though I didn't have enough experience and had to prove myself, over-researching information, driving myself relentlessly without working in self-care or taking time to play creatively, being afraid of what others would think of this book, comparing my writing to those whom I admire, like Malcolm Gladwell and Elizabeth Gilbert, and looking at friends' successful book launches with envy.

Yep, it's true: I did all of that stuff.

In addition to all that, I totally overprojected, and this book almost didn't make it. The working outline of this book was for twelve chapters up to three weeks before my writing deadline. At that point, despiting having only four or five of the chapters completed, I was still trying to achieve that goal. At the rate I was going, there was no way I would complete the book and also maintain my sanity. Fortunately, I received sage counsel and guidance in the nick of time. I hired a writing coach when I felt I was getting writers' block to help me get over the finish line.

I could share even more realizations and insights about my writing process, but I won't do so here. You can check them out on my blog at DeniseJacobs.com/blog/ and get the full story on some of my writing struggles.

## REALIZING DREAMS

A few weeks ago, I had a moment thinking about this book. My target date for completing the manuscript was rapidly approaching, and I'd been feeling anxious about the prospect of not being able to hit my deadline. I was starting to feel stressed and put upon, when suddenly several memories came to me.

I thought back to when I lived in Seattle and went to book readings by authors including Alice Walker, Octavia Butler and Bebe Moore Campbell at the Elliott Bay Bookstore. Sitting in the audience, I not only listened to the reading, but I also soaked up every possible detail of the whole scene to more clearly envision myself doing the same in the future: giving readings from my book to a crowd of appreciative readers.

I remembered also going to a reading of the book *Bud, Not Buddy* by Christopher Paul Curtis years ago, and how when I met him, I shyly mentioned that I was an aspiring writer.

This recent morning while I was washing dishes, I realized that I'm doing that very thing right now: getting up everyday to write a book makes me a de facto writer, something I've dreamed of being since my early twenties. Just like the writers I admire, I am a published author. Even though I thought it would feel and look different, I'm okay with the fact that this is simply my life.

You may recall the anecdote in Chapter 5 about my father's response to me when I said I wanted to be a writer. Sadly, my father passed away unexpectedly in 2002 at the young age of 65. I wish he could have been around to see me come into my own in the last ten years. I'm sure he would have been thrilled that I was able to prove him wrong about this whole writing and getting published thing. I like to think that wherever he is, he's proud of what I've accomplished.

## WHAT'S NEXT?

I'll let you in on a secret: I didn't get to cover all of the topics that I had planned to for this book. But that's okay – I now have the perfect excuse to write the next one! There is even more to learn about ourselves, the Inner Critic, and reaching our creative best. I still have tons of additional content to share about perfectionism, procrastination, impostor syndrome, burnout, and fear of failure and success — and how to deal with those forms of the Inner Critic. To enhance this information, I'll learn more about how to change habits and also how to truly embrace play, creative or otherwise. The Inner Critic can be heavy stuff, so as a counterbalance, I'll be researching how we can become happier through creativity. So stay tuned: the next book is going to be great!

I hope you get as much out of reading this book and putting the tools in it to use as I have had bringing the book into being. Thank you!

## Take the Work Further

In Chapter 8, I mentioned that you don't have to go through this process alone. So for the readers of this book, I've set up an exclusive Facebook group where you can connect with others who have read the book and are doing the work to banish their Inner Critics: creativedo.se/byic-community.

As a bonus, group members will have access to my upcoming projects, courses, and beta reading before anyone one else.

## Work With Me

If you'd like to go deeper into this work with guidance and accountability, I'd be delighted to be your coach, to work with you one-on-one to transform your inner critical voice into one of support and appreciation.

Also, I'd be happy to come to your company and give a reading from the book, do a keynote style presentation, and/or run a workshop on creativity and the Inner Critic, getting creatively unblocked, or creative collaboration. I also provide coaching to teams.

Contact me and let's set something up and start busting through those creative blocks!

## Connect With Me

I want to hear from you – please share with me your journey and tales of triumph of banishing your Inner Critic. I'd love to hear of your struggles and insights as well.

You can email me directly at denise@denisejacobs.com.

If you want to stay up to date with my work and get quasi-regular infusions of creative tips, inspiration, book recommendations, and news on my upcoming events, then sign up for my newsletter! With my newsletter, you'll also get announcements on projects and products in the works, such as

- *Banish Your Inner Critic* Journal and notebooks
- *Banish Your Inner Critic* Creative Dose cardset
- online creativity courses and speaking masterclass
- creative inspiration subscription service
- training programs
- A Creative Dose podcast
- events and retreats
- mastermind and coaching groups
- and upcoming books!

Sign up here: creativedo.se/email-list-subscribe

## Connect with me online

- Websites: DeniseJacobs.com | TheCreativeDose.com | InnerCriticBook.com
- Twitter: twitter.com/denisejacobs
- Facebook: facebook.com/denisejacobsdotcom
- Instagram: instagram.com/denisejacobs
- Pinterest: pinterest.com/denisejacobs

# Share the Love

If you enjoyed this book, I'd love to hear what you think! Please leave a review on Amazon.com or BarnesandNoble.com and share your impressions and thoughts.

Also, if you found it useful, please share the love. Give this book to a friend, write a blog post about *Banish Your Inner Critic* and your own experience, and share it on Twitter, Facebook, Instagram and other social media using the hashtag #byeinnercritic.

Again, thank you so much for reading this book, embarking on this journey, and being willing to go deep and do this work!

# ACKNOWLEDGMENTS

When I'm not in research mode, I read avidly for pleasure. One thing I actually love reading is an author's acknowledgements. Seeing names of all the other people who helped bring the book that I just read into being both warms my heart and shows me that the process of writing a book is never a solo endeavor. While writing this book, I was bound and determined to not to fall into my old patterns of trying to be superhuman and do it all myself. I took to heart the words my dear friend Debbie said to me, that this book was never meant to be my sole responsibility, and I put them into action. I reached out to people for assistance and guidance and took help when offered so I would have plenty of people to thank at the end.

First, I want to thank my mother, Deloria Jacobs, not only for being my proofreader extraordinaire and catching errant typos, but also for being my most enthusiastic beta reader. One of my favorite parts of writing this book was to finish a chapter, send it to Mom, and talk on the phone and discuss the content while fixing the typos. It's one of the best feelings in the world to have your mother 100 percent supportive and genuinely interested in the work that you're passionate about. I hit the mom jackpot! I want to thank my sister Diane for being such a source of creative wonder all of my life. There is nothing creative that she can't master, and she holds extraordinary creative power.

I have dubbed my writing coach, Rosanne Bane, "my creativity fairy godmother." I ordered her book, *Around the Writer's Block,* a year ago as a research source, but when the stress of meeting my untenable writing goal gave me writer's block, I turned to the book for answers. I was so impressed with the content that I reached out to her to get emergency coaching for the last several weeks of my writing schedule. Even though she reminds me that I was the one who did the work, it was Rosanne's guidance and phenomenal program to help writers move through creative blocks that produced both this book and five fabulous pairs of earrings that I made as my creative therapy. And if Rosanne was my creativity fairy godmother, then Debbie Rodriguez was personal power fairy godsister. Debbie helped me get back in touch with my creative power, gain a new appreciation of my skills and talents, and feel more confident about my writing – likening it to a warm gooey delicious cinnamon bun that you don't want to stop eating.

My editors were fantastic: Andrea Mather has been there from the beginning, prompting me to start with an outline and a sample chapter when I signed on with Mango Media. She has long had the talent of taking my verbose writing and cutting it down to more succinct and accessible prose, and she's had the patience of Job when working with my overly optimistic time estimates for getting completed chapters to her. Jean Cook, who came in at the eleventh hour during my final big push, helped to clarify my thoughts and the resulting writing. She additionally provided the service of being a cheerleader when I started getting word-weary at the end.

I can't say enough wonderful things about my web designer/developer, project manager, and the first member of the Denise Fan Club, Jim True. Jim has tirelessly worked with me since 2013, providing far more value to me than a highly functional updated website. Jim has been my business confidant, cheering squad, advisor, and friend. I literally would not be as far as I am in my business without Jim's insight, crazy smarts, problem-solving, loyalty, enthusiasm, encouragement, and belief in me. I truly feel fortunate to have met him and to work with him.

The newest member of my team, Rosalin Delgado, quickly showed me how much more I'll be able to do with a personal assistant. She was instrumental in making my final speaking trips of 2016 a hundred times easier, doing preliminary research for several chapters of this book, and generally helping to streamline my business. I'm looking forward to seeing what we do this year and how the business will continue to grow with her help.

The team at Mango Media has been great to work with. Thanks to Chris McKenney for being open to working on this project, Hugo Villabona for hanging in during my mulitiple deadline speculations. Marva Hinton for her initial editing and enthusiastic response to the first few chapters, Michelle Lewy for her marketing expertise, and Elina Diaz for the book design and Roberto Núñez for his styling genius.

My ace, Jessie Shternshus, was an enormous support; she checked in on me regularly, was always game to bounce around ideas, gave input on exercises, and shared her experience of being creative. One of the biggest gifts that Jessie has given me, however, was a piece of advice that has totally changed my world and helped me to see myself more clearly, let my creativity flow more, and devise ways to restructure and run my business. I feel so fortunate to have found such a kind and loving person to be my colleague and my friend.

Deep heartfelt thanks go to Jason Cranford Teague, who went above and beyond being one of my book buddies by offering to help me with anything that was stumping me. It's Jason you can thank for the Inner Critic Achilles Heel Questionnaire. Jason has been a fellow writer I could kvetch with, a fount of ideas and creative solutions, and a true friend.

Speaking of book buddies, I amassed a cadre of them. My very first one, Donna Lichaw, came early in my writing process – in fact, while I was still in the planning stage, before I actually wrote my first chapter. Donna had recently completed her own book, and we met regularly for a month or so to chat about progress, plans, and concepts. When I did start writing, Donna was available for quick, sometimes longer, conversations and advice. Donna got me over the hump with my deep revamp of Chapter 1, telling me to cut almost everything and move the content elsewhere, which was wise and sanity-saving advice.

Adam Constantine was always open to giving feedback and listening to my thought process and mini writing triumphs. One paragraph was added to Chapter 8 because of Adam's initial response to it, when he wrote me in chat, "WELL GO AHEAD AND GET ME HYPED AT 3:28 ON A TUESDAY. What a fantastic thought." Martin Hynie checked in, offered help and ideas, and had a Skype Indian dinner with me, which was just brilliant. When I caught up with Armando Cruz and we met for lunch, our conversation turned into a mini-coaching session in which he helped me clarify my goals for the book and proposed alternatives for generating content.

My trips overseas last summer brought me international book buddies. At a conference in Norway, I met the wonderful Kylie Hunt, who, when I asked for a book buddy on Twitter, wrote back, "Pick me! Pick me!" I loved our weekly meetings and her insightful feedback on what I had written, plus her suggestions to help it resonate with readers even more. While in Melbourne, I connected instantly with Max Adler, and we spent several conference evenings talking about life. Max's experience as a facilitator and his capacity for processing thoughts and feelings deeply was invaluable in helping the chapters hit the proper emotional tone. Patrizia Bordignon attended my workshop at UX Australia and then gifted me afterward with beautiful beads to make earrings and an offer to help me with anything I needed with the book. I was delighted to receive both, and Patrizia has thrown herself wholeheartedly into reading the chapters for typos, sharing her initial reactions with me, and brainstorming possibilities for taking my work beyond this book. Thanks to Susie Ting for her amazing brain that generates so many ideas on how to help people be more creative and her generosity.

I'd like to thank Stephanie Rieger, Janine Hartmann, Matthew Jackson, Adrian Zumbrunnen, Toni Van Eden, Lindsay Crenshaw, Sarah Cooper, Aimee Gonzalez, and Shaka Brown for sharing their stories of creativity, working through blocks, and inspiring me. I want to thank Johannes Mollø-Christensen for two great conversations both during and after a chance meeting at a restaurant in Oslo. Talking to Johannes helped me find the courage to stop hiding behind what other people say about the importance of creativity, find my own voice, and make my own stand about reclaiming our Creative Power. Thanks to Ted DesMaisons who inspired me to think of how banishing could be softened and who also found many typos. Thanks to Ariel Garten and her lovely family for having lunch during their visit to Miami, talking about the Inner Critic, giving me exercise ideas, and listening to book excerpts. Thanks to Lauren Bacon, Maria Molfino, and James Taylor for interviewing me for their courses and podcasts. Many thanks to Dynamo De Jesus for starting Action Club, giving me insight on its underlying philosophies, and inviting me to experience it for myself. Thanks also goes to Donna Hughes for doing energy work on me when I was depleted and giving me the idea for the Three+3 exercise.

My literal home team was amazing. I can't give enough thanks to my chosen sister and dear friend Amber Zimmerman for being the best housemate I could ever have. Amber respected my need for quiet, gave me space to work, picked up groceries for me during my final big push so that I didn't have to leave the house and lose writing time, and kept the garden going to boot. Amber has also been my impromptu marketing and social media advisor, giving great feedback. Amber's fiancé Kevens Celestine – a creative himself – was supportive, expressed interest in the writing itself, and showed deep respect for my creative process. Amber and Kevens also gave me the best birthday/winter holiday/congratulations on completing the book present: a brand new washer and dryer! I still get a little teary when I look at my new appliances.

Shante Haymore-Kearney, another amazing source of support, did not pooh-pooh my idea that this book is the equivalent of writing a master's thesis. I will be forever grateful to her husband Derek Kearney, who gave me the phrase, "We're going to go deep" when talking about emotional issues. Byron Tokarchuk, Andy Lambert, Elizabeth Williams, and Wanda Benvenutti checked in on me and my progress regularly and sent writing well-wishes from afar. Julia Wakefield sent writing well-wishes from near and was instrumental in helping me to leave the house on occasion for brunch.

I want to thank the organizers who invited me to their conferences to present my "Banish Your Inner Critic" keynote to audiences both in the United States and abroad. Thanks go to Hanne Josefin at MakingWeb.no in Oslo, Norway; Sara Hurley at MinneWebCon in Minneapolis, Minnesota; Rene Thomas at BCAMA Vision in Vancouver, British Columbia, Canada; Trey Mitchell at edUI in Charlottesville, Virginia; Colleen Chow at Adobe Max; Hannah Fletcher at Facebook through its Design Lecture Series; Laura Fitton at Inbound in Boston, Massachusetts; Andi Galpern at Cascade SF in San Francisco, California; Steve Fischer at Design Content in Vancouver; Val Head at Web Design Day in Pittsburgh, Pennsylvania; Julie Ng at UX Munich in Munich, Germany; Jakob Bradford at NDC Oslo; and Joel Hughes (with a special thanks for the phrase, "Well, bless their cotton socks!") at Port80 in South Wales. Special thanks to Darren Cooper for taking the chance on having me speak at TEDxRheinMain only two days before the event, which helped me to achieve the dream of speaking at a TEDx and to develop a talk that became the core of the "Banish Your Inner Critic" keynote.

Retroactive thanks go to Krista Stevens, my original editor for the article "Banishing Your Inner Critic" in the webzine *A List Apart* in 2011, Jeffrey Zeldman for giving the article the green light, and Carolyn Wood for inviting me a year earlier to submit an article idea. Deep thanks go to Alec Matias and his heartfelt email to me about how much my 2014 *Web Standards Sherpa* article "Breaking the Perfectionism-Procrastination Infinite Loop" helped him actually change his habits and perspective.

Many thanks to Stephanie Fernandez and Cristina Nostra at Books and Books for starting the process of creating a really different and wonderful book launch event for the book. I'm so excited! Thanks to Mitchell Kaplan for great conversations about the writing scene in Miami, and for having an awesome independent bookstore and giving Miami's intelligentsia a place to gather. Thanks to Rebekah Monson of Miami New Tropic for being a friend and for being willing to support the book event.

Even though she wasn't a part of this book process, I have to thank Nivi Morales for introducing me to the artwork of her brother, Americo Morales. He is the maestro behind the watercolor art that graced the cover and influenced the interior chapters. In fact, his piece "Untitled" has inspired me from the very first moment I saw it, and is the energy and spirit that I hope will permeate my work and my brand forever. I encourage you to visit AmericoMorales.net to be inspired by this remarkable artist yourself.

Deep thanks go to all of the people who have attended my keynotes, talks, and workshops through the years. I do this work because I love it, and your interest and participation inspire me to keep going, and to want to give you even more content that will help make your lives better.

And last, but not least, even though they can't read, I'd like to thank my office feline moral support staff members, Aashika and Zealand. They have been the ones who have worked (read: slept and been petted) tirelessly, spent late nights at my side, and been adoring and loyal companions.

# ABOUT THE AUTHOR

Denise R. Jacobs is a Keynote Speaker + Author + Creativity Evangelist who speaks at conferences and consults with companies worldwide. As the Founder + CEO of The Creative Dose, she promotes techniques to unlock creativity and spark innovation in people, teams, and workplaces, particularly those in the tech world. She teaches game-changing techniques for busting through creative blocks, developing clear and effective communication, cultivating collaboration, and up-leveling productive creativity.

Through speaking, writing, training, and consulting, Denise shares big concepts that challenge the status quo and lead to "ahas" that translate into immediate actions, skills, and new habits to transform all aspects of people's work lives with focused creativity and improved productivity. Her objective is real-world results where teams work better, produce more, and skyrocket their company's success. Denise has presented at events and organizations worldwide such as Google, Facebook, Automattic, GitHub, the BBC, South By Southwest Interactive, NDC Oslo, UX Week, The Society for Technical Communications, various chapters of The American Marketing Association, Creative Mornings, The Future of Storytelling, The Future of Web Design, Inbound, CREATE Fest, AdobeMax, and TEDxRheinMain.

Denise is a Web Design & Development industry veteran and is the author of *The CSS Detective Guide*, the principal book on troubleshooting CSS code. She co-authored the *Smashing Book #3: Redesign the Web* and *InterAct with Web Standards: A holistic guide to web design*, and was nominated for .Net Magazine's 2010 Best of the Web "Standards Champion" award.

Denise is also the founder of Rawk The Web, a movement focused on changing the face of the tech industry by increasing the numbers of visible diverse tech experts, and the Head Instigator of The Creativity (R)Evolution, a movement to spread the force of creativity around the world as a vehicle for positive change.

When not traveling for speaking, leading workshops, coaching or writing, Denise tends to the organic garden that is her whole backyard, designs and makes handmade earrings, dreams up and produces new handmade herbal soap flavors, and gets lost in speculative fiction and magical realism books. Denise resides in Miami, Florida.

# NOTES

## Notes: Introduction

[1] Gwendolyn Bounds, "How Handwriting Boosts the Brain," Wall Street Journal, accessed January 10, 2017, http://www.wsj.com/articles/SB10001424052748704631504575531932754922518.

## Notes: Chapter 1 – Why Banish the Inner Critic?

[1] Kotler, Steven. "Flow States and Creativity." Psychology Today. Accessed December 16, 2016. https://www.psychologytoday.com/blog/the-playing-field/201402/flow-states-and-creativity.

[2] Mihaly Csikszentmihalyi, *Flow: The Psychology of Optimal Experience* (New York: Harper & Row, 1990), 48-67.

[3] Kotler, "Flow States and Creativity."

[4] Kotler, "Flow States and Creativity."

[5] Anne McIlroy, "Neuroscientists Try to Unlock the Origins of Creativity." The Globe and Mail. Accessed December 16, 2016. http://www.theglobeandmail.com/technology/science/neuroscientists-try-to-unlock-the-origins-of-creativity/article565081/.

[6] McIlroy, "Neuroscientists Try to Unlock the Origins of Creativity."

[7] Firestone, Robert, Lisa A. Firestone, and Joyce Catlett. *Conquer Your Critical Inner Voice: A Revolutionary Program to Counter Negative Thoughts and Live Free from Imagined Limitations.* Oakland, CA: New Harbinger Publications, 2002.

[8] David Kelley and Tom Kelley, *Creative Confidence: Unleashing the Creative Potential Within Us All* (2013), 6.

[9] W. Timothy Gallwey, *The Inner Game of Work* (New York: Random House, 2000), 7.

## Notes: Chapter 2 – Take Back Your Creative Power

[1] Sharon Begley, *Train Your Mind, Change Your Brain: How a New Science Reveals Our Extraordinary Potential to Transform Ourselves* (New York: Ballantine Books, 2007), 244.

[2] Judah Pollack and Oliva Fox Cabane, "Your Brain Has A "Delete" Button--Here's How To Use It," Fast Company, accessed January 24, 2017, https://www.fastcompany.com/3059634/your-most-productive-self/your-brain-has-a-delete-

button-heres-how-to-use-it.

[3] Rick Hanson and Richard Mendius, *Buddha's Brain: The Practical Neuroscience of Happiness, Love, & Wisdom* (Oakland, CA: New Harbinger Publications, 2009).

[4] Begley, *Train Your Brain*, 157.

[5] Begley, *Train Your Brain*, 160.

[6] W. Timothy Gallwey, *The Inner Game of Work* (New York: Random House, 2000), 44.

[7] Begley, *Train Your Brain*, 237.

[8] Begley, *Train Your Brain*, 147.

[9] Begley, *Train Your Brain*, 140.

[10] Paul Gilbert and Sue Procter, "Compassionate mind training for people with high shame and self-criticism: overview and pilot study of a group therapy approach," Clinical Psychology & Psychotherapy 13, no. 6 (2006): 371, doi:10.1002/cpp.507.

[11] Begley, *Train Your Brain*, 254.

[12] Begley, *Train Your Brain*, 149.

[13] Carolyn Gregoire, "How To Wire Your Brain For Happiness," The Huffington Post, accessed January 21, 2017, http://www.huffingtonpost.com/2013/10/17/how-tiny-joyful-moments-c_n_4108363.html.

[14] Begley, *Train Your Brain*, 150.

[15] Hanson and Mendius, *Buddha's Brain*.

[16] Hanson and Mendius, *Buddha's Brain*.

[17] Begley, *Train Your Brain*, 141.

[18] Begley, *Train Your Brain*, 148.

[19] Kristin Neff, *Self-Compassion: Stop Beating Yourself Up and Leave Insecurity Behind* (New York: William Morrow, 2011), 101.

[20] Begley, *Train Your Brain*, 139.

[21] Begley, *Train Your Brain*, 148.

[22] Begley, *Train Your Brain*, 229.

[23] Begley, *Train Your Brain*, 146.

[24] Begley, *Train Your Brain*, 9.

[25] Gilbert and Procter, "Compassionate mind training for people with high shame and self-criticism," 357.

[26] Andrew Plotkin, "Jane McGonigal Talk: "Reality is Broken"," The Gameshelf | Independent Game Criticism and Other Interesting Stuff, accessed January 4, 2017, http://gameshelf.jmac.org/2011/02/jane-mcgonigal-talk-reality-is/.

[27] Collen M. Story, "7 Ways to Overcome Destructive Self-Criticism," Writing and Wellness, accessed January 4, 2017, http://www.writingandwellness. com/2016/03/21/7-ways-to-overcome-destructive-self-criticism/.

[28] Sandra Bienkowski, "5 Ways Self-Compassion Can Turn Your Life Around," The Huffington Post, accessed January 4, 2017, http://www.huffington-post.com/sandra-bienkowski/5-ways-self-compassion-can-turn-your-life-around_b_9040752.html.

[29] Neff, *Self-Compassion*, 47.

[30] Michelle McQuaid, "3 Ways to Turn Self-Criticism Into Self-Compassion," Psychology Today, accessed January 4, 2017, https://www.psychologytoday.com/ blog/functioning-flourishing/201604/3-ways-turn-self-criticism-self-compassion.

[31] Story, "7 Ways to Overcome Destructive Self-Criticism."

[32] Story, "7 Ways to Overcome Destructive Self-Criticism."

[33] Robin Nixon, "Self-Compassion: The Most Important Life Skill?," Live Science, accessed January 4, 2017, http://www.livescience.com/14165-parenting-compas-sion-life-skills.html.

[34] Gilbert and Procter, "Compassionate mind training for people with high shame and self-criticism," 358.

[35] Kristin Neff, PhD, "What Self-Compassion is Not: Self-esteem, Self-pity, Indul-gence," SelfCompassion.org, accessed January 23, 2017, http://self-compassion. org/what-self-compassion-is-not-2/.

[36] Gilbert and Procter, "Compassionate mind training for people with high shame and self-criticism," 357.

[37] Gilbert and Procter, "Compassionate mind training for people with high shame and self-criticism," 364.

[38] Paul Gilbert and Deborah A. Lee, "The perfect nurturer: A model to develop a compassionate mind within the context of cognitive therapy," in Compassion: Conceptualisations, Research and Use in Psychotherapy (London: Routledge, 2005), 326-351.

[39] Melinda Smith, M.A et al., "How to Stop Worrying: Self-Help Tips for Re-lieving Anxiety, Worry, and Fear," HelpGuide.org, accessed January 24, 2017,

https://www.helpguide.org/articles/anxiety/how-to-stop-worrying.htm.

## Notes: Chapter 3 – Judgment Dread

[1] Timothy A. Pychyl Ph.D., "Procrastination and Flow Experiences: A Tale of Opposites," Psychology Today, accessed January 14, 2017, https://www.psychologytoday.com/blog/dont-delay/200805/procrastination-and-flow-experiences-tale-opposites.

[2] "Our Approach — The Compassionate Mind Foundation USA," The Compassionate Mind Foundation USA, accessed January 13, 2017, http://www.compassionfocusedtherapy.com/new-page/.

[3] Carolyn Gregoire, "How To Wire Your Brain For Happiness," The Huffington Post, accessed January 21, 2017, http://www.huffingtonpost.com/2013/10/17/how-tiny-joyful-moments-c_n_4108363.html.

[4] Roy F. Baumeister et al., "Bad is stronger than good," Review of General Psychology 5, no. 4 (2001): doi:10.1037//1089-2680.5.4.323.

[5] Rick Hanson, "Confronting the Negativity Bias - Dr. Rick Hanson," Dr. Rick Hanson: The Neuroscience of Lasting Happiness, accessed January 13, 2017, http://www.rickhanson.net/how-your-brain-makes-you-easily-intimidated/.

[6] "When a Stranger Calls (1979 Film) - Wikipedia," Wikipedia, the Free Encyclopedia, accessed January 18, 2017, https://en.wikipedia.org/wiki/When_a_Stranger_Calls_(1979_film).

[7] "After Earth," Wikipedia, the Free Encyclopedia, accessed February 8, 2017, https://en.wikipedia.org/wiki/After_Earth.

[8] Alison Poulsen, PhD, "Criticism and Contempt," So what I really meant..., accessed January 14, 2017, http://www.sowhatireallymeant.com/articles/conflict/criticism-and-contempt/.

[9] Malcolm Gladwell, *Blink: The Power of Thinking Without Thinking* (New York: Little, Brown and Co, 2005).

[10] Paul Gilbert and Sue Procter, "Compassionate mind training for people with high shame and self-criticism: overview and pilot study of a group therapy approach,"Clinical Psychology & Psychotherapy 13, no. 6 (2006): 363, doi:10.1002/cpp.507.

[11] Gilbert and Procter, "Compassionate mind training for people with high shame and self-criticism," 358.

[12] Julia Galef, "Surprise Journal: Notice the Unexpected to Fight Confirmation Bias for Science and Self-improvement," Slate Magazine, accessed January 14, 2017, http://www.slate.com/articles/health_and_science/science/2015/01/surprise_journal_notice_the_unexpected_to_fight_confirmation_bias_for_science.html.

13  W. Timothy Gallwey, The Inner Game of Work (New York: Random House, 2000), 117.

14  Lida Citroen, "3 Reasons to Create a Kudos File," Unleashing Your Brand, accessed January 14, 2017, http://www.unleashingyourbrand.com/3-reasons-to-create-a-kudos-file/.

15  Michael Gavin, "Do you have a kudos file? Do you contribute to someone else's?," LinkedIn, accessed January 14, 2017, https://www.linkedin.com/pulse/do-you-have-kudos-file-contribute-someone-elses-michael-galvin.

16 Kristen Tobias, M.A., "Awfulizing time," The Albert Ellis Institute, n.d.albertellis.org/awfulizing-time.

17  Marelisa Fabrega, "Ten Strategies for Overcoming the Negativity Bias and Increasing Your Quality of Life," Daring to Live Fully, accessed January 13, 2017, https://daringtolivefully.com/overcoming-negativity-bias.

18  Meryl Streep, "A Conversation with Meryl Streep" (lecture, Chancellor's Speaker Series, University of Massachusetts Lowell, Lowell, Massachusetts, April 1, 2014).

19  Eric Maisel, *Mastering Creative Anxiety: Twenty-Four Lessons for Writers, Painters, Musicians, and Actors from America's Foremost Creativity Coach* (Novato, Calif: New World Library, 2011), 37.

20 Phil Hansen, "Phil Hansen: Embrace the Shake," TED: Ideas Worth Spreading, n.d.https://www.ted.com/talks/phil_hansen_embrace_the_shake?language=en.

21  Jessica Stillman, "5 Ways to Get the Most Out of Criticism," Inc.com, accessed January 21, 2017, http://www.inc.com/jessica-stillman/5-ways-to-get-the-most-criticism.html.

22  Lori Deschene, "How to Deal with Criticism Well: 25 Reasons to Embrace It," Tiny Buddha, accessed January 21, 2017, http://tinybuddha.com/blog/how-to-deal-with-criticism-well-25-reasons-to-embrace-it/.

23  Hugh MacLeod, *Ignore Everybody: And 39 Other Keys to Creativity* (New York: Portfolio, 2009).

24 Margaret Paul, PhD, "Do You Compare Yourself to Others?," The Huffington Post, accessed January 14, 2017, http://www.huffingtonpost.com/margaret-paul-phd/self-worth_b_2855751.html.

25 James Clear, "Haters and Critics: How to Deal with People Judging You and Your Work," James Clear, accessed January 14, 2017, http://jamesclear.com/haters.

## Notes: Chapter 4 – High Self-Criticism

[1] Holly VanScoy, Ph.D, "The Many Faces of Shame," Psych Central, accessed February 6, 2017, https://psychcentral.com/lib/the-many-faces-of-shame/.

[2] Theodore A. Powers, Richard Koestner, and David C. Zuroff, "Self–Criticism, Goal Motivation, and Goal Progress," Journal of Social and Clinical Psychology 26, no. 7 (2007): 827, doi:10.1521/jscp.2007.26.7.826.

[3] Elizabeth Bernstein, "'Self Talk': When Talking to Yourself, the Way You Do It Makes a Difference," Wall Street Journal, accessed February 1, 2017, https://www.wsj.com/articles/SB10001424052702304831304579543772121720600.

[4] Pamela Weintraub, "The Voice of Reason," Psychology Today, accessed January 28, 2017, https://www.psychologytoday.com/articles/201505/the-voice-reason.

[5] Weintraub, "The Voice of Reason."

[6] Adam Phillips. "Against Self-Criticism." London Review of Books 37 no. 5 (2015): 13-16, http://www.lrb.co.uk/v37/n05/adam-phillips/against-self-criticism.

[7] Rick Hanson, "Confronting the Negativity Bias," Dr. Rick Hanson: The Neuroscience of Lasting Happiness, accessed January 13, 2017, http://www.rickhanson.net/how-your-brain-makes-you-easily-intimidated/.

[8] Matthew May, "Ideacide: The Perils of Self-Censoring (And How You Can Stop It)," 99U by Behance, accessed January 28, 2017, http://99u.com/articles/53751/ideacide-the-perils-of-self-censoring-and-how-you-can-stop-it.

[9] Michael Bergeisen, "The Neuroscience of Happiness," Greater Good, accessed January 16, 2017, http://greatergood.berkeley.edu/article/item/the_neuroscience_of_happiness.

[10] Collen M. Story, "7 Ways to Overcome Destructive Self-Criticism," Writing and Wellness, accessed January 4, 2017, http://www.writingandwellness.com/2016/03/21/7-ways-to-overcome-destructive-self-criticism/.

[11] Kimberly Nichols, "Tools of Transformation #18: The Master Emotions: Shame, Guilt and Fear," Newtopia Magazine, accessed February 3, 2017, https://newtopiamagazine.wordpress.com/2013/05/15/tools-of-transformation-18-the-master-emotions-shame-guilt-and-fear/.

[12] Beverly Engel, L.M.F.T., "How Compassion Can Heal Shame from Childhood," Psychology Today, accessed February 3, 2017, https://www.psychologytoday.com/blog/the-compassion-chronicles/201307/how-compassion-can-heal-shame-childhood.

[13] Hanson, "Confronting the Negativity Bias."

[14] Paul Gilbert and Sue Procter, "Compassionate mind training for people with high shame and self-criticism: overview and pilot study of a group therapy approach, "Clinical Psychology & Psychotherapy 13, no. 6 (2006): 358, doi:10.1002/cpp.507.

[15] Melinda Beck, "Silencing the Voice That Says You're a Fraud," Wall Street Journal, accessed January 4, 2017, http://www.wsj.com/articles/SB124511712673817527.

[16] Susie Steiner, "Top Five Regrets of the Dying," The Guardian, accessed January 15, 2017, https://www.theguardian.com/lifeandstyle/2012/feb/01/top-five-regrets-of-the-dying.

[17] Hanson, "Confronting the Negativity Bias."

[18] Robin Nixon, "The Neuroscience of Self-Esteem, Self-Criticism and Self-Compassion," Live Science, accessed January 30, 2017, http://www.livescience.com/14151-neuroscience-esteem-criticism-compassion.html.

[19] Engel, "How Compassion Can Heal Shame from Childhood."

[20] Engel, "How Compassion Can Heal Shame from Childhood."

[21] Gilbert and Procter, "Compassionate mind training for people with high shame and self-criticism," 358.

[22] Gilbert and Procter, "Compassionate mind training for people with high shame and self-criticism," 361.

[23] Phillips, "Against Self-Criticism."

[24] Nixon, "The Neuroscience of Self-Esteem, Self-Criticism and Self-Compassion."

[25] Gilbert and Procter, "Compassionate mind training for people with high shame and self-criticism," 361.

[26] Homaira Kabir, "Letting Go Of Shame And Self Criticism," The Huffington Post, accessed January 30, 2017, http://www.huffingtonpost.com/homaira-kabir/letting-go-of-shame-and-s_1_b_10525506.html.

[27] Kristin Neff, *Self-Compassion: Stop Beating Yourself Up and Leave Insecurity Behind* (New York: William Morrow, 2011), 63.

[28] Olivia Longe et al., "Having a word with yourself: Neural correlates of self-criticism and self-reassurance," NeuroImage 49, no. 2 (2010): 1849, doi:10.1016/j.neuroimage.2009.09.019.

[29] Gilbert and Procter, "Compassionate mind training for people with high shame and self-criticism," 368.

[30] Neff, *Self-Compassion*, 53-54.

[31] Laurence Hirshberg, "Do Your Thoughts Have You?" The NeuroDevelopment Center, accessed February 7, 2017, https://www.neurodevelopmentcenter.com/do-your-thoughts-have-you/.

[32] Bergeisen, "The Neuroscience of Happiness.".

[33] Scott B. Kaufman, "The Real Neuroscience of Creativity," Scientific American Blog Network, accessed January 12, 2017, https://blogs.scientificamerican.com/beautiful-minds/the-real-neuroscience-of-creativity/.

[34] Magdalena A. Ferdek, Clementina M. Van Rijn, and Miroslaw Wyczesany, "Depressive rumination and the emotional control circuit: An EEG localization and effective connectivity study," Cognitive, Affective, & Behavioral Neuroscience 16, no. 6 (2016): doi:10.3758/s13415-016-0456-x.

[35] Engel, "How Compassion Can Heal Shame from Childhood."

[36] Christopher Bergland, "Squeeze a Ball With Your Left Hand to Increase Creativity," Psychology Today, accessed January 31, 2017, https://www.psychology-today.com/blog/the-athletes-way/201304/squeeze-ball-your-left-hand-increase-creativity.

[37] Marelisa Fabrega, "Ten Strategies for Overcoming the Negativity Bias and Increasing Your Quality of Life," Daring to Live Fully, accessed January 13, 2017, https://daringtolivefully.com/overcoming-negativity-bias.

[38] Eric Barker, "The 8 Things The Happiest People Do Every Day," Barking Up The Wrong Tree, accessed January 29, 2017, http://www.bakadesuyo.com/2014/06/happiest-people/.

[39] Weintraub, "The Voice of Reason."

[40] Weintraub, "The Voice of Reason."

[41] Weintraub, "The Voice of Reason."

[42] Weintraub, "The Voice of Reason."

[43] May, "Ideacide."

[44] W. Timothy Gallwey, *The Inner Game of Work* (New York: Random House, 2000), 117.

[45] Lisa Firestone, PhD, "The Critical Inner Voice that Causes Depression," Psychology Today, accessed January 30, 2017, https://www.psychologytoday.com/blog/compassion-matters/201009/the-critical-inner-voice-causes-depression.

[46] Weintraub, "The Voice of Reason."

[47] Weintraub, "The Voice of Reason."

[48] Kim Ranegar, "Using Your 'other' Hand Benefits Your Brain," NWITimes.com, accessed January 29, 2017, http://www.nwitimes.com/niche/shore/health/using-your-other-hand-benefits-your-brain/article_6da931ea-b64f-5cc2-9583-e78f179c2425.html.

[49] Kali Munro, "The Inner Critic: Accepting Ourselves," KaliMunro.com |

Toronto Therapy & Online Counseling, accessed January 28, 2017,

[50] Carrie Barron and Alton Barron, *The Creativity Cure* (New York: Scribner, 2012), 44.

[51] Jeffrey Davis, M.A., "Science of Creativity Moves Into the Body," Psychology Today, accessed January 12, 2017, https://www.psychologytoday.com/blog/tracking-wonder/201211/science-creativity-moves-the-body.

[52] Susan Goldin-Meadow, Hearing Gesture: How Our Hands Help Us Think (Cambridge, Mass: Belknap Press of Harvard University Press, 2003).

[53] Bridget Murray Law, "Gestures give learning a hand," American Psychological Association, last modified November 2005, http://www.apa.org/monitor/nov05/gestures.aspx.

[54] Goldin-Meadow, "TEDxUChicago 2011 - Susan Goldin-Meadow - What Our Hands Can Tell Us About Our Minds.".

[55] Scott D. Williams, "Self-esteem and the self-censorship of creative ideas," Personnel Review 31, no. 4 (2002): 496, doi:10.1108/00483480210430391.

[56] May, "Ideacide."

[57] May, "Ideacide."

[58] Lynn Newman, "5 Immediate and Easy Ways to Silence Your Inner Critic," Tiny Buddha, accessed January 28, 2017, http://tinybuddha.com/blog/5-immediate-and-easy-ways-to-silence-your-inner-critic/.

[59] Katy Bourne, "Our Creative Lives: My Letter to the Critic," Katy Bourne | I Sing Jazz. I Write Stuff, accessed January 29, 2017, http://katy-bourne.com/our-creative-lives-my-letter-to-the-critic/.

[60] Newman, "5 Immediate and Easy Ways to Silence Your Inner Critic."

[61] Phillips, "Against Self-Criticism."

[62] Jason Bardi, "How Selective Hearing Works in the Brain: 'Cocktail Party Effect' Explained," ScienceDaily, accessed January 29, 2017, https://www.sciencedaily.com/releases/2012/04/120418135045.htm.

[63] Jeremy Dean, "The Cocktail Party Effect," PsyBlog, accessed January 29, 2017, http://www.spring.org.uk/2009/03/the-cocktail-party-effect.php.

[64] Stephanie M. Foote, "Tame Your Inner Critic," Inside Higher Ed | Higher Education News, Career Advice, Jobs, accessed January 29, 2017, https://www.insidehighered.com/advice/summer/summer7.

[65] Mark McGuinness, "Why Your Inner Critic Is Your Best Friend," 99U by Behance, accessed January 29, 2017, http://99u.com/articles/6971/why-your-inner-

critic-is-your-best-friend.

## Notes: Chapter 5 – Deficiency Anxieties

[1] Patrik Edblad, "How to Deal With Negative Emotions: Cognitive Reappraisal," Selfication, accessed January 12, 2017, http://www.selfication.com/how-to-deal-with-negative-emotions/.

[2] "Improve Your Perspective Using Cognitive Reappraisal," Cognitive Behavioral Therapy Los Angeles, accessed February 8, 2017, http://cogbtherapy.com/cbt-blog/2014/5/4/hhy104os08dekc537dlw7nvopzyi44.

[3] Michael Sun, "Psychological Skills: Changing Your Emotions – An Intro to Cognitive Reappraisal," Psychology In Action, accessed February 8, 2017, http://www.psychologyinaction.org/2014/02/17/psychological-skills-changing-your-emotions-an-intro-to-cognitive-reappraisal/.

[4] Amy Morin, "Taming Your Inner Critic: 7 Steps To Silencing The Negativity," Forbes, accessed February 8, 2017, http://www.forbes.com/sites/amymorin/2014/11/06/taming-your-inner-critic-7-steps-to-silencing-the-negativity/#545378656316.

[5] Emily Nickerson, "How to Silence the Voice of Doubt," The Muse, accessed February 8, 2017, https://www.themuse.com/advice/how-to-silence-the-voice-of-doubt.

[6] Marcia Reynolds Psy.D., "How To Feel Good Enough," Psychology Today, accessed February 8, 2017, https://www.psychologytoday.com/blog/wander-woman/201312/how-feel-good-enough.

[7] Margarita Tartakovsky, M.S., "3 Ways to Develop Self-Trust," PsychCentral.com | World of Psychology Blog, accessed February 8, 2017, https://psychcentral.com/blog/archives/2013/10/17/3-ways-to-develop-self-trust/.

[8] Paul Gilbert and Sue Procter, "Compassionate mind training for people with high shame and self-criticism: overview and pilot study of a group therapy approach," Clinical Psychology & Psychotherapy 13, no. 6 (2006): 365, doi:10.1002/cpp.507.

[9] David Russell Schilling, "Knowledge Doubling Every 12 Months, Soon to Be Every 12 Hours," Industry Tap, accessed February 8, 2017, http://www.industrytap.com/knowledge-doubling-every-12-months-soon-to-be-every-12-hours/3950.

[10] JA Mangels et al., "Why Do Beliefs About Intelligence Influence Learning Success? A Social Cognitive Neuroscience Model. - PubMed - NCBI," National Center for Biotechnology Information, accessed January 12, 2017, http://www.ncbi.nlm.nih.gov/pubmed/17392928.

[11] Gwen Knowles, "Why Feeling Incompetent Is All Part Of The Career Change Process – And What To Do About It," Careershifters, accessed February 8, 2017,

http://www.careershifters.org/expert-advice/why-feeling-incompetent-is-all-part-of-the-career-change-process-and-what-to-do.

[12] Knowles, "Why Feeling Incompetent Is All Part Of The Career Change Process – And What To Do About It."

[13] Nir Eyal, "Three Steps To Get Up To Speed On Any Subject Quickly," Nir and Far, accessed January 12, 2017, http://www.nirandfar.com/2016/07/three-steps-get-speed-subject-quickly.html.

[14] Josh Kaufman, "5 Secrets to Learning New Skills More Quickly Than You Ever Thought Possible," Business Insider, accessed February 8, 2017, http://www.businessinsider.com/5-secrets-to-learning-new-skills-more-quickly-than-you-ever-thought-possible-2013-7.

[15] Corbett Barr, "Deliberate Practice: What It Is and Why You Need It," Expert Enough, accessed February 8, 2017, http://expertenough.com/1423/deliberate-practice.

[16] James Clear, "What Do Experts Do For 10,000 Hours? How Experts Practice Better Than the Rest," James Clear, accessed February 8, 2017, http://james-clear.com/deliberate-practice-strategy.

[17] Drake Baer, "Why "Deliberate Practice" Is The Only Way To Keep Getting Better," Fast Company, accessed February 8, 2017, https://www.fastcompany.com/3020758/leadership-now/why-deliberate-practice-is-the-only-way-to-keep-getting-better.

[18] Brenda Ueland and Cynthia Miller, *Tell Me More: On the Fine Art of Listening* (Tucson, Ariz: Kore Press, 1998).

[19] Bruce Nussbaum, *Creative Intelligence: Harnessing the Power to Create, Connect, and Inspire* (New York: Harper Business, 2013).

[20] Steven Johnson, *Where Good Ideas Come from: The Natural History of Innovation* (New York: Riverhead Books, 2010), 10.

[21] Daniel Gogek, "How Pixar Transformed Their Criticizers into Creators: The Magic of "Plussing"," Think Like An Innovator, accessed February 8, 2017, http://www.thinklikeaninnovator.com/how-pixar-transformed-the-criticizers-into-creators-the-magic-of-plussing/.

[22] Kirby Ferguson, "Everything Is a Remix," Everything Is a Remix, accessed January 12, 2017, http://everythingisaremix.info/.

## Notes: Chapter 6 – Comparison Syndrome

[1] Shane Parrish, "Mental Model: Bias from Envy and Jealousy," Farnam Street, accessed February 9, 2017, https://www.farnamstreetblog.com/2016/08/mental-model-bias-envy-jealousy/.

[2] Parrish, "Mental Model: Bias from Envy and Jealousy."

[3] Henrik Edberg, "How to Overcome Envy: 5 Effective Tips," Practical Happiness Advice That Works | The Positivity Blog, accessed February 9, 2017, http://www.positivityblog.com/index.php/2010/07/13/how-to-overcome-envy/.

[4] Jeremy Golden, "6 Apps to Stop Your Smartphone Addiction," Inc.com, accessed February 10, 2017, http://www.inc.com/jeremy-goldman/6-apps-to-stop-your-smartphone-addiction.html.

[5] Emily Nickerson, "How to Silence the Voice of Doubt," The Muse, accessed February 8, 2017, https://www.themuse.com/advice/how-to-silence-the-voice-of-doubt.

[6] Sonya Derian, "Stop Comparing: An Alternative to Competing with People," Tiny Buddha, accessed February 9, 2017, http://tinybuddha.com/blog/stop-comparing-yourself-to-others/.

[7] Henrik Edberg, "How to Stop Comparing Yourself to Others (and Start Empowering Yourself)," Practical Happiness Advice That Works | The Positivity Blog, accessed February 9, 2017, http://www.positivityblog.com/index.php/2014/09/03/comparison-trap/.

[8] Sonya Derian, "Stop Comparing: An Alternative to Competing with People," Tiny Buddha, accessed February 9, 2017, http://tinybuddha.com/blog/stop-comparing-yourself-to-others/.

[9] Nilofer Merchant, "Onlyness (The Topic and the Talk at TEDxHouston)," Nilofer Merchant, accessed February 9, 2017, http://nilofermerchant.com/2013/01/17/onlyness-the-topic-and-the-talk-at-tedxhouston/.

[10] Nilofer Merchant, "What Color Is My Weird? (How to Find Your Onlyness, Part I)," Nilofer Merchant, accessed January 12, 2017, http://nilofermerchant.com/2015/01/20/what-color-is-my-weird-how-to-find-your-onlyness-part-i/.

[11] Theodore A. Powers, Richard Koestner, and David C. Zuroff, "Self–Criticism, Goal Motivation, and Goal Progress," Journal of Social and Clinical Psychology 26, no. 7 (2007): xx, doi:10.1521/jscp.2007.26.7.826.

[12] Mike Robbins, "Are You Threatened by Other People's Success?," The Huffington Post, accessed February 9, 2017, http://www.huffingtonpost.com/mike-robbins/overcoming-insecurity_b_3295802.html.

[13] Alexander H. Jordan et al., "Misery Has More Company Than People Think: Underestimating the Prevalence of Others' Negative Emotions," Personality and Social Psychology Bulletin 37, no. 1 (2011): xx, doi:10.1177/0146167210390822.

[14] Daniela Tempesta, "Why You Should Stop Comparing Yourself to Others," The Huffington Post, accessed February 9, 2017, http://www.huffingtonpost.com/daniela-tempesta-lcsw/comparing-yourself_b_4441288.html.

[15] Kristin Neff, *Self-Compassion: Stop Beating Yourself Up and Leave Insecurity Behind* (London: Hodder & Stoughton, 2011), 62.

[16] Parrish, "Mental Model: Bias from Envy and Jealousy."

[17] Susie Moore, "How to Overcome Social Comparison," The Huffington Post, accessed February 9, 2017, http://www.huffingtonpost.com/susie-moore/comparison_b_4646013.html.

[18] Cal Newport, "The Steve Martin Method: A Master Comedian's Advice for Becoming Famous - Study Hacks," Cal Newport - Study Hacks Blog, accessed February 9, 2017, http://calnewport.com/blog/2008/02/01/the-steve-martin-method-a-master-comedians-advice-for-becoming-famous/.

[19] Denise Jacobs, "Acknowledge Accomplishment," The Pastry Box Project, accessed February 9, 2017, https://the-pastry-box-project.net/denise-jacobs/2012-july-21.

[20] "Know Your Brain: Reward System — Neuroscientifically Challenged," Neuroscientifically Challenged, accessed February 10, 2017, http://www.neuroscientificallychallenged.com/blog/know-your-brain-reward-system.

[21] Patrik Edblad, "The Power of Small Wins: Why Celebrating Your Progress is Crucial for Long-Term Success," Selfication, accessed February 10, 2017, http://www.selfication.com/motivation/the-power-of-small-wins/.

[22] Emma-Louise Elsey, "Take Time to Review and Celebrate Your Success: You'll Be Glad You Did!," Life Coach On The Go, accessed February 10, 2017, https://lifecoachonthego.com/review-and-celebrate-success-youll-be-glad-you-did/.

[23] "Reward Effort, Not Just Achievement - Engaging Minds Online," Boston Learning Center & Tutoring Services, Executive Function Coaching - Engaging Minds - Engaging Minds Online, accessed February 10, 2017, http://engagingmindsonline.com/blog/26-blog/249-reward-effort-not-just-achievement.

[24] "Celebrating is Key to Success," Lead Fearlessly, accessed February 10, 2017, http://leadfearlessly.com/celebrate-success/.

## Notes: Chapter 7 – Creativity Denial

[1] Isabel Allende, *Eva Luna* (New York, New York: Bantam Books, 1989), 187.

[2] Steven Pressfield, *The War of Art: Break Through the Blocks and Win Your Inner Creative Battles* (New York: Black Irish Entertainment, 2012), 39.

[3] Jane McGonigal, Reality Is Broken: Why Games Make Us Better and How They Can Change the World (New York: Penguin Press, 2011), 32.

[4] Neil A Fiore, *The Now Habit: A Strategic Program for Overcoming Procrastina-*

*tion and Enjoying Guilt-Free Play* (New York: Tarcher/Penguin, 2007), 68.

[5] Shaka Brown, "Why I Run," ShakaBrown.com, accessed February 10, 2017, http://www.shakabrown.com/home/why-i-run/.
[6] Fiore, *The Now Habit;* 59, 62-63, 71-72.

[7] Pamela Weintraub, "The Voice of Reason," Psychology Today, accessed January 28, 2017, https://www.psychologytoday.com/articles/201505/the-voice-reason.

[8] Scott D. Williams, "Self-esteem and the self-censorship of creative ideas," Personnel Review 31, no. 4 (2002): 498, doi:10.1108/00483480210430391.

[9] Andy Clarke, "Out of Our Brains - The New York Times," Opinionator - New York Times, accessed January 29, 2017, https://opinionator.blogs.nytimes.com/2010/12/12/out-of-our-brains/.

[10] Amy Cuddy, "Amy Cuddy: Your Body Language Shapes Who You Are," TED: Ideas Worth Spreading, n.d.https://www.ted.com/talks/amy_cuddy_your_body_language_shapes_who_you_are.

[11] Jane McGonigal, *Reality Is Broken: Why Games Make Us Better and How They Can Change the World* (New York: Penguin Press, 2011), 33.

[12] Christopher Philip, "The Culture Of Nonverbal Triumph," Body Language Project, n.d.bodylanguageproject.com/articles/culture-nonverbal-triumph/.

[13] Cuddy, "Amy Cuddy: Your Body Language Shapes Who You Are.".

[14] Cuddy, "Amy Cuddy: Your Body Language Shapes Who You Are.".

[15] James Altucher, "The Ultimate Guide for Becoming an Idea Machine," Altucher Confidential, accessed January 12, 2017, http://www.jamesaltucher.com/2014/05/the-ultimate-guide-for-becoming-an-idea-machine/.

[16] Jessie Shternshus and Mike Bonifer, *CTRL+Shift: 50 Games for   50 **** Days Like Today* (Atlanta, GA: BDI Publishers, 2015).

[17] Tom Kelley and David Kelley, *Creative Confidence: Unleashing the Creative Potential Within Us All* (London: William Collins, 2013), 118.

[18] Altucher, "The Ultimate Guide for Becoming an Idea Machine."

## Notes: Chapter 8 – Step Into Your Creative Power

[1] Abayomi Jegede, "Top 7 Regrets of People Who Are Dying," Lifehack, accessed February 10, 2017, http://www.lifehack.org/articles/communication/top-7-regrets-people-who-are-dying.html.

[2] Michael Bergeisen, "The Neuroscience of Happiness," Greater Good, accessed

January 16, 2017, http://greatergood.berkeley.edu/article/item/the_neuroscience_of_happiness.

[3] Mary Ardito, "Creativity: It's the Thought that Counts," Bell Telephone Magazine, Volume 61, Number 1, 1982, 32.

[4] Rosanne Bane, *Around the Writer's Block: Using Brain Science to Solve Writer's Resistance : Including Writer's Block, Procrastination, Paralysis, Perfectionism, Postponing, Distractions, Self-Sabotage, Excessive Criticism, Overscheduling, and Endlessly Delaying Your Writing* (New York: Jeremy P. Tarcher/Penguin, 2012).

[5] Bane, *Around the Writer's Block.*

[6] David Kelley, "You Are the Creative Type .com," CNN, accessed January 16, 2017, http://www.cnn.com/2012/07/15/opinion/kelley-creativity/.

[7] Jegede, "Top 7 Regrets of People Who Are Dying."

[8] Simon T Bailey, *Release Your Brilliance: The 4 Steps to Transforming Your Life and Revealing Your Genius to the World* (New York: Harper Collins, 2008).

[9] Malcolm Gladwell, *The Tipping Point: How Little Things Can Make a Big Difference* (Boston: Little, Brown, 2000).

[10] Tom Kelley and Jonathan Littman, *The Ten Faces of Innovation: IDEO's Strategies for Beating the Devil's Advocate & Driving Creativity Throughout Your Organization* (New York: Currency/Doubleday, 2005).

[11] Brené Brown, "Brené Brown: Listening to Shame," TED: Ideas Worth Spreading, n.d. http://www.ted.com/talks/brene_brown_listening_to_shame.

[12] "Schoolhouse Rock - 3 Is A Magic Number," YouTube, n.d.https://www.youtube.com/watch?v=aU4pyiB-kq0.

[13] Maureen O'Connor, "Addicted to Likes: Social Media Makes Us Needier," The Cut, accessed January 14, 2017, http://nymag.com/thecut/2014/02/addicted-to-likes-social-media-makes-us-needier.html.

[14] Tia Ghose, "What Facebook Addiction Looks Like in the Brain," Live Science, accessed January 14, 2017, http://www.livescience.com/49585-facebook-addiction-viewed-brain.html.

CPSIA information can be obtained
at www.ICGtesting.com
Printed in the USA
BVOW08s1605080917
494193BV00004B/4/P